Change and Continuity in Adult Life

Marjorie Fiske
David A. Chiriboga

Change and
Continuity in
Adult Life

Jossey-Bass Publishers

San Francisco • Oxford • 1990

CHANGE AND CONTINUITY IN ADULT LIFE
by Marjorie Fiske and David A. Chiriboga

Copyright © 1990 by: Jossey-Bass Inc., Publishers
350 Sansome Street
San Francisco, California 94104
&
Jossey-Bass Limited
Headington Hill Hall
Oxford OX3 0BW

Library of Congress Cataloging-in-Publication Data

Lowenthal, Marjorie Fiske.
    Change and continuity in adult life / Marjorie Fiske, David A.
Chiriboga.—1st ed.
        p.   cm.—(The Jossey-Bass social and behavioral science series)
    Includes bibliographical references.
    Includes index.
    ISBN 1-55542-249-7 (alk. paper)
    1. Aging—Psychological aspects—Longitudinal studies.
2. Adulthood—Psychological aspects—Longitudinal studies.
I. Chiriboga, David Anthony. II. Title. III. Series.
    [DNLM: 1. Adult—psychology. 2. Aging—psychology. 3. Human
Development—in adulthood. 4. Life Change Events—in adulthood.
BF 724.5 L917c]
BL724.55.A35L68   1990
155.6—dc20   67620
DNLM/DLC
for Library of Congress   90-4966
                                   CIP

Manufactured in the United States of America

The paper in this book meets the guidelines for
permanence and durability of the Committee on
Production Guidelines for Book Longevity of the
Council on Library Resources.

JACKET DESIGN BY WILLI BAUM

FIRST EDITION

Code 9057

The Jossey-Bass
Social and Behavioral Science Series

Contents

Preface

It is a universal truth that aside from those who suffer a premature death, most people grow up, grow older, and die. Not so universal is the way in which we negotiate the occasionally rocky road from infancy through adulthood and beyond. There are many variations of this passage, some leading to lives of inspiration and challenge, others leading to lives of quiet desperation, boredom, or mental dysfunction. What factors determine how people fare during the adult years? Is there room for growth and change, or are our personalities immutably fixed, as some would suggest? No one today can answer these questions—owing to the scarcity of longitudinal studies of adulthood, the frequent use of highly educated and affluent samples in those few studies, and the length of time required to study adult development.

This book explores the multiple ways in which people grow older by examining the lives of ordinary men and women from the lower- to middle-class spectrum of society. Recognizing that changes during adulthood may take a long time to evolve, respondents were interviewed repeatedly over a twelve-year period, thereby providing a unique opportunity to witness lives in progress. Recognizing that no one individual or discipline could do justice to the wealth of data provided, a group of investigators was assembled that included sociologists, psychologists, and anthropologists. Meetings conducted on a monthly basis for over twelve years forged this group into a true interdisciplinary team.

The uniqueness of the study is accentuated by the fact that we sampled not for age but for progress along the life course. Each subject was facing a normative transition: subjects included high school seniors who soon were to enter adult life, newlyweds who were facing decisions about parenthood, parents about to face the proverbial empty nest, and men and women within two to five years of retirement. By selecting people on the basis of critical—but ex-pected—role transitions commonly experienced at different stages and ages of life, we were able to look at people's lives before they entered these critical periods as well as after. This allowed us to conduct a truly prospective study of continuity and change in adult life.

We have written for a broad range of people interested in the study of lives over time. For the most part this audience consists of professionals and graduate students in the fields of psychology, so-ciology, anthropology, and social work. Professionals from the health and allied health sciences will also find the results of interest, since one of the major strengths of the study resides in its use of state-of-the-art indices of life stress as a means of predicting the well-being of subjects. For the older participants we were especially interested in how social and physical loss affects people's lives.

In the interest of readability we have limited the use of tech-nical jargon in order to focus on the central issues. The book relies heavily on the use of case studies, and we follow a representative group of respondents over a significant segment of their lives. Ther-apists and other helping professionals may find these case studies especially useful for their clients, and readers of all backgrounds and orientations may find themselves spontaneously identifying with one or more of the 216 members of the sample.

Organization of the Book

We have organized the chapters around the internal processes and external circumstances that govern continuity and change over time. The overarching theme is that the way adults live out their lives depends on the interplay between these internal processes and external conditions. Chapter One sets the stage for our discussion by introducing the study and the people we interviewed. Designed to counterbalance the investigations of elite samples that pervade the literature on life-span development, we focused on an area that in the late 1960s was just emerging as an issue of importance to life-span development: social stressors. In fact, embarking on our investigation shortly after the initial publication of the landmark Holmes and Rahe (1967) Schedule of Recent Events, we had the opportunity not only to incorporate the life-events methodology but to expand and improve upon it. One of our greatest satisfactions has been that our measures of social stressors—including life events, hassles, and societal pressures—not only have proved their relevance to adult development but continue to be as timely today as they were some ten to fifteen years ago.

The book is divided into three parts. Part One, "How Adults View Themselves at Different Ages," focuses on the self-images of participants, because it is generally recognized that our identities as individual human beings are strongly associated with our health and sense of well-being. Chapters Two and Three explore these conceptions most directly. In Chapter Two we use an objective measure—the Adjective Rating List—as one way of answering the question Who am I? The rating list includes seventy personal characteristics that respondents rate as "like me," "not like me," or "undecided or in-between." Given that our rating list is very structured and forces people to respond to a fixed number of adjectives, we sought to balance the picture of complex lives by asking respondents for their own impressions of themselves. In Chapter Three, therefore, we consider subjective descriptions of the self. As in Chapter Two, we focus on the self, but here the methodology is very different. Respondents are handed a piece of lined paper and asked to describe themselves in twenty different ways as quickly as possible. As in Chapter Two, we consider how people change over the twelve years of the study.

The next two chapters summarize change in domains other than self-concept, but each provides its own answers to the question Who have I become? over the dozen or so years of the study. In Chapter Four, "Being Flexible Versus Rigid," we move from what people think of themselves to what they think about and do. This chapter is based on McCrae and Costa's (1984) Experience Survey. Of the original instrument's sixty statements, we selected fourteen, seven reflecting flexibility and seven rigidity. The key topics include the relationship between flexibility and expansivity versus rigidity and constriction. In Chapter Five we consider reactions to social change. Our information is based on a social change checklist that asks respondents about the impact on their lives of a variety of social conditions, including new ways of doing things at work, changing roles of women, changes in rights of minorities, crime in the streets, and changes in the economy and employment. To test the strength of social concerns we also asked our respondents for their reactions to the international situation, nuclear dangers, and new life-styles.

In Part One we considered some of the ways in which people see themselves or are viewed by other people. We turn next to an in-depth consideration of stress in Part Two, "How Stress Affects Development and Adaptability." In Chapter Six we examine the effects of childhood deprivation on adult adaptation. As might be expected, this chapter deals with the distant past and its impact on the present. A childhood events scale designed for this study included twenty items ranging from death of one or both parents to problems at school, but three categories emerged as especially critical: death or prolonged absence of one or both parents, cruel punishment, and death of a sibling.

It is only within the last two decades or so that stress experiences have been of interest to scholars concerned with adult development. Previously the focus was on special stressors or traumas relevant to short-term changes in physical and social functioning. In Chapter Seven, "Impact of Life Stress: Crisis or Challenge?," we find that exposure to stress may have a positive or negative impact on all aspects of life, including health, sexuality, cognitive functioning, and personal relationships. As the title of the chapter implies, what challenges one person may overwhelm another; in other words, the resources of the individual determine the outcome of stress. We also present a typology of stress that classifies stress exposures into three categories: micro, meso, and macro.

Chapter Eight, "Influence of Mythical and Forgotten Stressors," considers some of the more unusual stressors of the life course. Two are perhaps overstudied: intergenerational conflict and the so-called midlife crisis. The two remaining stressors are perhaps more understudied than studied: boredom and hassles. We report evidence that, despite student protests and the Vietnam War, intergenerational relations seemed to work out just fine for the majority of participants. No discussion of stress and loss in adult life would be complete without some reference to the midlife crisis. After the youngest children leave home, one expects parents to have a lot of time on their hands and to miss them. Not so for our parents! We then report evidence for what may well be the critical stressor of the retirement years: boredom. The final section of this chapter discusses day-to-day stresses, here called hassles, that have a subtle way of eroding the quality of life.

In Chapter Nine, "Resources and Deficits: Clues to How Adults Handle Stress," we present a lifespan model of adaptation predicated on the relative balance between a person's resources and deficits. The first section is devoted to change, for better or worse, in such situations as marriage, work, and goal satisfaction. The second deals with assets and liabilities ranging from creativity to self-centeredness. The chapter concludes with an analysis of a complex and interesting topic: solitude. The fact that people are exposed or not exposed to stressors clearly represents only one of the factors underlying change and continuity in adult life. Part Three deals with what matters most at the four stages of adulthood. Here we consider additional factors that have been hypothesized as important to well-being. Chapter Ten tests the important hypothesis that people who are satisfied with their goal achievement have a more positive self-image than those who are not. Findings from two of our groups—the second oldest group of women and the oldest men—support this thesis, whereas all other groups varied considerably. The chapter concludes with responses to the question: Looking back over your life thus far, how successful have you been in getting what you want out of life?

In Chapter Eleven, the principal theme is commitment in four aspects of life that the literature suggests are central to human motivation: moral, interpersonal, mastery, and self-concern. These commitments represent fundamental issues and are examined at each of the five interviews in the course of nearly twelve years.

Our last topic deals with the basic quality of life. Chapter

Twelve considers an innovative approach to measuring whether our needs and desires in major aspects of life are being satisfied. We present an overview on whether participants, both men and women, at each of the four stages of life feel that they are getting enough satisfaction (or more or less than enough) in their work, recreation, love, and companionship.

We conclude the book, in Chapter Thirteen, with a discussion of the central theme not only of this book but also of the numerous other works that are based on our study. This theme is simply that social stressors play a dominant role in shaping the trajectory of adult lives. Here we pay particular attention to the still understudied and underappreciated influence of what we call macro-level stressors—those that occur at the societal level, such as threats of war, news of economic decline, toxic spills, and the like. From a practical point of view, our findings underscore the need for development of an applied psychology of the adult life course.

To help those who may wish to investigate our empirical findings in greater detail than presented here, we include in the Resources sections a list of published documents from the study, as well as copies of the instruments that formed the basis for our analyses. Please note that not all instruments are included, since some are standard. Moreover, all bibliographic citations refer to works listed in the References—not the works listed in the Resources.

Acknowledgments

In a study spanning nearly twelve years of data collection and fifteen years of data analysis, it would be next to impossible to mention all the wonderful friends and colleagues who have played important roles in the research effort. A few are particularly deserving of recognition. Majda Thurnher, the sole anthropologist on the project, has always served as a source of inspiration and continues to do so now that she has retired. Phyllis Olsen served in a number of capacities, beginning as project secretary and ending as departmental administrator. Without her warmth and humor we would never have survived all those many years. Christie Kiefer, Robert Pierce, Irving Rosow, Judith Stein, and the whole multidisciplinary team of researchers that together constituted the Human Development Program in Psychiatry should also be recognized: they provided an intellectual context that made our research experience all the more satisfying.

And finally, on a more personal note, we acknowledge our families: Carol Lissance, June Rowson Squarebrigs, Barbara Wai Kinn Yee, Carlos Daniel Chiriboga, and David Anthony Chiriboga II. How could we ever have done this without them?

August 1990

Marjorie Fiske
San Francisco, California
David A. Chiriboga
Galveston, Texas

The Authors

Marjorie Fiske is professor emerita of social psychology of the University of California, San Francisco. She received her B.A. degree (1935) from Mount Holyoke College in sociology and economics and her M.A. degree (1938) from Columbia University in social psychology. She holds an honorary doctor of science degree, honoris causa, from Mount Holyoke College.

Fiske's main research activities have been in library science and in interdisciplinary studies of adult development and aging. Her experience in library science includes work with the U.S. Department of State and a statewide study in California of censorship in public and high school libraries. From 1958 to 1984 she directed a series of interdisciplinary studies on adult development and aging at the University of California, San Francisco. In 1960 she received the Library Literature Award of the American and International Library Association; in 1973 she received the Robert W. Kleemeier Award for Outstanding and Meritorious Contributions to Research in Aging from the Gerontological Society; and in 1987 she received a Distinguished Contributions in Research Award from the American Psychological Association. Among Fiske's nine books are *Middle Age: Prime of Life?* (1979), *Four Stages of Life* (1975, with M. Thurnher and D. Chiriboga), *Crisis and Intervention: The Fate of the Elderly Mental Patient* (1970, with A. Simon and L. Epstein), *Book Selection and Censorship* (1968), *The Focused Interview* (1989, with R. K. Merton and P. Kendall), and *Mass Persuasion* (1946, with R. K. Merton and A. Curtis).

Fiske was research director of the National Federation of Business and Professional Women; senior research associate and subsequently research director of Columbia University's Bureau of Applied Social Research; deputy director of research, U.S. Department of State; research consultant for the Fund for Adult Education; and director of the Human Development and Aging Training and Research Program, University of California, San Francisco.

David A. Chiriboga is associate professor of allied health sciences and chair of the Department of Graduate Studies, School of Allied Health Sciences, University of Texas Medical Branch. He received his A.B. degree (1964), magna cum laude, from Boston University with distinction in psychology and his Ph.D. degree (1972) from the University of Chicago in human development. He holds a joint appointment in the Department of Preventive Medicine and Community Health, University of Texas Medical Branch.

Chiriboga's main research activities have been in the area of stress, coping, and adaptation. In addition to serving for fourteen years as coinvestigator on the Longitudinal Study of Transitions on which this book is based, he served as principal investigator of a life-span study of how people cope with different stages of marital dissolution. He is principal investigator of a panel study that evaluates how adult children and their aging parents cope with issues of dependency and care. He also is principal investigator of a project designed to evaluate an innovative geriatric day hospital and a project designed to evaluate the effectiveness of health promotion programs for the elderly. Chiriboga is coauthor of *Four Stages of Life* (1975, with M. [Fiske] Lowenthal and M. Thurnher) and has written more than sixty articles and book chapters that deal with life-span issues in stress and adult development.

Chiriboga was director of research in the Center for Aging and Health, University of California, Davis, from 1984 to 1986. From 1985 to 1986 he served as director of the Gerontology Education and Training Center, San Jose State University. He is past president of Division 20 (Adult Development and Aging) of the American Psychological Association and serves on the editorial boards of *Generations, Psychology of Aging,* and the *Journal of Aging and Health.*

Change and Continuity in
Adult Life

1

Introduction:
The Complexities
of Adult Lives

The focus of this book is on how adults change—or do not change—as they grow up and grow old. What kinds of people, under what past and present circumstances, grow, stagnate, or regress? These intriguing questions emerged in an earlier study of persons aged sixty and older conducted between 1958 and 1967. (See Lowenthal, Berkman, and Associates, 1967; Lowenthal, 1964.) Some of the six hundred people who were interviewed (three or four times) felt trapped, in a rut, and depressed, while others were full of zest and curiosity. About halfway through this first study, many of us on the research team began to realize that to understand such paradoxes of growing older, we needed to know more about the processes of change in earlier periods of adulthood and to study them in depth while they were taking place. We also realized that the study of adult lives could not be based on cross-sectional "snap-shots" or even panel studies conducted over two to five years.

Thus was born the research project on which this book is based. The following pages tell about the project and the people we studied. At the time we began our efforts, much was known about the growth and development of infants, children, and adolescents. The same was true of the old and very old. But except for a few studies of infants and children that had been extended into adult-

1

hood, little was known about the development of adults, the care-takers of both the young and the old.

Our research team recognized that the study of lives involves the collaboration of experts from many different fields. In the late 1960s, as we surveyed the literature on adult development, we found that interdisciplinary studies were quite rare. From clinical psychology to psychiatry and psychoanalysis, theory was deeply rooted in infant and child development and its assumptions of sequential stages and crises. In the few studies conducted by sociologists and anthropologists, the focus was on socializing forces such as ritual or work in one or more cultures. There had been few attempts to portray sociohistorical perspectives in studies of adulthood, yet these perspectives are of critical importance.

Our objective in writing this book is to portray the life course as a complex transactional process that evolves over time and to fill in some of the unexplored regions of adulthood—to chart, in other words, what Neil Smelser (1980, p. 1) has called the "white parts on the map" of adulthood. The wealth of interdisciplinary information we have gathered from our respondents in five in-depth interviews over nearly twelve years enables us to trace continuities and discontinuities in specific aspects of living considered significant by people who ranged, at the outset, from high school seniors to pre-retirees (216 persons in all). The use of both qualitative and quantitative data enables us to provide rich descriptions of what Rosow (1978) has called "the experiential uniqueness" of men and women who were living through different phases of their lives and generously shared them with us.

A Study of Lives

The study was conducted by a team of social and behavioral scientists. The core staff included Marjorie Fiske (social psychology), Majda Thurnher (anthropology), and David Chiriboga (life-span psychology); Don Spence, Elinore Lurie, Carroll Estes, and Richard Suzman served in succession as project sociologists. The staff had the advantage, especially during the planning year, of frequent collaboration with psychoanalysts and psychiatrists in the development of innovative adaptive measures not based on the prevailing medical model. These collaborators included Alexander Simon, Robert Butler, and Leonard Micon. Our interview schedule included structured, quantifiable instruments, rich qualitative data, and, at the first contact, very detailed life histories. The models we developed for the study simplify this complex body of information—including a model of stress and stress perception/preoccupation, a model of adaptation that takes resources as well as deficits into account, a commitment model, and a model of role change as transition that provided an overarching theme to our studies. All will be described in due course; those desiring further information may wish to read cited works, including our book reporting the results of the first interviews (Lowenthal, Thurnher, Chiriboga, and Associates, 1975).

A Life-Span Study. Although most of the research team were gerontologists by training, our sampling design was based on the premise that to appreciate fully how a person grows into old age, one must also appreciate how a person grows from adolescence into young adulthood and from young adulthood into middle age. For this reason we opted for a life-span sample approach. Recognizing that age acts as a spurious or "carrier" variable, however, we also opted for a unique set of inclusion criteria. Instead of sampling according to age, we sampled according to where people stood in relation to one of four normative (and therefore predictable) life transitions. Two of the respondent groups were in the early stages of adulthood: (1) high school seniors who were facing graduation and entry into adult status and (2) men and women whose first marriage was less than one year old and who would presumably be dealing with parenthood within the next few years. We also included persons at earlier and later stages of middle age: (3) men and women whose youngest child was a high school senior and who therefore were likely to face the proverbial empty nest and (4) men and women who either were expecting to retire within five years or had a spouse about to retire.

Since we studied respondents for up to twelve years, it would be confusing to refer to them in terms of their phase of life when first sampled. For example, all the high school seniors had progressed far beyond high school by the time of even the first follow-

up contact. To avoid confusion, we will often refer to those originally in the high school phase of life as the *youngest* sample and
those who started out as newlyweds as the *second youngest* group.
Similarly, the middle-aged parents facing the empty next phase will
be called the *second oldest* group while those initially facing retirement are called the *oldest* group.

A Study of Ordinary People. One of our major concerns was to
study ordinary people. Longitudinal studies of the adult life course
in the late 1960s were, for the most part, continuations of contact
with elitist and above-average children—the Berkeley Child Guid-
ance Study, the Oakland Growth Study, the Grant study of Harvard
undergraduates, and Terman's Study of Gifted Children, for example. Because subjects were generally above average, many rather
optimistic theories of adult development emerged from these
groups. We hoped to balance them by studying a mainstream sample. Inasmuch as we planned to do so in depth, and with many
variables, we sought to simplify the demographic characteristics by
selecting the most homogeneous district of one West Coast city: San
Francisco. The district we selected was composed at that time (with
a few exceptions) of lower-middle-class and blue-collar workers.
The neighborhood was then almost exclusively white. With the
hard-won cooperation of the city's school board, and encouraged by
a faculty colleague who happened to be a board member during the
planning phase of our study, one sampling base became the senior
class of a large high school in that district.

From school records we identified high school seniors who
were the youngest members of their families, thereby also locating
parents who were about to enter the empty nest phase. With one
exception, they were not parents of the high school senior sample.
Using public vital statistics, we identified newlyweds of less than a
year with at least one of each pair living or having lived in this
district; for all this was their first marriage. The oldest people, who
planned to retire within two or three years, were located through
records of firms or agencies in the area or suggested by people in
the other three groups. Thus everyone in the sample could be expected to undergo a transition to a new life stage. How they nego-
tiated these changes was one of our major interests. Another was

how such changes differ in impact from the unexpected events and circumstances that most people encounter as they grow older.

The Beginnings. In October 1968 we began interviewing respondents for what turned out to be the first of a five-interview longitudinal study of how people adapt to the challenges posed at different stages of life. For the next fifteen months we set about collecting the sample, ending up with 216 subjects who were willing to put up with an average of six hours of interviewing and at least three contacts. They consisted of the following:

- 25 high school males aged 16–18 (average = 17)
- 27 high school females aged 17–18 (average = 17)
- 25 newlywed males aged 21–38 (average = 26)
- 25 newlywed females aged 20–34 (average = 23)
- 27 empty nest males aged 44–61 (average = 52)
- 27 empty nest females aged 39–57 (average = 48)
- 30 preretirement males aged 53–65 (average = 61)
- 30 preretirement females aged 45–67 (average = 58)

The Remaining Interviews. Each of the four remaining interviews was designed to fit within a single three-hour session. The second interview was conducted between April 1970 and November 1971. The third interview was conducted between February and November 1974; the fourth was completed between February and August 1977. The fifth and final set of interviews was completed between April and August 1980. During these multiple contacts we lost some respondents, and by the time of the last contact our sample had shrunk to 168 persons. Not unexpectedly, some respondents had died, eighteen in all, primarily the older ones. To allow for mortality, the older groups were oversampled to begin with. A few respondents of all ages dropped out at one or another contact and stayed out; some missed one or two interviews. Table 1 may be helpful in keeping track of where respondents were at different contacts. It also conveys a sense of how far they progressed in their life course during the time they participated in our study.

The retention rate of about 78 percent over twelve years of study reflects a high degree of commitment to the project on the part

Table 1. Developmental Stages of Respondents.

Initial Life Stage of Respondents	Interview Contacts and Age of Respondents					Final Life Stage of Respondents
	First (1968-1969)	Second (1970-1971)	Third (1974)	Fourth (1977)	Fifth (1980)	
Late adolescence (high school seniors)	16–18	18–20	22–24	25–27	28–30	Young adulthood
Young adulthood (newlyweds)	20–38	22–40	26–44	29–47	32–50	Early middle age
Early middle age (empty nesters)	39–61	41–63	45–67	48–70	51–73	Late middle to old age
Late middle age (pre-retirees)	45–67	47–69	51–73	54–76	57–79	Old age

of the respondents. Their cooperation was sustained by the many ways we found to stay in touch with them: progress reports, birthday and holiday cards, and gift copies of a small book based on data from the first interview. Curiously, there was little evidence of bias in who did or did not complete the study; dropouts did not differ in mental health, sociodemographic characteristics, self-reported health, or any of thirty-six other variables we included in an analysis of attrition.

The Interview Tools. The reader may find that some of the questions and instruments used in this study are unfamiliar. Not many researchers these days use the Barron Creativity Scale, for example, but life events and hassles are very fashionable in current research and Costa and McCrae's Experience Survey (Costa and McRae, 1976; McCrae and Costa, 1984) is still growing in popularity. The reason for this curious co-existence of scales is that longitudinal research often involves trying to predict, or even shape, the course of research instrumentation and development. Sometimes one gets lucky and the research tools prove to have lasting value. Sometimes one is not so lucky. In the Longitudinal Study of Transitions, as our project came to be known, we fared relatively well from a historical perspective: most of our research instruments are still in use and have established their value as well. For those interested in the scales we developed or modified, the Resources section contains all instruments and questions that were unique to the project. Since standard research tools are described in cited works, they are not duplicated here.

The Lives We Studied

One unique aspect of this book is that we emphasize the themes and aspects of living to which respondents themselves attach most importance and, moreover, examine how change and continuity in those spheres interact with their sense of well-being. Whatever the time perspective in a longitudinal study, studying change in several dimensions of the lives of four groups of men and women, young and old, is a complex undertaking. The difficulties are compounded by the fact that each person lives in a unique configuration of past, present, and future that also changes. Because we must convey both the generalities of gender and phase-of-life differences and the uniqueness of individuals, the book embraces two supplementary modes of presentation. One mode is quantitative: derived from sophisticated methods, it constitutes the backbone of the book, telling us what is most significant and why. The second mode is qualitative: important findings are illustrated by vignettes, quotations, individual change charts, and biographies. In addition, four key individuals are followed through most chapters. These four represent differing ways of life that can help us understand how individuals deal with stressful experiences. Before introducing them it is appropriate to describe the settings, life-styles, and personal characteristics of the four groups when we first interviewed them.

To begin, our respondents in general represent that segment of society descended from traditional blue-collar workers. For the most part upwardly mobile, their ways of living resemble those of the middle and lower middle classes. They live in their own small homes in a neighborhood distinguished by the homogeneity of its architecture. Very few have leadership roles in their district or in the city; for most, the primary concern is the family, both nuclear and extended. Aside from the high school seniors (at the first interview), a majority have had some technical or general education beyond high school—few have completed college. Not surprisingly, the newlyweds are better educated than the middle-aged, who in turn have had more schooling than the pre-retirees. Also reflecting national trends, the older the respondents, the more likely they are to have many siblings, while they themselves have an average of two or three children. Most profess some religious affiliation, and, again reflecting the population at large, more women than men attend services; many parents who do not participate themselves send their children to Sunday school or synagogue. More than three-fourths of the women have jobs, usually part time, to supplement the family income.

The High School Seniors. As with all four groups followed in this book, it is difficult to describe high school seniors as an entity. At the first interview the boys and girls differ from each other more than they do from the older people of the same sex. The characteristics they share include negative feelings and images of themselves—timidity, restlessness, dissatisfaction—and many are unhappy, far more so than people in the older cohorts. School problems represent the biggest stress for the majority, especially passing the tests to graduate in order to qualify for a job or more schooling. Looking back on our own lives, we might easily conclude that these characteristics are par for the course at seventeen or eighteen. The world around them, however, was in more than usual flux. The boys were worried about being drafted and the girls about racial conflicts (which had been rare when they were freshmen but became frightening in the course of their high school years). Over half of the boys worked part time, and more of them were unhappy than those who did not. Very few girls had jobs, and they enjoyed a broader range of activities than boys. While the boys had more friends of long standing, girls' descriptions of their friendships (of the same or opposite sex) were more likely to convey a sense of mutuality, reciprocity, and warmth.

The boys' principal long-term goals were to find interesting jobs, at the same time retaining plenty of freedom for other things they enjoyed doing—but many were apprehensive about reaching the goals they were tentatively establishing. Girls were not interested in occupations: they wanted to find self-fulfillment and to develop a way of life uniquely their own, but they were as vague as the boys about how to go about it. Though many parents were impatient with such vague aspirations, most of the students had fairly warm relationships with their families. The majority were not yet caught up in the activism developing in nearby colleges and universities in the late 1960s and early 1970s.

The Newlyweds. The newlyweds, all in their first marriages, ranged from age twenty to thirty-eight at first contact; because of our sampling criteria, none as yet had children. These men and women had much more in common than did the high school seniors, and they shared a complex life-style with a variety of interests and activities, as though to make the most of the preparenthood phase. Some men worked part time and were attending junior or community colleges. A large majority of both sexes worked, some of the women helping with their husbands' college expenses. In speaking of their mar-

riages, both sexes emphasized emotional involvement and respon-
siveness, understanding, and enjoying each other. Compared to respondents of the opposite sex, men felt less anxious and more
mature in sex relationships and women more satisfied emotionally.
Some men and women felt more distanced from one or both of their
parents. (As we will see, the advent of children often improves these
generational relationships.)

Most surprising was the fact that men and women agreed
that "he" should be the boss in the newly established family—
another circumstance that would change, for some very quickly.
The newlyweds had more friends and saw them more often than
people in any other group except the pre-retirees. They had the
strongest sense of growth and were happier and more satisfied than
others. They often felt proud and confident. The principal difference between men and women was in their concepts of themselves.
More newlywed women described themselves as warm, jealous, and
not energetic than did other women in the sample. The newlywed
men were dramatically different: highly energetic, flamboyant, im-
pulsive, versatile, and unconventional were typical self-descriptions
rarely found among younger and older men.

The Empty Nesters. Despite the fairly normal adolescence of high
school seniors in our sample, the middle-aged parents worried
about their children's aspirations (vague) and behavior (both lazy
and frenetic). As a group these parents were polar opposites of the
newlyweds. Men focused on money, maximizing security for their
retirement. Women had the lowest range of activities in the sample.
Several of them told interviewers they "should" get out of their
house and do something, but they were as vague as high school
seniors about how and what. At the same time they were the most
concerned about social issues and thought "people" should do
something about them. Men believed in law and order and placed
responsibility on government. Many of these men and women described themselves as rather dull people. The men were the antithesis
of male newlyweds: orderly, cautious, hardworking, and self-
controlled. Women were unhappy and absentminded. Like the high
school seniors, many "empty nesters" were dissatisfied with their
lives. About half of them reported some deterioration in sex rela-

tionships. Husbands described their wives in terms of their competence as homemaker and mother; wives first acknowledged the pro-
vider role of husbands, and many went on to say that their spouses
need a great deal of understanding and indulgence. Both men and
women spent more time rehashing past decisions than did people
in other stages of life.

The Pre-Retirees. The pre-retirees were, on the average, about ten
years older than the middle-aged; the women in both groups were
generally three or four years younger than the men. Only about a
third of them had any education beyond high school. Children of
the Depression, a few had not finished grade school. Some observed
that they had learned more in two or three years at high school than
their children did in the junior and community colleges. Nearly all
of the men still worked full time, as did over half of the women.
Several men, especially those in civil service jobs, were developing
small businesses or other ventures of their own to work on at least
part time after they retired.

Both men and women were apprehensive about retirement,
their own or their spouses', for a variety of reasons. Nonworking
women who had no children at home feared they might have to give
up their well-established social life with women friends or that
husbands would hang around the house and interfere with their
domestic routines. Some people of both sexes suspected that more
togetherness might exacerbate friction. Like the middle-aged men,
however, the pre-retiree males were quite positive in describing
their wives. And in contrast to the middle-aged women in the study,
their female counterparts were equally positive in describing their
husbands. The men were more likely than those in other groups
to consider their marriages egalitarian, while the pre-retirement
women were for the most part at the extremes, viewing their marriages as either male dominant or female dominant. Half of the men
noted a decline in sexual relationships and potency but thought it
was normal at their age, whereas over half of the women said they
had either improved or not changed, and more than twice as many
women as men expected no change in the future.

The interpersonal relationships of this oldest group were
notable: they were closer to their children than the middle-aged

were, and they had more friends and richer friendships than people
in other stages. They were also positive about themselves. The men
were the least dissatisfied or unhappy, more patient, interested, and
comfortable with others and themselves than other men; the women
felt more competent, independent, and assertive than did the other
women being studied. They were also happier than younger
women, but not as happy as their male counterparts. Pre-retirees
were as future-oriented as younger people and far less concerned
with the past; their philosophies of life were more humanitarian
and their goals less materialistic. This brief summary reflects their
golden years. As they grow older over the course of the study, we
find that the glow dims—drastically for a few, moderately for most.

Selecting the Cases

In selecting cases to be followed intensively throughout the
book, we first had to decide on how many people to use. Anything
fewer than four seemed insufficient to illustrate the complex transactions between individual and environment; anything more than
four seemed likely to overwhelm the reader; four cases seemed just
right. Having settled on four cases, then, our next decision concerned whether we should include a representative from each stage
of life. After reviewing the pros and cons, we decided to draw these
four people from the two older groups. The reasons were twofold.
First, the need to comprehend the "developmental" part of adult
development is most evident when we consider the older adult.
Some have in fact questioned whether there can be a developmental
science of later life (see Flavell, 1970), while others note the particular vulnerabilities of older persons (see Kohut, 1977). Second, the
entire research team was composed of specialists in the second half
of life and thus we felt particularly qualified to delve into the issues
of older adulthood in the way these case studies demanded.

Our overall desire was to choose individuals who could illustrate the many ways in which people deal with the challenges and
threats posed by progression along the life course. We drew upon
a working model of commitments (Fiske, 1980) as a basis for selecting the cases. One of the four categories of the commitment model
is self-concern, which embraces preoccupations with the self rang-

ing from self-protectiveness to a carefree hedonism. Our earlier
work (Fiske and Chiriboga, 1985, for example) indicated this
category is quite appropriate to the study of stress response and so
we based our screening process on this category. We first identified
all of those middle-aged and older people who, at the first contact,
ranked self-concern the highest or lowest of their commitments.
The next step was to locate subgroups of changers and nonchangers
and finally, among the changers, to locate people who had changed
in specific ways at subsequent interviews—for example, from low
to high to low or from high to low. Since we wished to have one
man and one woman in each of the two older groups, the last
screening was of stage and sex groups.

Nine people fit our requirements. Of these, we selected the
four whose education, marital status, and occupation were most
typical of the two older groups as a whole. The remaining five are
introduced in later chapters as "alternates" whose lives help us to
round out some of the points we make in this book. Of The Four,
the primary cases to be followed, one is an empty nest male who was
consistently low in self-concern, a female counterpart who changed
from high to low, a pre-retirement man who began high and moved
to very low, and a woman in the same stage who remained consistently low except for the final interview. Their names, and the
names of all persons described in this book, have been changed to
preserve anonymity.

Olav Olavsen, in the empty-nest phase, was chosen because
he was consistently low in self-concern. He is sixty-one when we
meet him, a machinist with seven years of education. As a young
man he had come from Sweden to the United States to visit relatives,
met his future wife, and decided to stay. She is college-educated and,
like him, a staunch Lutheran. They have four children, his wife has
never worked, and he considers himself very happily married. He
describes his philosophy of life in what the interviewer called "Protestant Ethic, nineteenth-century style" terms. His own description
may be summed up as: Do the best you can now and prepare for
the life hereafter. His goals at the first interview are to live a meaningful, peaceful, and happy life while making others happy too. He
feels closest to his wife, next closest to his children, and has a few
good friends. His major resource is religion, and he is serving his

church both as deacon and as a member of the choir. His sense of creativity both at work and as a hobbyist with metalworking is very fulfilling. As we follow him over the ensuing years, we will see how well these resources serve him in periods of severe stress.

Hazel Sutter, also in the empty nest group, is fifty-one years old and highly self-concerned when we first meet her. By the fifth interview, this is the lowest of her commitments (lowest of all middle-aged women) for unexpected reasons. After a long, unhappy marriage she has been divorced for four years at the time of the first interview. Her daughter is in high school and her son in Vietnam. Through most of her adult life she has worked hard as manager and cook in the cafeteria of a large corporation. Her mother, always in poor health, has recently become part of her household. While she would like to have gone to college and managed an "experimental kitchen," she clearly enjoys being mother confessor to the staff, consisting primarily of young men. Although she describes herself in quite positive terms, at the same time she feels "dull." Her work is a resource because "it keeps me exhausted and at least I sleep good." She likes serving on committees and is involved in two food-related organizations. A liberal, she is interested in unions and other public issues and feels frustrated that she does not have time to do very much about them. She lives in a modest house and is not at all materialistic, occasionally enjoying simple short trips. The interviewer finds her very self-controlled until she asks Hazel about her friends, at which point she says her closest woman friend has recently died and tears roll uncontrollably down her cheeks. Her interviewer for the second contact describes Hazel as "a small energetic woman with red hair in curls. She smiles all the time and is a warm open person." By the final interview Hazel is happily involved with, and living with, a male friend.

Max Schindler, a pre-retiree, scores at the top of the list on self-concern when we first meet him. He changes up and down subsequently, and it is his second lowest commitment when we last see him. He is fifty-three at the outset; his wife is forty-five and working full time as a paralegal secretary. They have three children. He did not quite finish high school, has long been a factory supervisor, but quickly identifies himself as a gun collector, fisherman, and hunter. Although he dislikes his job, he approves of the workers' union, one of his few liberal concerns. He is "antiwar" but also calls himself a racist. His wife, according to him, does whatever he wants. His main goal is to make more money and build a house "up north where taxes are cheaper." One interviewer, female, describes him as a "macho" Hemingway type, likable and flirtatious, cheerful but quick to anger and able to use his fists. (He used to "belt" his children.) He is not religious and finds it odd that his older daughter has become very much so. His friends are a group of "thirty or more" men with whom he goes hunting or fishing.

Pre-retiree *Adelaide Stone* is fifty-two, young for her group, when we first talk. She has a business school education and works as a secretary for a city agency. Ten years younger than her husband, she plans to work for another fifteen years. Mr. Stone works as a foreman at a local cement company and is expecting to retire within a month of the first interview. Widowed in her late thirties, with two teenage children, Adelaide has been married about six years before we meet her. She describes her husband in glowing terms. A widower with adult children of his own, he seems to fit right into the household. Adelaide feels closest to him, her children, two women friends, and three siblings. She grew up under very stressful circumstances that may have strengthened her for the future. Her father, an alcoholic, died when she was sixteen, and her mother died five years later. During the Depression the family was often on relief. The traumatic experiences of her childhood and adolescence still haunt her. The interviewer finds her to be full of energy, fortitude, and determination, healthy, quite attractive, and a warm, receptive person. She is liberal and, remembering her past, is concerned about welfare for the poor and "the general fear" of war. Her work, which she likes, is a major resource. Nominally Catholic, she does not, at first contact, attend services, but during the dramatic tribulations to come, her religion becomes a source of strength. She remains consistently low in self-concern until the last contact, when she becomes one of the highest.

Summing Up

Studying change and continuity in adult life presents a challenge. Unlike the developmental progressions of early childhood, where each day or week may witness the unfolding of a new ability or behavior, adult development and aging may take years to become noticeable and measurable. There is even some debate about whether the term *development* is appropriate to the conditions manifested during adulthood, since the course of adult life often seems to depend heavily on chance factors.

Our attempt to assess change and continuity was unique in several ways. First, we sampled not by age but by place in the life course. This we accomplished by identifying persons who were facing likely normative transitions. This sampling strategy allowed us to match people for stage of life without ignoring factors such as chronological age. Second, we made an effort to include ordinary men and women, and did not focus on the well-educated and middle-class elite who often volunteer for social and behavioral science projects such as ours. Third, we had multiple interview contacts over a period of approximately twelve years, which seemed long enough to capture evidence of change if indeed change were to occur. Finally, our sample included men and women from both the early and the later stages of adulthood; this provided an opportunity to contrast life experiences.

We were also fortunate to have assembled an interdisciplinary team of researchers that remained relatively stable over the years of study, and to have included a number of instruments that continue to hold scientific credibility years after the initiation of the project. In the chapters to follow we will see how all these facets of study, subjects, and interviews came together to furnish some intriguing perspectives on adult life. Our first concern is how adults view themselves at different ages.

Part One
How Adults
View Themselves
at Different Ages

2

Exploring the Self: Objective Impressions

When talking about their lives, older clients rarely describe themselves as having changed in any major way since early adulthood. Their hair may be whiter, their bodies may have grown older, but not the inner core, the "me" of selfhood around which the personal universe pivots. This chapter focuses on the many ways in which adults view themselves and how their self-images change over time. Before we report on our study, though, a brief review of the premises and key issues is appropriate.

Key Issues

The self-views we will be considering here represent the ways in which participants rated themselves on a relatively structured Adjective Rating List. Since participants were restricted in the adjectives they could use and our interpretation of their ratings reflects our own thinking on the concept of self, the findings in this chapter do not necessarily indicate how the participants might describe themselves if given the chance to do so freely. We did in fact give them the chance, and the results are discussed in the next chapter. Here we deal not with the described self so much as what some might call the "essence" of the human being: the personality. Personality refers to that grouping of characteristics that makes one a unique and identifiable person. Many would agree that personality, broadly defined, is the objective component of the individual's self-concept. (See, for example, Bengtson, Reedy, and Gordon, 1985.) In other words, each of us carries around a self-image, or set of images about the self, that makes up what we see as the self. While these images may appear highly individualized and perhaps chaotic, certain patterns do emerge. These patterns constitute the individual's personality, the self-concept as viewed from outside the self.

Stability and Change. Regardless of whether one is studying the objectively or subjectively defined self, a critical question emerges: how complicated is the adult self? Some time ago Bernice Neugarten, a pioneer in adult development, pointed out several vital but often ignored differences between studying adults as compared with the well-established fields of infant and child development. For Neugarten the study of adult lives is inherently more complex because adults have a longer experiential history: "The self-concept of the adult has elements of the past contained within it. . . . The blending of past and present is a psychological reality" (Neugarten, 1969, pp. 125–126). One consequence of this greater complexity and richness, according to Neugarten, is that well-rounded views of adults are more likely to require a multidisciplinary orientation embracing not only psychology but social psychology, sociology, anthropology, and social history as well. (We would add psychiatry and psychoanalysis to her list.)

The longer experiential history of adults raises another issue for Neugarten: the importance of considering change over time. In the area of selfhood, a number of researchers have considered the question of personal continuity and change in detail. Their results seem to support the notion that the self is a relatively stable aspect of the human condition (see McCrae and Costa, 1984). But most empirical studies have a major flaw: they simply have not studied the lives of their subjects over the span of time necessary to detect change. In other words, studies of two to four years in duration (the most frequent period covered) may fail to capture any significant change in a construct as complex as the self since the rate of change during the adult years tends to be quite slow.

A Broader Perspective. Scholars other than social scientists, including philosophers, historians, and psychoanalysts, have addressed the question of changing selves. Kenneth Burke (1977, p. xlvii), updating his study of the Depression era, emphasizes the long-term consequences of major social change. Such change may lead to an "unsettling" of the individual since it can undermine a person's basic assumptions about life. That this unsettling may affect the self-concept is clear from our own findings: some older people (just reaching their twenties during the Depression) continue to feel insecure forty to fifty years later, although others consider themselves lucky because they are better off now than in their childhood years.

Another type of change related to self-concept is postulated by David Norton (1976), who suggests that awareness of growing old is timed by shrinking options in one's culture. Philosopher Christopher Lasch (1984), referring specifically to aging in the United States, finds that newer cohorts of older people are becoming more and more concerned with themselves. The change encompasses a sense of emptiness, isolation, and loss of faith in generational continuity. He sees the struggle against growing older developing in earlier periods of life than formerly because today's young and middle-aged people sense that they have fewer resources than did their parents' generation. Both Norton and Lasch implicitly or explicitly link these changes in self-concept to a pervading—and historically recent—awareness of the possibility of human extinction.

Psychoanalyst Heinz Kohut reports, from clinical evidence, a new type of concern with self (or narcissism) developing. He predicts that it will become the typical self of Western society (Kohut, 1977). His reasoning is complex, but it may be summed up like this: the new narcissism results from increasing parent/child distancing, both physical and emotional, over the past two or three decades, which has deprived children of adequate role models. Kohut asks for the cooperation of social and behavioral scientists in seeking to determine how long it will take for specific social changes—such as the increased participation of women in the work force and the more frequent absence of fathers—to alter the structure of the self-concept. Old people should be included in their research, for Kohut

(1977) finds them especially vulnerable to changes of this magnitude.

Robert J. Lifton, another psychoanalyst, also speaks of a "new narcissism" that looks like self-love but in fact embraces negative self-views. Like Norton and Lasch, he attributes the changing self-concept to fear of biological destruction. Lifton (1979) notes a cleavage between generations: people who grew up in the prebomb era seem to maintain positive images of fulfilled selves and human continuity that are lacking among the young of today. One hypothesis for this chapter, then, is that among our two older groups, self-concepts are quite positive and become more stable with time, whereas the young continue to have diffuse and changing images of themselves.

As we begin to address the question of selfhood in this chapter, it should be recognized that there is more than one way to study this elusive concept. On the first page of his award-winning book *Conceiving the Self*, Morris Rosenberg (1979, p. 5) writes that "the self stands as a concept foremost in the ranks of confusion." One problem may be that the self-concept is not necessarily stable; as both Lifton (1971) and Louis Zurcher (1977) have noted, the modern self may in fact be quite mutable and change with the demands of the environment. Zurcher concludes that any single approach to studying the self may fail to grasp the complexities of this elusive concept. Thus he calls for studies that draw on more than one way of assessing the self-concept and trace people as they change or do not change over time.

The Rated Self

The design of our study permitted us to act upon Zurcher's exhortation to study people over substantial lengths of time and to draw on at least two ways of examining the self-image and how it changes. This chapter is based on one of these ways: an Adjective Rating List that includes seventy different attributes of the self. In Chapter Three we examine information obtained from a less structured instrument—the Twenty Statements Test (Kuhn and McPartland, 1954) used by Zurcher and others—and learn what spontaneously described selves are like.

As we considered the literature on selfhood and adult life, we realized that our data confirm what others have postulated. The impression we obtained, after reading the multiple interviews for each of the cases, was that images of former selves can provide a comforting sense of continuity or, especially in periods of stress, a challenge for change. New social norms provide yardsticks by which, consciously or not, self-images develop. Ways of living that become commonplace in the course of our twelve-year study include premarital living together, increase in divorce, delayed marriage, decisions to have no children, and young middle-aged women returning to school and embarking on new careers. Time lags in acceptance of such new life-styles were common among our older groups: many expressed dismay about the changes in the early phases of the study but had come to tolerate them by the last interview.

Naturally, the impressions one gleans from reading the 200 to 300 pages of text on each participant may differ from the objective impressions gained from quantitative analyses of data. In this section we present the outline of a quantitative perspective; in the following section we will examine change and stability among eight people having positive or negative self-images.

At each contact point, all of the study participants were asked to rate themselves on the seventy-item Adjective Rating List. Adjectives on this list were taken from the 300-item Gough Adjective Checklist and represent those suggested by Block (1971) as constituting a reasonably comprehensive array. We differed from Gough in having participants rate each adjective as either like themselves, in-between or unclear, or unlike themselves. We also asked them to circle self-attributes they wished they did not have. Rather than provide results in extensive and perhaps tedious detail, we offer here a summary of what we learned. Most of the analyses were based on factor analyses of the original list as well as (in the case of what we called self-criticism and self-ambiguity) simple counts of items.

At the first contact, a comparison between all men and all women showed general agreement about characteristics in the Adjective Rating List they considered desirable: both sexes valued confidence, self-control, cooperativeness, and sincerity; both rejected hostility, indecisiveness, and touchiness. Examining the older people, in general we find that self-concepts are likely to become more negative as people grow older. Subgroups, however, differ considerably in how they change. Among the middle-aged men, nearly as many had a more positive image at the fifth contact as had become more negative about themselves at that point. Some had not changed at all. The same was true of their female counterparts except that self-ratings of a higher proportion revealed no change. More people in the oldest group revealed change: many of the men had become more negative about themselves, while women were more equally divided between improvement and deterioration.

The adjective cluster we have called dysphoria (Pierce and Chiriboga, 1979) adds a different dimension. Dysphoria is represented by a cluster of adjectives related to dissatisfaction and malaise. The young were generally more dysphoric than older people. Looking just at the four older groups, we find a general trend toward reduced dysphoria over the course of the twelve-year study. Reductions in the dysphoria of middle-aged women were particularly dramatic, while many of the men in that group did not change. Both men and women in the oldest group became less dysphoric, on the average, as time went on. Those in the two younger groups were not only more dysphoric than older participants, they were also more hostile—a difference sustained through all the interviews. Women in all stages were less satisfied than men at all contacts, and they felt less secure. Over the years of the study, the empty nest males became less assertive in their self-views and the second youngest group of men became more assertive. These findings accord with Jung's notions concerning the second half of life and with Gutmann and Neugarten's thesis that a shift from assertive to accommodative styles of mastery occurs as males move through middle to old age.

Apart from looking at specific clusters of adjectives that reflected such attributes as hostility and self-satisfaction, we also considered another dimension of the self: the clarity of the self-image. As noted earlier, our instrument was a rating list rather than a checklist and we asked participants to tell us whether each of the seventy adjectives was like them, in-between and uncertain, or unlike them. By counting the number of times a participant was unwilling or unable to report a given adjective as distinctly like or unlike him or her, we obtained a measure of what in fact was the reverse of image clarity: ambiguity of self-view. In other words, those who said they were uncertain about adjectives were in some sense reflecting ambiguity about who they were. Greater ambiguity, in turn, was found to correlate with a greater number of psychological symptoms (Lowenthal, Thurnher, Chiriboga, and Associates, 1975; Chiriboga, 1984).

At the first contact, men in the two youngest groups were the most vague and women in the two older groups were less certain than their male counterparts. The older women were not unduly unclear, however. In fact, pre-retirees of both sexes ranked lowest on self-ambiguity at the outset and continued to have the clearest self-views throughout. The middle-aged of both sexes had changed very little at the third contact, but by the last interview they were more certain of their identity. Younger groups changed in the direction of more clarity, but their self-images remained more diffuse than those of older people at all interview points.

There was yet another way in which we considered our participants: we asked them to tell us how many of their self-ascribed characteristics they were unhappy about. They did this by circling undesired characteristics, and then we simply counted up the number of circled items. At our first contact, we found to our surprise that there were no differences between the two younger and the two older groups. While women tended overall to be more critical of themselves, there was some evidence of increased convergence over the life course: sex differences in self-criticism were highly significant among the youngest group but almost nonexistent among the oldest group. In time these initial similarities and differences in self-criticism began to change. Younger people generally increased more in self-criticism than the two older groups, but the difference was not significant. One group stood out: the second oldest group of women increased most in self-criticism over the years.

One of the reasons why social scientists have been interested in people's self-images lies in the pivotal role the self is presumed to play in what transpires. There was indeed some evidence that the self-views of participants, as expressed at our first interviews, were influential in shaping their later trajectories in life. Men and

women of all ages who were less assertive, for example, were more
likely to undergo transitions such as parenthood or retirement at an
earlier date. Men who entered these transitions early were likely to
be more clear-cut in their self-views, more amiable, but higher in
perceptions of control. Women who entered transitions early were
initially less hostile, more insecure, less polished, and less self-
critical.

A Closer Look at Selfhood

In order to illuminate the changes and consistencies discussed in the preceding section, we have selected eight people from
the two older groups—four of whom had become more positive in
self-view and four more negative—to examine in depth. Here we are
concentrating on older participants for much the same reasons we
drew our four intensive cases from the older groups: less is known
about them, overall, and our work has been focused primarily on
middle and later life. The eight cases include one man and one
woman in each subgroup who, when we first met them, thought
well of themselves and four who did not. As we follow them over
nearly twelve years, we find a wide array of biographical explanations for their self-images and why they do or do not change.

Positive Self-Concept. Lionel Wilcox is forty-nine when we first
meet him and does not change his remarkably high opinion of
himself at all during the twelve years of study. He is one of the few
college graduates in the sample (he majored in engineering); a summary of his protocols shows him to be a personification of the
Protestant Ethic: he works very hard, he makes as much money as
possible, and he attends church on a regular basis. Lionel sells
electronic equipment and in the course of the study becomes manager of sales and eventually reaches the top of the career ladder. His
success in business is the major satisfaction of his life. His wife, who
has two years of college, works part time as a clerk. He speaks well
of his wife, describing her as loving, social, and outgoing, but notes
that she is not very good with the family budget. They play golf and
canasta together when he has time.

The Wilcoxes have two daughters. At first meeting, the family sees little of Lionel, for he travels three weeks out of four (and likes his schedule). His descriptions of family are what one might call "detached-positive" with no indication of emotion or spontaneity. His father has died just before the first interview, for example, but Lionel dismisses the death as a statistic. "Death in the later years is not a big thing," he says with no sign of regret. He speaks at great length about a business setback, however, making clear that it was quite traumatic for him.

Lionel's assumed role in life seems to be that of Organization Man, as much in church as in business. He describes his relationship with his two daughters as "friendly but not close." Five years later he has become sales manager and travels less. His older daughter married after college graduation and the younger is still in college. (She later drops out.) While he continues to fulfill his "organizational" responsibilities at church, he is too busy at work for other service activities. He does, however, join a new business organization and has become vice-president of the company by the seventh year into the study. He says his only stresses are self-imposed and related to business, which he much enjoys. The major satisfaction in Lionel's life is making big sales. During the last interview he reports all is well with the family, which now includes two granddaughters. Work "takes 70 percent of my time," he says, and he may or may not retire when sixty-five. He is still satisfied with his marriage but continues to complain of his wife's ineptness with the family budget and now her lack of punctuality as well. His opinion of himself remains very high.

Cora Leary, also at the empty nest stage at first contact, has a clearly positive view of herself— though never as strongly as Lionel Wilcox and though she changes more than Lionel during the time she participates in the study. Her father left home shortly after she was born, her mother had to go to work (as a secretary), and she was brought up by her maternal grandparents, whom she loved. Described by the interviewer as an attractive, receptive, and charming woman when we first meet her (she is forty-two), Cora is a high school graduate whose main occupation before marriage had been as a clerk-typist.

Now that her only child, a son, is in high school, Cora is back at work again: she is employed part time in a school cafeteria where she enjoys the company of young children. Her husband, a college graduate, works as a tax accountant. Unable to have more children, she wants to adopt one or even two but her husband refuses on the grounds that he could not possibly like someone else's child. She is very active in her church (Episcopalian) and, unlike Lionel Wilcox, she is very religious. That and a few close friends are her major resources. Mr. Leary is stingy and has not been easy to live with. The anniversary present he recently gave her, a coat, is his first gift to her in twenty-five years.

By the second interview Cora Leary's closest friend has died and she still mourns for her. Her mother has bought a trailer and moved to a nearby town, but she lives independently. Cora's main goals are to see her son through college, improve her relationship with her mother, and help others. She had been taking care of the grandmother who brought her up, but the grandmother has recently died. Cora mourned a bit, then consoled herself with the thought that her grandmother had lived a rich life with many blessings. Being elected deaconess at her church for three years pleases her greatly, and she continues to work on church committees as well. She has also become a volunteer for the PTA and at election time worked at a polling booth.

By the third interview her son, whom she alternately calls brilliant and difficult, is still in college and financially dependent. She looks forward to his marrying and having children as "fulfillment of family life," adding that it is the will of God, her "dear, loving father," that she have only one child. The interviewer notes that she has become more matronly in appearance and laughs a lot. By the fourth session, Cora Leary has become an elder of the church and spends more time there. Her husband strongly objects, saying she has to choose between church and him, so she is planning to curtail her time at church in order to go to auctions and garage sales with him (his favorite hobby). She continues to enjoy helping others and considers her son her closest friend.

The highlight of the final interview is the news that for the first time in forty-three years Cora has had a reunion with her father and the pleasure of introducing him to his grandson. She plans to stay in touch with him and feels that her life is more complete. Cora Leary is fifty-four and, because of her husband's money worries, now works full time at the school cafeteria. Since the last contact she has had a health problem; still quite ill, she takes medication and reports feeling fine. She took a course similar to est, learned a lot from it, and would like to take more courses, including physical exercises. Her spare time is filled with activities such as visiting the handicapped and listening to their life stories. She has been abroad with her husband, who was on a business trip, and, with him, has now joined a jazz society. Liberal and politically aware, she prays for world peace. Serving communion on Easter Sunday recently was the highlight of her life. For more humble reasons than those of Lionel Wilcox, one feels that Cora Leary's good opinion of herself is very appropriate.

Retirement stager Byron Poole maintains the most positive self-concept of these four positive people, and one suspects that this may be due to comparisons he makes with his former self. His father was a shipping clerk for a trucking firm, and the Depression was traumatic for his family. In contrast, the sixty-year-old Byron has had two years of college and is a systems program analyst, quite healthy when we first meet him. He had a serious heart attack some twenty years earlier, but his health is now excellent.

Rather late in life Byron married a woman of his own age, a college graduate who used to be a teacher. They have one child, a son, who gives a major purpose to his life, he says. Like Cora Leary, he is genuinely religious and active in his Protestant church. By the second interview he is retired and misses his colleagues, but he does not miss getting up early. Now treasurer of the church "in order to have something to do," he takes care of church property as well as his own. After retirement he and his wife take a long trip around the country to visit old friends. Though he finds he is tiring more easily, he would like to find a paid job so that he can help his son and daughter-in-law buy a house.

By the third session, Byron Poole has spent six months as interim pastor of his church and has also acquired a grandson. Always a giving person, he is working three months a year for United Way. His brother and a close friend have died, and he himself was hospitalized for hernia surgery. His marriage improves with time (it was good to begin with) and, despite his declining agility, the Pooles have taken a European holiday. He reports that he enjoys his religious and genealogical research at all the interviews.

Before the last interview Byron's excellent health begins to deteriorate: he was hospitalized for heart problems and still has angina pain when walking. Surprisingly, these difficulties do not influence his self-concept. He remains the most positive of the four, happy to be alive, enjoying what life has to offer, giving of himself to others.

Dora Romano, the fourth person in the group of positives, is a sixty-one-year-old woman of Italian ancestry. Originally a very devout Catholic, she now attends church only twice a year. A high school graduate with one year's training in business school, she worked before marriage but has not wanted to since. Her husband, also a high school graduate, worked as equipment purchaser for a bank. They have one child, a daughter with two children. Unlike the majority of people in the study, Dora Romano is an avid reader of serious books and journals, especially those relating to peace and the environment. Her primary goals are independence of mind and peace in the world; she feels useful in her volunteer work with retarded girls. Her elderly parents are living nearby, but she does not feel very close to them or to her three siblings. She describes her husband with great warmth and in turn is pleased to report that he appreciates her. She goes to baseball games with him, and they usually entertain friends on Saturday nights.

By the second contact, Dora Romano's husband has retired; her daughter has finished her degree and is teaching, which pleases Dora very much. This circumstance also solves the problem of her husband's spare time, for on weekdays the two of them now stay with their grandchildren at their daughter's house about twenty miles away. Dora is also trying to smooth relationships with her own mother. (Both her parents are becoming more dependent on her, though not financially.) Her activity level is about the same as before, and in general Dora is very satisfied with her life, especially her good health. The only important change she reports at the third and fourth interviews is that she has to spend much more time caring for her ill parents. Though some husbands resent such diversion of attention from themselves, Mr. Romano is supportive and she continues to consider her marriage much better than most.

When we last talk with Dora Romano, life is proving more difficult for her. Her parents' health has deteriorated even further, and taking care of them demands much of her time. She herself has been hospitalized, and though she is now recovered, there are many things she can no longer do. She feels guilty if she does not spend all her time with her parents. While at the fourth interview she reports herself to be "quite happy," at the fifth and final contact she is "not very happy." Her daughter gives her much pleasure, and her main goal now is to see her granddaughter graduate from college. Though her parents' care is stressful and she rates the current year very low, her opinion of herself remains quite positive, perhaps because of her husband's devotion and support.

In summary, then, except for Lionel Wilcox of the one-track mind, these people, like everyone else, have health problems, periodic or chronic, over the twelve-year period we talk to them. They have other problems as well. Cora Leary has a very difficult husband, but instead of feeling intimidated she pursues her own well-rounded interests, strong and independent. Despite illness and constant pain, Byron Poole is happy to be alive. Dora Romano's life has become very difficult, but she maintains her healthy self-view. What these three have in common is optimism and a lifelong pattern of concern and giving to others.

Negative Self-Concept. As we turn to consider four people with very negative self-views, we find further support for the thesis that there is not necessarily a strong relationship between life circumstances, self-concept, and happiness or unhappiness. Sam Meyer, for example, is Lionel Wilcox's opposite number in that he too is in the empty nest stage. Sam has an extremely negative self-image, by far the most negative of this group of four. During the study he has changed more than any of the eight, however, thinking somewhat better of himself as time goes on. Forty-nine at the outset, he tells of an exotic early life. Ethnically he is a mixture of Scotch, Armenian, and Jewish but is not religious. Born in Thailand (his father owned a large corporation there), he has five brothers and sisters and they were brought up primarily by servants. Sam as a young child had severe migraine headaches and many "flus and fevers" as he was growing up in Thailand, and he wanted more attention from his mother than he received. He was sent to a boarding school in that country and was very unhappy about being away from the family, especially his siblings, with whom he had close relationships: "We were very much together and we were always concerned about each other." By the time he was twelve, his father had become a heavy drinker, his business had suffered losses, and the family was deeply concerned and embarrassed.

When we become acquainted with Sam for the first time, he is earning his living as a lower-level bank manager (he has a high school education), occasionally supplementing his income by playing the saxophone. Music is his first and real love, and he still wishes he had become a professional musician. He did not marry until he was thirty-nine, a woman his own age, who had two children. She had an eighth-grade education and worked as a teller in another bank. At the first interview Sam's stepdaughter is pregnant; the father of the child is a convicted felon and in jail. The girl has broken the relationship but wants to keep the child when it is born. Upset and angry, Sam feels that putting it up for adoption would be the right solution, but he will let his wife work it out. Otherwise he enjoys his work, hopes to become a bank officer, and has recently been elected "marshal" in an Elks lodge. Sam has a warm and close relationship with his wife, and they are very supportive of one another, able to talk over anything that disturbs them. He has a temper that he knows distresses his wife, and he hopes to become more considerate.

Despite a heart attack serious enough to keep him hospitalized for one month and at home for two more, many aspects of Sam Meyer's life have improved by the second interview. Now a bank officer as he had hoped, he works longer hours but finds the job very rewarding financially and stimulating as well. His pregnant stepdaughter has now had her baby boy and, still not married, has moved to her own apartment. The stepson graduated from high school, works hard as a grocery clerk, and lives at home. Home is now a new house in a better and safer neighborhood.

By the third contact the stepson has decided to move to Burma, where he was born. The two are good friends, and Sam regrets the move. His stepdaughter had moved to Burma a year or two earlier and married there. Sam's marriage, good all along, is even better. "Quite happy" at the first interview, he now considers himself "very" happy, fortunate in reaching the goals he has worked toward with diligence. His self-concept has improved considerably, putting him on a par with the other three who attribute negative characteristics to themselves.

Two and a half years later Sam Meyer is angry about being passed over for a promotion and, as usual, blames himself; he thinks it was because he is too open about his feelings. The work is still challenging. Finding errors in accounts and discovering more creative ways of handling accounts by hunches and fitting together bits and pieces of information are satisfying, promotion or not. His health is good, but he checks many symptoms on a mental health list (the forty-two-item California Symptoms Checklist; Chiriboga and Pierce, 1981) that suggest depression. The fact that he has contemplated suicide does not accord with his feeling "pretty happy," frequent references to enjoying his job, and his excellent marriage. (She is the "driving force" of this life.) His stepson now lives in Bermuda, having married in Europe while training to be a gourmet chef. Sam is very proud of him. The stepdaughter has become a psychiatric counselor and will soon return to work in this country.

At the last encounter the stepdaughter and her family have returned and so has Sam's stepson. These developments are related to the interviewer before Sam reports that he has received his overdue promotion, suggesting that interpersonal relationships have a new, and higher, priority in his life. Later in the interview Sam says he thinks he has become more lenient and less volatile. Although he still reports several psychological symptoms, he is "very happy" and his wife gets most of the credit. He still greatly enjoys music, both playing and listening. Fewer negative traits are checked on the self-concept list, and he is now slightly more positive than the other three people in this group who do not think very well of themselves. Sam may be interpreting himself correctly in saying he would probably have been more successful if he had been diplomatic rather than outspoken.

Irma Clark has changed less than the other three negative people during the twelve years of study, and overall she is a bit more positive about herself than they. Forty-six at the beginning of the project, she has lived in her neighborhood since she was five months old. Her parents, Russian-Jewish immigrants, moved there from Canada in order to have her treated for polio. Her father was a shipping clerk and not well paid. Altogether she was hospitalized four times as a child, and each treatment lasted for six months. When we first meet her, she walks with a severe limp. (One might be tempted to conclude: "Aha! That's why her self-image is on the negative side.") She was raised in the Jewish tradition and is proud of her Russian background, but she does not consider herself religious. Like several other women in the empty nest group, she graduated from high school and went to business school for a year, finding a job as secretary before she married.

Off and on through the several years we talk with her, Irma expresses regret that she never went to music school. Her husband (also forty-six but not Jewish) did not finish high school, but he has a good position as a civilian foreman in the navy. They have a daughter who is married and has a daughter of her own; the other daughter is a high school senior. About ten years before the first interview, when she was in her mid-thirties, Irma had what she calls a "nervous breakdown" and was in psychotherapy for depression. She continues to take medication for depression throughout the study, but she nevertheless ranks quite high on mental health symptoms.

Paradoxically, all interviewers find Irma Clark to be a warm, friendly, and very outgoing person, a "Jewish mother" par excellence, and her house is always open. She is also one of the most socially concerned people in the middle-aged group, intelligent and well read. Irma has close relationships not only with family but with several friends. As for her husband, she says that for the first twenty years of the marriage they did not communicate well with each other, and it is still a problem.

By the second interview Irma's husband has had an aortic clot, is in pain, and tires easily. They continue to have frequent guests, and they have taken a few pleasure trips. Together they celebrated her parents' fiftieth anniversary, during which there were some family reconciliations. She continues to be optimistic, expecting her husband's health to improve and both daughters to be more settled. (They are currently taking care of a cheetah that belongs to one of them.) Most of all she wants to have more grandchildren. She rates herself as "pretty happy," even though her dislocated hip tires her more than it used to. She feels somewhat closer to her husband (his illness makes her feel needed), enjoys her handiwork hobbies, and has joined the Democratic National Committee and Mothers for Peace. Mr. Clark does not understand his wife's interest in world affairs and her liberal political stance. For Irma these views are simple and straightforward. As she tells her interviewer, "I agree with Joan Baez, and if you know her views you don't have to ask me anything else."

By the third interview, Mr. Clark has had three operations but recovered well. Irma is now concerned lest they get on each other's nerves after his retirement. Still politically active, she has more grandchildren and rates herself "happy with exuberance." Irma's life has become less exuberant by the fourth contact: her mother and father have died within a few months of each other, and her husband now has both diabetes and cancer. She cares for him at home, and, wanting to be near her, he is present at this interview. Irma lives from day to day, enjoying her new cat, her family, and their families, and is outraged about many political developments. She feels she has been fairly successful in life.

Her husband dies at home several months before the last interview, but Irma has had three happy years before that, feeling needed. She continues to enjoy her hobbies and looks forward to a trip with her daughter and son-in-law. On the negative side she often finds herself daydreaming about the past, her husband's death, and her own serious childhood illness. Her social life has deteriorated because most of her friends still live in the world of couplehood. She has fewer symptoms than at the prior contacts (though still many), and there is a slight improvement in her self-concept. One would like to know how things are going for Irma Clark a year or two later. Still in her fifties, she may well have bounced back. One explanation for her sustained negative self-image is that she is crippled. Through all the interviews she sometimes brooded about her early illness and about her appearance as well. She also feels her childhood illness and deformity altered her parents' feelings for her. From her own friends and family she mentions no negative comments.

Fifty-nine-year-old Jake Winters, a pre-retiree, does not have a strongly negative perspective on himself when we first meet him, but he has developed one by the third interview. He is a police officer and quite proud to be the first high school graduate in his family. His wife, also a high school graduate, is fifty-eight, and they have three children. Jake, who admires his father (owner of a liquor store) very much, patterns his own parenting to fit the way he was brought up. He sees himself as a stern disciplinarian: physical punishment was frequent when his children were younger, and communication was through the mother, as in his own childhood. He regrets that his children did not go to college and that none are yet married. His older son, thirty, works for the police department; Jake thinks he is too gullible. His older daughter is "serious" and the younger, who is seventeen, is a "mischief-maker"; so far, he muses, "they have stayed out of trouble." He admires his wife, and their conflicts, none of them major, revolve mainly around the children. He finds his job adventurous, is glad he does not have more responsibilities, and expects to retire at the same rank he first had, at which time he hopes to take a trip around the country. Aside from work, he spends time watching television, reading magazines, and puttering. Several of his co-workers are his "pals." In the past he had been active in church, American Legion, and PTA. His interviewer thinks him quite modest and very confident but a bit smug.

The most important thing in Jake Winters's life by the second interview is that "my son went to Hong Kong where he met a girl whom he recently married." The new wife already had a three-year-old son, "so now I am grandfather of a Chinaman." The ethnic trappings surrounding this new role seem to bother him. One of his daughters has also married. He finds himself becoming more "short-fused" and "things" bother him more now. Planning to retire in a few months, he has made no plans "except to wake up breathing every day." He rates himself as very happy, with no complaints.

The next interview finds Jake still working because he has received a substantial raise. He now has a granddaughter (not Chinese). Feeling closest to his wife, he also has a few men friends. Jake considers himself quite happy. The only new development that might account for his much more negative self-concept is that he has had surgery for a benign tumor and now suffers from hypertension. He worries more about inflation as he anticipates retirement.

Two years later a heart attack forces him to retire. He must now exercise more to lose weight, and he feels he has become even more short-tempered. At the last interview, he makes an about-face in self-view, now saying that his children and grandchildren have made him more responsible and tolerant. At this time Jake Winters rates himself as "pretty happy" on the Bradburn Morale Scale, but his self-concept ratings remain very negative. There seems little doubt this macho man's ego is deflated by his physical disabilities, which now include wearing a hearing aid.

The fourth person who rated herself very negatively on the self-concept list is Amelia Booth, and she sustains this poor self-image throughout the study. One of the few women in the sample who has had no children, fifty-four-year-old Amelia was born in Texas (her father was a pottery manufacturer); she is "American from way back," a churchgoing Presbyterian who went halfway through college. Her childhood was privileged and happy. She did not finish college because she did not like being away from home, calling herself a "homebody." Amelia's husband, whose education stopped after high school, is a successful businessman, and for the first part of their marriage he traveled a great deal. Both his and her parents live nearby. She is active in her church and a few lodges and enjoys keeping house and handiwork. She describes herself and her life-style as "Victorian" and speaks warmly of her husband, adding that they are selfish because they have no children. Her friends are women who share her interests.

By the second interview the Booths are both anticipating retirement, which they expect within the next fifteen months, with both excitement and some trepidation. She reports that the most important thing that has happened since the first interview is that she and her husband have both kept their health. Essentially there has been little change and everything is going smoothly. One problem, she reports, is that her mother is still alive and living with them: as long as her mother continues to live, Amelia thinks that her own life will be somewhat restricted. Amelia also finds that she tires a bit more easily now than before; she rates the present year

relatively low on the Life Evaluation Chart, primarily because of
her mother.

The Booths are retired by the third interview. Amelia's
mother continues to live with the couple and Amelia continues to
feel that her life is not her own. In this interview and the next one
we find essentially the same story: the mother is living and thriving;
Amelia is growing more and more discontented. She reports feeling
hassled about dealing with her mother "fairly often" at the third
and fourth interviews, feels that she does not have the time to visit
and be visited by friends, rarely has the time to lose herself in anything she finds enjoyable, and generally lacks the time and energy
to enjoy life. The interviewer at the third contact reports that Amelia at some fundamental level still expects to be "taken care of" by
her mother and resents the need for her to provide care. The interviewer's terse synopsis of the case: "A spoiled brat grows old."

By the fifth interview, her mother has finally died. But now
Amelia is beginning to experience health problems herself, and she
views these as a barrier to the things she would enjoy doing if she
were able. For the first time she lists several complaints about her
husband as well, seeing him as another source of her woes: his
health has declined even more than her own and she has to do more
things for him now than ever before.

A distinctive feature in the lives of these four negatively rated
selves is the strong influence of the past. Jake Winters's parents were
cold and distant; they relied heavily on physical punishment to keep
the children in line. Amelia Booth's life is notable for its downward
mobility, not limited to social status. Her parents were not only
upper middle class but overly indulgent, and their household included many servants who catered to the children's desires. Despite
his six brothers and sisters, Sam Meyer felt lonely as a child because
he rarely saw his highly social mother. Irma Clark, although not
downwardly mobile, throughout her life felt that her parents' attitudes toward her were strongly and negatively influenced by her
serious illness and its consequent deformity. In Chapter Six we
explore the effects of childhood deprivation on adaptation in adult
life.

The Four

The people we follow through the book help to clarify the relationship between their self-descriptions on the Adjective Rating List and their degree of self-concern (or narcissism)—the basis for their selection as central figures in this book. Olav Olavsen, the happy and creative machinist, is not overly concerned with himself in any of the five interviews we have with him; he consistently, though modestly, rates himself positively on the adjective list. Strong religious beliefs and a sense of personal creativity are powerful inner resources that carry him through very difficult times, including the death of his dearly loved wife. By contrast, Max Schindler's self-ratings depict an arrogant and conceited person, macho and materialistic. At first he circles no negative attributes to describe himself. At the third meeting he is still rating himself as highly self-assured. But at the last contact he acknowledges some uncertainty and says he feels more concerned about the well-being of his family and his relations with them. Having recently undergone a coronary bypass, he may well be experiencing intimations of mortality, but he has also developed an extremely satisfying retirement life.

The two women present vivid contrasts as well. Hazel Sutter, a long-divorced, hardworking cafeteria manager, changes from being self-concerned and diffuse about her identity to being practically outgoing in her self-ratings. At first she considers herself dull and cannot decide whether certain adjectives are like or unlike her. By the third encounter she is both more specific and more positive— almost certainly because there is now a man in her life, a neighbor (and widower) she is seeing quite often. At the last session her opinion of herself is exuberantly positive and she announces that she is very much in love.

Adelaide Stone is a young pre-retiree, fifty-two at the outset, a secretary who expects to work another fifteen years. Widowed with two children when in her late thirties, she has remarried a widower with adult children of his own. Despite many past and present misfortunes, she ranks consistently low on preoccupation with herself. At first she is both positive and realistic in filling out the

Adjective Rating List, but by the second interview she has learned of her son's drug addiction and by the fourth she herself has had a severe stroke. She has also divorced her husband during this interval, calling it a major turning point: "The stroke changed me for the better and the divorce changed a poor marriage into a good friendship." She is still not preoccupied with herself, but her rated self is not as cheerful and optimistic as it used to be.

In her optimism and high spirits, Adelaide resembles Olav Olavsen. Hazel Sutter's self-ratings improve after a series of positive experiences, and Max Schindler becomes more tolerant as he undergoes some of the inevitable insults of aging. All four of these cases seem to hold a positive view of themselves or to move in that direction as time goes by, regardless of how they differ in self-concerns.

Summing Up

To gain a broad perspective on changes in the self, we asked high school seniors at the last interview (now averaging twenty-eight years) and the parent generation (now averaging sixty-one) how they have changed during the past ten years or so. Unlike the change assessed by means of a structured instrument, a considerable majority in both groups feel they have become better people: more patient, tolerant, and mature. Both young and old generally add a few negative observations, the older group reporting physical changes, the younger hoping to improve in one or another aspect of their lives. Sam Meyer, for example, says he has become more lenient and liberal. "I used to be a stickler for details . . . but now I can see it's not that important. And of course some physical changes: I've lost my teeth, and I see more wrinkles now." High school senior Alvin Locke thinks more about the future and what he will be doing twenty years from now and also sees "a need to get into some kind of situation, either emotional or financial, that will be interesting as well as rewarding. I see a need for further challenge in my life." A few people in all groups say they have not changed, and about as many have mixed feelings: they have in some respects improved and in others deteriorated.

None of the young people feel they have changed for the

worse, and only three of the older group think they have deteriorated. All of the latter three are women, and they have what appear
to be sound reasons for reporting a change for the worse. Daphne
Randall, one of the more exotic people in the sample, grew up in
a well-educated and quite prosperous family in Berlin. Because of
their Jewish blood, with the advent of the fascist regime the family
emigrated to Columbia, which they all disliked. Her father soon
died. Friends visiting from the United States persuaded them to
move here, and the man Daphne soon married came with them.
Their only child, a son, proved to be epileptic, her husband was
unable to find work, and she is the family wage-earner during the
years of the study. She nevertheless manages to pursue her many
cultural and political (liberal) interests. By the fourth interview,
Daphne is widowed, retired, and living alone. These losses do not
lead to further problems. On the contrary, freed at last of all the
social constraints she has felt in her life, Daphne is exuberantly
enjoying cultural events, college extension courses, and political
activities. By the last interview she has terminal cancer, still lives at
home, and is pleased to report she now has a grandchild. In answer
to the ten-year change question she says: "Well, not much until I
got sick . . . now look at me, I'm a complete wreck. I have no
hope." After this brief observation she is unable to answer further
questions. She dies within the year.

Alice Rand is accustomed to changes for the worse. When
first we meet, her executive husband is in a coma and remains so
for over three years before dying. Alice has four sons. She rises to
the occasion by taking courses in fashion design. She enjoys the
work and eventually owns her own business. At the last interview
she is working full time as a fashion coordinator but is in a traumatized state, having been mugged and badly injured a year or so
earlier. She still suffers from vertigo. "I'm now just surviving. Everything goes back to that awful night when I was mugged. It
colored everything. If I had been my old self you would have found
me in my own apartment." (She now shares a house with another
woman.) "It's amazing how one event can change your life
completely."

Norma Neuman is married and has four children. The initial
interviewer observes that she seems somewhat self-deprecating

about the triviality of her existence. She plays the roles of wife and mother, but what she enjoys most is socializing and playing card games with her women friends. Widowed shortly before the second contact, she now has diabetes but controls it with medication. She complains of loss of memory and losing things, but tries hard to sustain some social life. Her main complaints at the last interview (she is now sixty-nine) suggest that senility may be involved: her memory is much worse than before and she has even more trouble searching for lost objects. She does not hear or see well either.

All three of these women, the only ones who unequivocally say they have changed for the worse, experienced sudden or gradual traumas of considerable severity. One can only be surprised, especially among people of late middle age and older, that there were so few who reported serious problems, physical, psychological, or situational, over the past ten years. Overall, however, the results discussed in this chapter suggest that it is not self-concept alone, not environmental context alone, and not progression along the life course alone that makes for stability and change in self-ratings. Rather, it is the self in transaction with life's circumstances and the personal and historical moment. In the following chapter, we continue reporting on dimensions of selfhood but will consider qualities that emerge only in spontaneous, free-flowing statements.

3

Further Explorations
of the Self:
Subjective Descriptions

In the last chapter we reviewed evidence for stability and change in self-concept as measured by ratings on seventy adjectives. As well, we examined the lives of several participants in an attempt to discover not only the reasons for change but also why some people have more positive views of themselves than others. Here we take a different perspective on the self. At the third interview, five years into the study, we introduced a less structured way for people to tell us what they are like. Using the Twenty Statements Test (Kuhn and McPartland, 1954), respondents were asked to identify themselves in up to twenty different ways and to do so quickly, as though they were talking to themselves.

The statements were initially separated into sixty distinct categories, but for the sake of simplicity these sixty can be merged into nine comprehensive groups:

- Biosocial givens (male, brown eyes, gray hair, American)
- Roles and membership (worker, housewife)
- Abstract (a person, a human being)
- Ideological (a Republican, a Methodist)
- Interests and activities (skier, sailor)
- Physical self (healthy, strong, deaf)
- Sense of self (outgoing, happy-go-lucky)

- Interpersonal characteristics (sensitive, aggressive)
- Personal characteristics (mood states, thinking states)

In the first section of the chapter we compare men and women and young and old in terms of their spontaneity, here defined in terms of the number of statements made. (The number ranged from one to twenty.) Vignettes of representative individuals illustrate conditions of constriction and expansion, the extremes of the spontaneity continuum. The next section is devoted to the surprisingly few people who made three or more negative statements as they recorded who they are, followed by a discussion of unusual people who reflect existential characteristics or whose self-concepts border on either the erratic or the bizarre. We next describe categories favored by each of the eight groups of younger and older men and women, and present vignettes of people who represent them. The chapter concludes with a discussion of The Four as well as four "alternates" whose personal stories expand on the basic themes that emerge in this chapter.

Overall, the intent is to flesh out our understanding of people's self-image and to examine the utility of this image in understanding people's lives. As well, we wish to explore the commonly held assumption that young people today have a vaguer image of themselves than does their parents' generation.

Constriction Versus Expansion: The Extremes of Spontaneity

One way to classify the information obtained from an instrument such as the Twenty Statements Test is simply to count the number of statements that are made. We found great variation in the number of responses, and this variation seemed to depend on the individual's makeup, by and large, rather than simply representing chance difference.

In general, men made fewer statements about themselves than did women. About twice as many males as females made five statements or fewer. Aside from people who refused to take the "test" for a variety of reasons, there were three men and two women who made only one or two statements. High school senior Tammy Middleton, now about twenty-three as we interview her in the third contact, describes herself only as "woman." The interviewer notes that, though cooperative, she has trouble comprehending most of the questions in this round and seems very anxious.

Art Cassidy, in the young adult group and now twenty-nine years old, has just had a second son. Never able to hold a job for more than six months, he has had several suicidal depressions. Art's homosexual and heterosexual desires compete for attention; he blames his father for the fact that he first had intercourse when he was eleven years old. (It is not clear whether it was incest.) Given the ambiguities of his life, it is not surprising that his one statement is that he is "a person."

Alice Rand, a member of the second oldest group, we know from Chapter Two; she is the woman whose husband was in a coma for several years. He is still being kept alive at the third interview, and she has become a workaholic, spending fourteen hours a day, seven days a week, on her now successful clothing store. She is now fifty and her four sons are working or away at college. Alice makes only one statement: "I don't know." Perhaps she does not have the time to find out.

One of the two constricted members of the oldest group of men, Mario Puccini, now sixty-seven, makes only two self-observations—"I am happy" and "I am satisfied"—even though he has many interests. A former printer, he is thoroughly enjoying retirement. His marriage is excellent and their only child, a college graduate, is temporarily living in Europe. That he misses him very much is his only negative feeling. His main satisfactions come from listening to classical music at the opera or symphony and serious reading. A friendly, outgoing man who enjoys the interviews, he is reticent about describing himself. In addition to being brought up not to brag or talk about himself, his life is oriented to the outside world and he is not very introspective.

The second pre-retiree, Ellis Wolf, is easier to understand. Now sixty-three, he is an insurance broker living with his fifth wife and pleased to report that he pays no alimony to the others. His rated self is very negative; his interviewers find him crabby, rude, and taciturn. His two self-statements are in keeping: "I don't know" and "I don't care."

Altogether, three of these five who appear constricted in describing themselves are also psychologically distressed: Tammy is very anxious, Art has suicidal depressions, and Ellis (in another context) anxiously anticipates senility. Alice finds effective sublimation in her work while Mario may simply be too bashful or modest to describe himself at length.

People making three to nine statements we labeled as moderately constrained. Forty participants fall into this group, and they include representatives of all stages of life. Pre-retirees account for about a third; the rest are quite evenly distributed except for newlywed women, of whom there are only two. The self-lists for this group suggest that their self-descriptions do not in fact differ in kind from the extensive lists made by other participants, and we conclude that they are merely somewhat more parsimonious.

Another way of considering the expansiveness/constriction continuum is simply to combine the data from all groups and look at the distributions. When this is done, we find that well over half the sample are on the expansive side, making at least eighteen statements. Among the four younger groups the range is from over half (newlywed males) to nearly three-quarters (high school women). The older people are less generous about describing themselves: the proportion listing eighteen or more ranges from two-fifths (pre-retirement men) to well over half among the empty nest men. A bit more than half of the women in these two groups list at least eighteen. Overall, the women are more expansive than the men at all stages of life.

Negative Self-Views

In contrast to the relative abundance of negative ratings on our Adjective Rating List, only half or so of the participants taking the Twenty Statements Test listed self-derogatory characteristics. This discrepancy supports the conclusions of investigators like Stephen Spitzer (1969) that the test, which involves people offering their own comments, has little in common with the more structured approaches. The point is that structured tests may not include the most personally salient adjectives; people only rate themselves from a limited sampling of potential descriptions of the self. Hence key descriptors may be omitted, and those that are endorsed may be only marginally relevant.

Looking at the sample as a whole, we find the men are less self-derogatory than the women in all subgroups except the second oldest stage. In the oldest group, both men and women outdid younger people in listing positive things about themselves: among the oldest group of men, for example, only two made self-derogatory observations. To illustrate the nature of their negative statements, we have selected four younger and four older participants, one man and one woman in each of the four life stages, whose lists include three or more negative appraisals of themselves. The range is from three to ten. They are quoted verbatim here and then examined in the context of each person's entire list—for obviously a person who lists four unpleasant characteristics and only a few others may differ from one who writes four negative statements but adds sixteen positive statements as well. Life circumstances that help to explain their self-views round out the vignettes.

The Younger. Former high school senior Buddy Peterson, now about twenty-three, records six negative statements: "frustrated," "not motivated enough," "disrespectable," "lazy at times," "greedy," and "lustful at times." Neutral self-observations include "looking for something definite," "could accomplish a lot," "concerned with myself," "concerned with what others think of me," and "sensitive." On the positive side, Buddy reports himself "thoughtful," "aware of others' feelings," "enjoys seeing life develop" (presumably his), and a few interests. The interviewer at the first contact notes that Buddy's rated self is quite negative; he seems young for his age but is generally likable in a mild and quiet way. By the second interview he is going part time to a community college and also working. He feels that the experience has "opened his mind" to problems relating to him and the rest of the world. He has made some friends at school and wants to "develop better traits" (unspecified).

While Buddy at first has no particular interest in girls, during the second interview he says he is not as moralistic as he used to be. (His parents are devout Lutherans and he was brought up quite strictly.) Two years later, at the time he is taking the test, Buddy is enrolled in an excellent out-of-town college. The most important event for him over the past few years is "just growing up." He now has a steady girlfriend and looks forward to getting an "outdoor job" after he graduates. He has forgotten that he had an appointment with the interviewer, and she finds him "flat," disinterested, and possibly on drugs. The consensus of interviewers at later contacts, as well as the male interviewer's impression at contacts one and two, is that Buddy is rather understated and shy, especially around women.

When we first meet high school senior Linda Norton, she feels closest to her boyfriend, who is "like a father to me." Her own father, a real estate broker, may at some time have been mentally ill, and she feels ambivalent toward him. She is close to her younger sister, but a former girlfriend's mother is her best friend. At this encounter the interviewer notes that Linda has ups and downs in mood; she is "remote" and possibly borderline schizophrenic. By the first follow-up Linda is unhappy about the boyfriend (with whom she now has problems), her boring job, and not being able to go to art school. She checks nearly all the items on the forty-two-item California Symptoms Inventory as applying to her. Two years later, at the third interview, Linda has married the boyfriend she has been dating throughout the study, partly because her mother wanted her to. At the time of the test, Linda has a routine job but hopes to get a better one. She is going to art school and also attends a Gestalt institute. She feels she has changed from dependent to independent, has better relationships with family and friends, and thinks she is finding out who she is.

On the Twenty Statements Test, half of Linda Norton's twenty statements are negative. She writes that she is "unrealistic," "hasty at making judgments," "cruel to those I feel superior to," "scatterbrained," "always late," "not objective," "sometimes hypochondriac," "childish" (she is twenty-three), "selfish," "and lazy." On the other hand, Linda also lists "romantic," "creative," "a dreamer," "kind to underdogs," "hopeful," "generous," and "adventuresome." She contradicts herself more than once, being both cruel and kind, generous and selfish, adventurous and lazy. One suspects that if her statements had been made during the first or second interview, there would have been even more negative ones.

Karl Koster is a twenty-nine-year-old newlywed at our first

encounter. He is a field surveyor and student living on unemployment insurance. His wife, who has a master's degree, is a physical therapist. Karl is a very intelligent person whom the first interviewer finds overly modest in his rated self and seeming to have "identity problems." By the second session he has his B.A. and is working on an M.A. He is ambivalent about his life at this time, finding it difficult to go to school, work, and keep up with his music, which he loves. (He sounds like a young Sam Meyers at times.) There is conflict in his marriage, too, because his wife wants to move out of state and he loves California. Karl has detached himself from some friends, met new ones, and still feels close to his parents. (His father is an advertising executive.)

By the third interview Karl has his advanced degree, is involved in music, and is "tuned in to psychic trips" and "the self-realization trip." Now doing odd jobs, he will soon teach. He has an alcohol problem but is getting help and considers it solved. He and his wife have separated; she now lives in another state, but he still feels close to her. Karl reports five negative characteristics: "unpredictable," "full of 'S' a lot of the time," "make snap judgments sometimes," "compromiser in a lot of situations," and "poor speller." He also calls himself an "old soul," "a musician," "a sculptor," and "teacher." He is "strong," "emotional," a "lover," "sometimes funny," and "religious," suggesting a rather well-rounded person.

Karl's female counterpart in the newlywed group is Connie Sherman, though her negative statements about herself are much milder than his. Her father is a farmer living in the southern part of the state, where she was brought up and where she belonged to 4-H clubs and the like. Both she and her husband are computer operators, and both have B.A. degrees, hers from a religious college. She is a devout member of the Baptist church. By the second interview the Shermans have bought a house in a new community and Connie enjoys creating a garden. She gets along better with her husband and does not feel as moody as she used to. They plan to have two children, and when they do she will no longer work. She is involved in more church groups than she used to be. By the third encounter the Sherman's first child has been born and Connie is indeed staying home. "I observe myself as mother and wife, instead of career woman and wife." She feels that she is not as good a wife as she hoped to be. On weekends they work on the house; her favorite activity is collecting antiques for it, a pursuit in which her husband joins her. This seems to be an excellent marriage; why she considers herself a poor wife is left unclear, but hints crop up in her free-spoken descriptions of self.

Connie is about thirty at the time of the Twenty Statements Test. Her four negative statements are mild but do suggest a self-image of someone who cannot be relied on: "not very energetic," "poor housekeeper," "slightly lazy," and "full of good intentions which aren't done." Neutral self-observations include "young mother" followed by "older than I think I am." She is "child-oriented," "educated," and a "middle-of-the-roader." Positive statements include "intelligent," "nice looking," "lucky," "fairly creative," "talented," and "patient."

In retrospect, all four of these self-negative young people are reasonably well educated, ranging from Karl, who has an advanced degree, to Linda, who went to college for two years. Three may have psychological problems: Linda checked most of the forty-two items on the symptoms list; Karl has had alcohol problems and reports "psychic trips" with drugs; Buddy may have at least experimented with them too. At the time of the last encounter, however, all four are doing well. Buddy has a steady job, is "more realistic," and thinks he is a much better judge of people than he used to be, presumably himself included. Linda likes herself better, is more self-confident and insightful, and reports that she now is a mature and happy person. Karl feels more "responsible" and "real." Like Linda, Connie is now sure of herself and also feels much more creative. In sum, as they have grown up, all have become more positive about themselves.

The Older. Turning to the older groups, we find that empty nest men are more laconic than younger ones and not so negative about themselves. Empty nester John Farrell is something of an exception. John is a police officer who admits that he loves violence. He has a high school education, as does his wife, a part-time secretary. The Farrells have three children, and they are all devout Baptists. Shortly before the second interview, John's wife had surgery for a

serious vascular problem and his younger son was fired because of
an arrest for speeding and driving under the influence of alcohol.

By the third session, John has received an award for being the
most friendly and helpful police officer in the force. His father-in-
law has given them twenty thousand dollars, and they give part of
it to John's oldest son, also a policeman, to help him buy a house.
John, now fifty-three, sometimes regrets that he did not study more
and move up in the ranks. On the other hand, the notion of relative
deprivation may be operative for him. By the time he was five his
father had become an alcoholic; his parents separated off and on;
he and his siblings were shunted around to live with various relatives. By comparison, his own family circumstances are excellent.
When his children were growing up he was an active and involved
father. All is not perfect, of course. For example, politically very
conservative, he is upset about the hiring of people in minority
groups, especially as policemen.

At this third interview John provides a full twenty statements
about himself, of which six are negative, some contradictory. He
says he is "sometimes cruel," for example, but on the other hand
is "kind," "considerate," and "protective of others." He reports
himself as "not very intelligent," has "a sharp tongue," is "preju-
diced at times," "resentful," and "a little conceited." In general he
is satisfied with his life, and the negative statements he lists seem
to reflect "honesty," his third statement in the list.

Mira Levitz is facing the empty nest stage when we first meet
her. Married to a bank manager with a B.A. degree in business
administration (she herself has had three years of college), Mira was
born in the Philippines; when she was about twelve her mother died
and her father sent her to a boarding school in a nearby city. She
is described as very intelligent, concerned about social issues, and
overly modest. Her husband is a difficult man, and she frequently
feels obliged to smooth relationships between him and their three
daughters. In that context she is described as an "appeaser" by her
interviewer. Mira has even stopped seeing some of her friends because he does not like them. She feels closest to her daughters, a few
friends, and her aunt, whom she dearly loves. Her husband is last
on the list. Her job, which she has done at home for many years,
is taking care of a few preschool children while their parents work,

and she loves it: "I think no one can be unhappy taking care of little children because they are a source of inspiration." Her principal anxiety is her complicated and moody husband.

By the time of the test, Mira is almost sixty. She rates the year quite low because of problems with her husband and her deep concern about world affairs, especially extreme nationalism because it dashes hopes for world unity. Mira records herself as "a procrastinator," "poor organizer," "somewhat meek," "an appeaser," "lazy," and "unimaginative." Several of her statements are of what we call the biosocial given type, such as "American," "Jewish," and "housewife." Roles include "mother," "wife," "grandmother," and "substitute mother." She "loves justice, nature, music, and art." The one personality characteristic she lists is "understanding." We agree with a comment made by her interviewer at this contact: Mira is a complex and interesting woman.

Jake Winters is a police officer we know from Chapter Two because he is one of the people whose rated self, while quite positive at the first contact, has become very negative by later ones. At the third contact, when he takes the Twenty Statements Test, Jake has some physical ailments and is worried about money as he approaches retirement. In contrast to several people who make negative statements, Jake reports himself as "very happy" when filling out the Bradburn Morale Scale—perhaps because he feels he is not a worrier. He lists three negative statements: the first one is "I am over the hill physically"; his second statement is "slightly overweight"; and the fifth is "sometimes stubborn." The remaining seventeen primarily involve interests and activities. He is "happily married," "handy with his hands," "not a worrier," and "had a satisfying life." Overall, the fact that he provides more negative statements than usual supports the findings from the Adjective Rating List, but the wealth of other material emphasizes that negativity is not characteristic of his self-view.

Retirement-stage participant Kate Armstrong is married and has four children, all boys, the youngest of whom is adopted. Kate has a high school education, and her husband, a college graduate, is a customs official. At the first session she is active in several church groups (Episcopalian) and the PTA and is also taking courses. By the second interview three of her four sons are married and one of them has two children. (The adopted son is still in school.) The sons, all college graduates, have recently set up a contracting firm in Oregon and hope their father will work with them summers to help supplement his retirement income. Kate is very happy at this time, feels close to her husband, and hopes to see the adopted son through college.

By the third interview there have been many changes in Kate's life. Her husband has retired and she herself is about to stop working as a nursery school teacher because she now suffers from asthma. The Armstrongs have sold their house and moved to Arizona (good for her ailment). They have spent three summers in Oregon and both enjoyed being with their sons. She feels less rushed and has more time to think, read, walk, swim, and attend study groups, though she does miss the children in nursery school and would like to teach again. (She is still only fifty, young for the retirement group.)

Kate's self-descriptive responses include five that are negative, and all of them fall toward the end of her list: "I am a procrastinator," "I talk too much," "I do too much mothering," "I don't do what I should do many times," and "I am not good in groups of women in a strictly social scene." Her positive attributes include being a "good worker with preschoolers" and a "good housekeeper, cook, and seamstress." Her twentieth statement is "I am O.K." Clearly Kate's self-image is not preponderantly negative, and those aspects that she reports do not in fact appear unduly self-derogatory. Perhaps this is because, as Kate reports in other parts of the third interview, she is very happy and gratified with life.

In summary, then, only one of these four older people who describe themselves in negative terms has more than a high school education; the exception is Mira Levitz, who went to college for three years. At our last contact, except for Kate Armstrong, whose negative self-views are mild, regrets are common. Ex-policeman John Farrell, now a widower, drinks too much, repeating his father's alcoholism; he is sorry he did not take courses and move up in the ranks. One of Mira Levitz's daughters has committed suicide, and Mira blames herself for the tragedy because she spends all her time taking care of her dying aunt. She has convinced herself that spending more time with her daughter would have prevented her death. Former police officer Jake Winters's rated self continues to be negative at our last interview, yet he seems on the whole to be fairly content. The explanation may be found in something he says toward the end of the final interview: "I had a very satisfying life." Now well over seventy, he can forget about his self-image and the difficult times at the station and reminisce about the good old days. And, finally, Kate Armstrong ages gracefully and realistically. Aware that she is slowing down, she says she has learned to be more "self-accepting."

Unusual People

Of special interest are two smaller groups whose statements are quite unlike those of their peers. A few seem confused and conflicted about themselves; the others may be called existential because they seem to be struggling with issues of who and why they are.

The Confused and Conflicted. Only six people made contradictory or confused statements about themselves; all are young and five were men. The woman, Pam Asarian, is in the youngest group and about twenty-three by the time of the third interview. Many of her statements are excessively positive; some are unrealistic. Her seventeenth is "sometimes I am a machine" and the nineteenth is "sometimes I want the whole world to be like me." Such statements are suggestive of inner conflict. Not surprisingly, Pam also scores high on multiple dimensions of dysfunction obtained from the forty-two-item California Symptoms Checklist (Lowenthal, Thurnher, Chiriboga, and Associates, 1975).

Interestingly, all five men in this group are newlyweds. Kim Gustavsen says, "I am Kim and Jane [his wife] or Jane and Kim and I am we." His four other statements include "things to do" and "independence." Tom Finn's fifth and last statement is "confusing who with what leaves my imagination where it usually is, blank." The four others are a "good fireman," "poor husband," "hard worker," and "hardheaded." Derek Mansfield first identifies himself as "someone who does not like this type of question" and his last statement is "enophile," probably meaning that he is very fond of wine. His few other statements are of the identification card variety.

Nate Martin simply writes "I don't know, I am me, whoever that is?" He wrote the statements at home because he was too tired to take the test during the interview. Gregg Marshall differs from the others in this group in that he completes his list. His first two statements are "who knows" and "who cares," another is "frustrated," and the twentieth is "a person who has finished this test." In between he declares some interests and activities.

While it is impossible to generalize about these six people because they are eccentric in different ways, their interviews convey an impression of people who are still very unsure about who they are or what they are becoming.

The Younger Existentialists. While the people we label as confused and conflicted are struggling with basic issues of who they are, other responses to the Twenty Statements Tests indicate a more accepting but still existential concern with identity. These existential statements express the idea that a person's essence is shaped by the life he or she leads; typically they include a few beliefs and a wide variety of states of being. Again it is the young who predominate. No one in the empty nest group appears, but three pre-retirees do, possibly because they, like the younger people, are struggling with questions of identity now that they have entered the retirement years. Altogether there are ten people: five men and five women.

High school senior Bonnie Osborne became engaged shortly before the third interview and is now living with her husband-to-be. She was recently fired as a secretary and says she would like to go back to school, though she is not at all sure what she wants to study. Living a disorganized life, at this time she is "not too happy" about herself. Her list of existential statements is one of the longest in the group. Here are a few examples: "I am things around me," "I am people I love," "I am my home," " a reflection of my childhood," "I am what I say and feel," and "I am contemplative of myself."

When we first meet her as a high school senior, Jeannie Reyes is keeping house for her mother and stepfather, both of whom work. Her mother is a secretary; he drives a cab. She herself works in a pub at night. Jeannie's existential statements include "I am happiness," "I want only truth out of life," "I am life," "I am death," and "I am nobody." At the time of the test she is married and a few months pregnant; she has been promoted but is not sure she wants more responsibility. In summing up her life at that third contact, she says, "I'm concerned with my life and that's about it," a conclusion that accords with her vague statements about herself.

When we first meet Carol Larson she is loquacious and many of her answers are tangential to the questions asked. Her relationships with family and friends are never made clear, no matter how many questions are asked. The interviewer comments that she did not consider the questions seriously, giggled throughout, and seemed vapid. By the second interview she is neither working nor going to school. At the time of the test, however, she is attending a community college secretarial program and works as a part-time secretary. She lives at home and has a boyfriend but is not contemplating marriage. On the test Carol lists herself as "a child of the universe," "one who needs," "one who gives." She is also "friend," "lover," "animal lover," "lucky child" (she is twenty-three), "loved child," and "poor thinker." This is all she writes, and it does seem to match the impression of several interviewers that Carol has a rather misty view of herself as a flower child philosopher.

No high school senior men list existential statements. Newlywed Barry Chambers, however, writes several. At the first contact, Barry is a college graduate and works as a school psychologist; his wife, who also has a degree, is a nurse. His father is an army officer and his parents were divorced when he was two. Devoted to his wife, who is Jewish, he joined her synagogue shortly after their marriage last year. By the second session they have bought a house and have a son. At the time of the test Barry's wife is pregnant again; he rates the year very high because of that. Barry enjoys making furniture, serious reading, and surfing. Among his self-descriptions are "I am a living, breathing soul," "I am Me with an exclamation point," "I am some dirt and some more," "I am what I am," "the air," "the wind," "a tiny molecule," "the littlest particle in the universe," "I am a Longhair," "weirdo," "whoever I want to be," "the understander," and "the understood."

Allen Petri is a college senior when we first meet. During this first interview he tells us that he used to be quite hedonistic but self-actualization is now his main goal. And, in fact, his interviewer

comments on Allen's "strong existential orientation." By the second
contact he has his degree and works as a drug abuse counselor—
whether this explains why he sometimes gets depressed is not clear.
He and his wife, an executive secretary, have bought a house near
a beach, and they walk there regularly. He works three days and two
nights, feels run down at this point, and has developed high blood
pressure. By the time of the test, Allen's wife has had major surgery,
but is recovering well, and they have had their first child. Allen is
now the probation officer he has long aspired to be, but he rates the
current year lower than others because he is not sure what direction
he wants to take in his career. Still interested in social problems, he
now worries most about "the population explosion" and world
hunger. Like Barry Chambers, he seems quite mature. His statements include "a mere mortal," "a groping individual," "a child
of the universal," "an illrational man," "a worrisome individual."
His other statements are the usual self-identifications.

Newlywed Hank Laird has had one year of graduate school.
Hank's wife, a college senior, teaches art. During the first interview
Hank tells us that he is waiting for a revelation to tell him what
his life's work should be. Like his wife, he too has training in art,
but his teacher has told him he is not good enough to teach. Hank
is very religious and active in a Catholic church where he sings in
the choir. Politically liberal, he belongs to many organizations and
is concerned about the moral and possibly physical destruction of
his country. In fact, nightmares about guns and violence disturb his
sleep. We do not learn much about his relationship with his family
of origin, but Hank's father is an army major, which may explain
Hank's nightmares.

By the second interview Hank reports that his relationship
with God has changed, but he does not elaborate. In any event he
is now a fire fighter. His wife has her advanced degree in art and
teaches. Hank hopes he will soon receive directions from God about
what his life's work should be. His main goal at this time is to
"please God." Shortly before the third interview there have been
some problems in his marriage, now smoothed out. At this time
Hank feels more settled and reports tremendous inner growth: "It's
the Lord's preparation for something." He works part time at the

postal service, goes to church three or four times a week, and also attends meetings of several church groups.

In this time of preparation and indecision, Hank describes himself as "an immortal soul," "a human—homo sapiens," and "a living organism." His other three statements are "male," "person with potential," and "husband"; fourteen spaces are blank. Since he does not yet know what he is going to do with his life, one can readily understand his fourteen blank spaces as well as the generalized descriptions.

Newlywed Sarah Levine had a very unhappy childhood. Her parents divorced when she was six (she says her mother was a prostitute and stripper), and she lived in many foster homes before moving in with an aunt and uncle. She went to an excellent college for two years but then had what she describes as a "schizophrenic" breakdown after her roommate was murdered. Sarah's husband is a graduate student and the two are having a lot of arguments about everything. She also worries a lot about her mental health and generally despairs at ever pulling things together.

By the time of the third interview, Sarah has just returned from living in Pakistan for several months, where she was converted to Bahai (an Oriental mystical religion). She and her husband have moved to Boston. Sarah has lost her despair, understands psychic phenomena, and does not think she is mentally ill anymore. She gets along better with her husband, now a special education teacher. She is not working but is doing some writing. Her greatest satisfactions are her marriage and Bahai; her main goal is to be a Bahai apostle. At this time her statements reflect her spirituality, her desire to grow, and a sense of oneness with the universe. They include: "a souie-rational [sic]," "a heart desiring to be kind, pure, and radiant," "a mind seeking to grow," "a spirit of discovery—the human spirit," "a wing on the bird of humanity," "a woman wing," "a servant of God and humanity," "fragile and struggling," "a member of a diverse family of man," "a coexister of a universe of other beings on other planets," "a coexister of the physical world," "a coexister of the spiritual world," "a person who strives to improve humanity." Sarah now feels less critical of others and more self-sacrificing, and her major concerns are discord and prejudice.

One can guess that the assurances of her new religion will help to allay any further breakdowns.

By the time of our last encounter with them, three of these young people have experienced some kind of conversion. Carol Larson becomes a "born again Christian" and is active in several church groups. Hank Laird, now thirty-four, has had an "intense religious experience" and is even more involved in his church groups. Though he now has a graduate degree, he still works at the post office. His marriage has improved because he is more "open." The Lairds have no children; Hank still feels he is in a transitional state waiting for God to tell him what to do with the rest of his life. Sarah Levine refuses the last interview, but at the next to last contact she reports that a highlight of her life was attending a Bahai national convention followed by Bahai summer school. She has separated from her husband, feels more self-confident, and has made new friends, and her "musical and writing abilities have unfolded." All three have acquired much-needed structure in their lives.

Bonnie Osborne is now happily married; she works as a bookkeeper in a doctor's office and looks forward to having children. Jeannie Reyes has a child. Both women feel very confident. Barry Chambers has two sons now; he has inherited money and despite his teaching credential is a commercial salesman. The Chamberses now own a large house and also two acres of land in the Tahoe ski area, where they plan to have a large cottage built. Barry's major social concern is "man's inhumanity to man." Allen Petri has a second son and has bought a house, having been promoted to Probation Officer III. He has separated from his wife twice and had affairs with other women, but he now feels guilty and hopes to save his marriage. By and large, most of these young people are at least trying to take charge of their lives.

The Older Existentialists. Of those we have categorized as being more or less existential in their self-images, the three older members of our study do not express the existential struggle for identity we see in the younger participants. Rather, their concern is with the search for meaning. Take Chester Bond, for example. Chester, in the retirement group, is not typical of people in the neighborhood we chose to study. He has an advanced degree from Duke University and before that went to elitist boarding schools. His father was a physician, and at the first interview one of his daughters recently graduated from Tufts University magna cum laude. He works as an electronics engineer. At the time of the test, Chester is taking some courses in preparation for his pending retirement. He is diabetic and like most people with that illness has mood swings, but the negative side is more irritation than depression. The Bonds recently sold their city house and bought one in the country along with a house trailer. His favorite activity is writing a novel based on his early life; his greatest concern is the possibility of war.

Chester's existential statements, if they may be called that, are of a different order from most of the others: "I think in terms of mathematics," "I am sure that man's mind was to improve his lot," "I am sure life is physical, mental, and moral—in balance, I think that I'm more than 'trailing clouds of glory from . . . etcetera.'" Other statements primarily concern interests and activities such as "fly-fisherman" and "a swimmer unafraid of water." He seems to be more philosophical than existential, at one point noting a personal characteristic to be "believing in the good that science can do for man" and that "the struggle to overcome obstacles keeps us young." He likes being a student and has studied for most of his life. "I really believe that the human mind is perhaps beyond our understanding."

In comparison with Chester, retirement stager Clyde Wheeler seems confused. At our first interview he is a public relations specialist for a large corporation and looks forward to retirement. By the second interview he is six months into retirement and finds that his retirement pattern has not resolved itself; he feels "scattered." He is, however, more relaxed and as a result his blood pressure has improved. The marriage is a good one and he feels close to their only child, a daughter. The Wheelers had recently visited Japan, where he joined a program of Zen for a week. The most important event between the second and third interviews is a two-week stay at a country Zen center, where he falls in love with a young man. He also contracts infectious hepatitis and later develops cancer. Clyde now meditates daily and feels it is "all coming together more." Gardening and sailing are his main enjoyments; his principal worries are inflation and moral decay. His existential statements are:

"one who doesn't know," "a small part of a living universe," "a decayed wasp," "an educated fool," "a solecist," and "Zen Buddhist." He lists only four other self-characteristics: "a skeptic," "an anarchist," "an uncertain bisexual," and "an intellectual."

Blanche Larkin is more religious than existential. In her early sixties when we begin talking to her, Blanche has had only two years of high school and is a receptionist in a department store. When she was thirty-five she had a conversion experience and became a Christian Scientist. Shortly before the first interview her husband, an alcoholic, was killed in an automobile accident. She has two married daughters and some grandchildren, with whom she often babysits. By the second interview Blanche has requested her retirement papers. Things have changed at work: she now has more responsibility than ever before and it has turned out to be more than she likes; she has just turned down an opportunity for promotion. Her main goal is to work in her religious organization.

At the time of the third interview Blanche has retired and is starting to work toward her main goal: she is attending ministry school. With financial aid from her daughters she has gone overseas to an international convention of the Witnesses, the highlight of her life. Bringing religion to others is her greatest satisfaction. She is convinced that Armageddon will come within five years. All of her statements are related to her beliefs and are presented in narrative form. For example: "I am a Christian Scientist; that means that I testify to the fact that there is a God; also that he is a God of love who is man's best friend; my work and desire is to testify to this"; "I am free to choose life or death; this freedom I have from God's word in the Bible"; "I am a humble servant of God."

Two of the older existential people do not fare as well as the younger ones as we look forward in time. By the next to last interview Chester Bond has undergone prostate surgery and suffered a serious insulin reaction. His marriage, however, is even more satisfying and the Bonds are planning to buy a much larger house. Chester is not so easily upset as he used to be but feels more vulnerable because of his health. By the last interview, in fact, he is so seriously ill that no contact can be made with him. Blanche Larkin, at the fourth contact, is very happy. Close to seventy, her hearing has deteriorated but she still does Bible education work and attends a ministry school. She feels "transformed by the renewing of my mind but not of my body." Blanche dies before the last interview. Clyde Wheeler reports, at the fourth interview, that he is not so tense and anxious as he used to be and says he is now more patient, secure, and less snobbish. Because of his Zen beliefs he has a sense of belonging. At the last session he says he is more serene and happier with himself and the world than ever before, despite the fact that he attends fewer Zen services.

Themes and Variations

To this point we have been reviewing two general characteristics of the described self: expansiveness and negativeness. We also had information on the inner basic categories that were used in self-descriptions. From the distributions we could conclude that, by and large, men and women in each subgroup shared one category as either their first or second choice. Among the youngest men, for example, *intra*personal characteristics was first choice and sense of self second. The reverse was true among their female counterparts, who put sense of self first and *inter*personal characteristics second. The newlywed men favored sense of self statements whereas the women preferred roles and memberships; the men ranked interpersonal second while the women put sense of self second. There was more unanimity in the empty nest group: their statements are very concrete, and most agree that interests and activities come first, roles and memberships second. The oldest men favor ideological statements and interests and activities about equally. The women rarely make ideological statements; among them interests and activities predominate.

In short, our hypothesis that the young tend to be introspective and sometimes vague while the older are specific and concrete is supported, with the exception of newlywed women. To illustrate these marked differences within and between subgroups we have selected one person from each to highlight differences in the described self.

High School Seniors: Focus on the Intrapersonal. High school senior Johnnie Baronie favors intrapersonal characteristics. An intelligent and enterprising young man, he has long had his heart set on becoming either a veterinarian or a medical doctor. By the second interview he has been rejected by a local vet school and works for a while as a night attendant at an SPCA animal shelter while going to community college. He studies hard, gets good grades, and by the third interview, at age twenty-three, he has been accepted at a first-rate university where he is majoring in biology. To help pay his expenses he works as a fry cook in one of the school's dining commons. His statements include "I am interested in learning," "I am knowledgeable," and "I'm not studious enough." Johnnie has temporarily given up some of his favorite athletic interests; study comes first so that he can attain his professional goal soon. At this point in his life intrapersonal concerns are highly appropriate; his primary focus is on personal development.

In contrast to Johnnie, former high school senior Trudy Rowe prefers the "sense of self" type of statement. Not a very good student, she drops out of nursing school just before the second interview. Given that she is a dependent, uncertain, diffuse, and rather anxious person, the Unification church of the Reverend Moon is providing a satisfying structure for her life. At the time of the test she has decided to go to New York and work for the church, hoping to become one of the many young "lay ministers" who help bring the message to others. After her religious education is completed, Trudy hopes to marry a man with similar beliefs and to have a family. Trudy is not the only young person in the sample who found this church appealing—it seems to help them in the difficult transition from late adolescence to adulthood. Several of her statements reflect her hope to become more mature: "an individual growing up"; "a striving for completeness"; "develop heart"; "searching"; "unfulfilled but with hope of feeling fulfilled."

Newlyweds: Focus on the Self. Former newlywed Charles Bonnet is also in the sense of self category, but for very different reasons than Trudy's. At the first interview he is almost completely indifferent to the needs of others, including those of his pregnant wife. He is excessively, one might almost say obsessively, engrossed in his monetary ambitions. Nevertheless he manages to combine two disparate roles: he is a graduate student and at the same time a suc-

cessful real estate agent. At the second session Charles reports fights
with his wife. (They have two very young daughters.) He finds it
reasonable to be a dictator in his own home—this is what being
"head of household" means to him. At the same time he is having
problems both at school and at work. When he is interviewed for
the third time, Charles is very well off financially and has decided
to put himself through law school. Now more introspective, he
thinks he knows himself better and says "I'm more on guard about
the ways I've screwed up," which may account for his many statements in the sense of self category. He feels much closer to his wife
and daughters, has made a few good friends, acquired satisfying
hobbies, and is "less hung up on money." That he tries to be honest
with himself is indicated by a few of his statements: "I have hurt
others sometimes"; "I sometimes screw up my priorities"; and "I
am somewhat egotistical."

Also in the newlywed group is Ann Laird—an exception
since roles are most important for her and account for the majority
of her sixteen statements. (Ann is Hank Laird's wife; they are the
only married couple who by happenstance fell into our sample.) At
the first interview she has nearly finished college and majors in art,
which she plans to make her career. She is already giving lessons
at home every Saturday. Ann's husband has a college degree and is
in the middle of his first semester in graduate school; he is majoring
in education. The Lairds are fundamentalists and very religious. By
the second session, Ann is teaching in an art school and learning
to work with children. Her other roles include keeping house, en-
tertaining, and teaching Sunday school. At the time of the test Ann
has three satisfying and related work roles that are mentioned in her
described self: "teaching in a music school for children," "teaching
adults" (in her home), and "playing guitar" (for a variety of events
at church, bazaars, and weddings). Most important at this time is
"discovering my true self," which includes being "less gullible" and
"speaking her mind." Also on her list are a few more roles: "cook,"
"seamstress," "conversationalist," "epicurean," and "traveler."

When we last talk with these young people they are far less
preoccupied with themselves. Johnnie has graduated from college,
is married, and now has a son and has bought a house. He works
as a quality supervisor for a restaurant chain, a far cry from his

earlier plans to be a vet or physician. He works hard, enjoys it, and has no time for introspection. Trudy is manager of the large printing company owned by a prominent newspaper. She feels mature, competent, and responsible. Engaged to a fellow church member, she plans to marry soon and hopes to have children. Charles Bonnet has matured. He says he is more "tuned in" to other people, including his wife and children, to whom he now listens. With more respect for others, he is also more honest about himself. Having passed the bar exam, he plans to build a law firm. Ann Laird is not in the best of health at the next to last interview, for tendonitis severely limits her activities. By the last contact she is healthy, more secure, and better organized as well as "independent and outgoing." In consequence she enjoys her work more (she is still teaching art), her marriage is more "settled and good," and she feels there is much more frankness and love in her relations with others. She looks forward to having children, and we suspect she will be a better mother than she could have been earlier. Looking back, it seems that the self-concerns paramount at the five-year follow-up represented a means of focusing on critical issues for these younger people.

Empty Nesters: Focus on the Concrete. We have already mentioned that the second oldest group, the former empty nesters, focused on concrete aspects of selfhood that concerned interests and activities, as well as roles and memberships. Marcus Buckley is an admirable representative of the interests and activities focus. He enjoys his job as teacher in an industrial arts high school because it is helpful to both students and industry. His overall goal, reported at the first interview, is "self-actualization in a way that contributes to society." He has several hobbies, some of which he shares with his son (a high school senior), a few with his wife. Before the second interview he has finished rebuilding a motorcycle and has taken a long-overdue vacation devoted to fishing, hunting, and hiking. His next activities will be to redo the plumbing in his home and help his brother finish his house in the country. Marcus looks forward to retirement, when he will have more time to devote to this sort of work, which is very different from that required by his profession.

At the time of the test Marcus is still about a year and a half from his retirement, but he is already expanding his list of future activities: he is going to add golf and more travel to his list. Only two of his twenty statements specifically mention hobbies: "I like antiques" and "I like my hobbies." The others reveal an exceptionally well-balanced and diversified human being: "doing a good job," "I like my home," "liked by those doing a good job," "hated by those doing a bad job," "I like to work," "I like to play," "I like cars and driving fast," "I enjoy designing new equipment," "love life."

We became well acquainted with empty nester Cora Leary in the preceding chapter. Like Marcus's her self-descriptions focus on interests and activities, but she is a much simpler and probably less talented person than Marcus. Her activities are numerous. She works in a school cafeteria, where she much enjoys her contacts with young children. She is also active in the PTA and a few church groups (Episcopalian). Cora loves to cook for church bazaars and in general to help other people when they need it. Her major interest is in national and international affairs, and she keeps herself well informed. She is pleased to be working up to becoming an elder of her church. Her statements include many enjoyments: "I am a person who enjoys music," "I am a person who enjoys good food," "I am a person who enjoys cooking," "I am a person who enjoys baking," "I am a person who enjoys crafts," and "I am a person who enjoys flowers." She also notes that "I am a TV viewer" and "I am a people watcher."

Retirees: Focus on Ideologies and Interests. To the concern with interests and roles typical of former empty nesters is added, with the oldest group, a concern with spirituality and religion. Abraham Brady fits the ideological category, being both a very religious Baptist—"God-fearing," as he puts it—and a passionate right-wing fanatic. On first acquaintance he is about to retire from his job as electronics engineer on a college campus. The Bradys have three grown children, two daughters and a son. Abraham is very family-oriented—he has a few acquaintances but no friends. During the interviews it is hard to keep him on track for he persists in proclaiming his politically conservative, Bircher ideology in response to nearly every question. By the third interview he feels that his religious faith has increased, and he seems almost paranoid about the state of the country and the city he lives in. All sorts of security devices have been installed in the two houses he owns and in his car as well. Age seventy at the time of the test, his first statement is "a religious person who thanks the good Lord for all he has done for me." Most of the others reflect his political stance: "I believe in stronger control of crime," "I believe in the death penalty," "no welfare" (underscored), and "death for drug peddlers."

Gladys Snyder, like Cora Leary, is a good example of the interests and activities choice. At the first interview she is still working as a legal secretary and is married to an auto mechanic who works only occasionally. Both are high school graduates. The Snyders have one married daughter and another who is engaged. Healthy when we first meet her, and a devoted grandmother, by the second interview she has been forced to retire: she has been hospitalized twice, once for hepatitis and once for a painful spinal problem. Added to her woes is the fact that the Social Security Administration has just turned down her application for disability. (She is now sixty-two and eligible for it.) Her husband has emphysema and they are living on his disability payments, which are inadequate. Life has greatly improved for Gladys by the third contact. Despite the painful back problem, she is satisfied with her activities and now rates herself as very happy on the Bradburn (1969) Morale Scale. The activities she enjoys most are needlepoint, hooking rugs, and reading. Her statements include many other enjoyments that are strikingly similar to those of Cora Leary: "I love to cook and bake," "I enjoy creating something out of nothing," "I enjoy giving presents and growing flowers," and "I love music."

In our last interview with these people we found that although much older than they were when describing themselves in the Twenty Statements Test, all had maintained some of their accustomed activities and a few had added others. Marcus Buckley has officially retired but works part time at an electric company he once owned. He now has some kind of "tremor" but nevertheless plays golf, fishes, volunteers as a voting inspector, has remodeled his house, and helped his son in building one. Still very enterprising, he plans to start a "fishing school." Cora Leary has been ill in the interim but is now back at work. Her active mother lives closer and they "do things" together. Having achieved her goal of being an elder in her church, she looks forward to more activities there. Still deeply concerned with political problems, she has added books and journals to her reading list. Her interests have expanded her horizons. Abraham Brady, remaining inflexible both politically and personally, is Cora's opposite. From a personal perspective he has become more than slightly paranoid, and his interpersonal relationships are confined strictly to his family. He worries much more about crime than he did, his security devices at both houses have multiplied, and he is more bombastic than ever. As if to provide some balance to his life, he also feels that his religious commitment has strengthened. The activity he likes best is fishing. Gladys Snyder's husband dies about two years prior to the final interview. Her mourning period is sad and protracted but she feels supported by reading inspirational books and having long talks with sympathetic friends. She has found an "inner peace" and tries to make the most of each day. To her versatile interests and activities she has added some academic courses "to broaden my mind."

As we got to know all these people who represent typical categories for their stage groups, we found that each has unique modes of living and coping. The less privileged and poorly educated prove to be at least as complex and interesting as those comfortably well off. Of particular interest was the finding that their self-descriptions, at each stage of life, seem quite appropriate. For people who are still struggling with who they are and where they are going, for example, a focus on inner concerns and self-descriptors seems quite fitting. Similarly, as the years stretch on and the self becomes established, it can now be characterized by givens: the activities and interests that have stabilized and now define the person. An interest in cars or music may not appear to be particularly descriptive of a twenty-year-old, for example, but to a sixty-year-old with a forty-year history of interest in cars or music, this interest may now represent a central theme in life.

An interest in religion and spirituality was another emergent theme in the lives of the older participants, although this concern may simply reflect cohort differences in the significance of religiosity. As we will see in subsequent chapters, however, this interest is reflected in many dimensions of living other than that of the described self and may well represent a developmental condition.

The Four and a Few Alternates

In the more empirical analyses, we find variations by age group in the perceived self that hint at a developmental progression, but a progression more dependent on social context than the kind of biological maturation that underlies development during infancy or even the teen years. The increasing importance of philosophical or spiritual considerations, for example, may rest upon experience with social loss and perhaps one's personal confrontations with illness and death. We now turn to a consideration of our four main cases but will supplement their stories with those of our alternates; the perceived self is simply too complex a topic to be illustrated solely by "The Four."

The Four. To follow up on the notion that a sense of spirituality has a special significance in the lives of our older respondents, it is perhaps no accident that empty nester Olav Olavsen's first and fifth statements are of the type we call ideological—in his case "I am a Lutheran" and "I have a strong faith in God." His second, third, and fourth identifications were "Swedish," "father of four children," and "man." The sixth, "I am happily married," is interpersonal (positive). The rest are interests and activities: "interested in music," "interested in good literature," "interested in crafts, drawing, painting," and "interested in gardening." Having listed these ten statements, he says "that's enough," and indeed they do provide a clear image of him. Again he reveals himself through his roles and interests and spirituality.

Hazel Sutter completes all twenty statements on her list, a list that is much less settled and related to roles and interests than those of most empty nesters. She notes only two identifications, "female" and "mother," and several intrapersonal statements, mainly negative, including "too quiet" (meaning she does not talk enough) and "too cross." Our experience has been that negative descriptions, while rare, are potentially more significant and revealing in the two older groups than in the younger—especially if, as in the case of

Hazel, the person seems to feel unable to change. Apart from the intrapersonal items, Hazel also brings up several interpersonal items, mainly familial, that also reflect a negative image: "I try to keep after my daughter's bad habits" and "I notice that my children lack what I lack." Personal characteristics are more negative than positive: "selfish in many ways," "too absentminded," and "growing old too fast." The test took place at the time she was just beginning to get acquainted with a widower neighbor, whom she liked very much, and this new relationship, at least for now, has not translated into a more accepting self-description.

Retirement stager Max Schindler reacts to the free-flowing test in predictable fashion. One of our least spontaneous respondents, he refuses to write anything down. The interviewer gives him the sheet and asks him to fill it in at home and mail it to her (also giving him a stamped and addressed envelope). He takes it, but despite a number of calls to him, nothing is returned. Since he accepts the rest of the interview questions, most of which are relatively structured, and continues in future interviews, his reluctance to take this particular test is especially revealing about his resistance to self-disclosure. Adelaide Stone, Max's female pre-retiree counterpart, was hospitalized with a stroke and too ill to be interviewed.

When we talk with them at the final interview, all four of these people are still very active. Olav, now a widower and retired, enjoys the same activities and has added wood carving. At age seventy-three one of the oldest of the former empty nesters, he is grateful to be healthy and independent. Hazel still works full time, likes it, and has much enjoyed a trip to Europe with the man she loves. Max has had heart surgery but has fully recovered. He has bought a farm, and his favorite activities now are hunting, fishing, and "building things." Adelaide's health is now much better than it has been, but she hesitates to make plans and is generally afraid to do a lot of the things that used to give her pleasure. With the exception of Adelaide, The Four share a capacity for resilience and demonstrate considerable continuity in activities reflective of their self-descriptions.

The Alternates. Given that the self-concept, as defined objectively and subjectively, lies at the core of our study of lives, a few more case vignettes may help to fill in the picture of how people perceive themselves and what self-descriptions suggest about people's lives. These additional cases include our "alternates." Of particular interest is the extent to which they reflect the same patterns of self-description previously described.

Among these alternates, Winston Faust is parsimonious in his statements. (The interviewer notes, however, that it was given late in the interview and late in the day and he probably was tired.) At the time of the test Winston is fifty-four and recovering from a car accident; both his speech and hearing are affected. Partly because of the accident, he has lost his principal job, and he and his wife now own a variety store. He finds the work relaxing and is now less active in his Masonic lodge and other groups. When he is fully recovered he hopes to travel and have more of a social life. As for his described self, he is "a person," "enjoying life," "believing in life," and "looking forward to a very pleasant life." All these self-descriptions are very positive and reflect spirituality rather than religiosity.

We became quite well acquainted with Irma Clark, empty nester, in Chapter Two, where she was one of the people whose rated selves are very negative. We were surprised to learn that her described self is quite positive. After identifying herself as "a woman," "married," "a mother," "grandmother," and "friend," her statements are those of a caring, well-rounded, and liberal person. She "cares about injustice," is "fairly creative," "enjoys cultural activities," "abhors racial bias," and is "a reverse snob at times." One might say that, in a very general way, her self-image matches that expected of a person who has successfully dealt with Erikson's stage of generativity.

Although retirement stager Cyrus Campbell has had only a high school education (at a private school), he is vice-president of a pharmaceutical company when we first meet him. At age sixty-four, he is just beginning to think of retirement; his wife, ten years younger than he, works part time as a postal clerk. They have two grown children, a boy and a girl, both of whom have been recently divorced. Cyrus's eighty-nine-year-old mother lives with them. His main goal is to "die with my boots on"; to spread happiness is his second goal in life. By the next interview Cyrus has retired and is enjoying his woodworking hobbies. He has bought an organ and plays it every day. He is very pleased that both of his children have remarried. A few months after the second interview, Cyrus goes to work for a lithographic company, where he puts in three hours a day. At the time of the test he is working a few more hours in the printing firm, has traveled extensively (his favorite activity), and still has had time to spend in his woodworking shop. His wife now works full time and his mother has been moved to a convalescent home, so he is alone more but has more time for himself. Since he has been released from his caregiving responsibilities, he now has a renewed interest in social and retirement groups. We are not surprised to learn that his self-statements are very positive, but his descriptions are somewhat like those of younger subjects in that they generally deal with interpersonal and intrapersonal qualities. He lists himself as "very happily married," "a proud parent," "friendly," "honest," "thoughtful of others," "satisfied," "energetic," and "successful in work."

Annabelle Whitman is a woman with an advanced degree in German who has never worked and now sometimes regrets it. She falls into our retirement category, therefore, primarily because of her financially successful salesperson husband. Annabelle's interests and activities are somewhat traditional and include attending meetings with her sorority group and various functions in the Eastern Star. Her husband has considerably less education (he is a high school graduate), and the couple has two daughters, one of whom is married. Sixty-five at the time of the third interview, Annabelle and the whole family have recently taken a trip across the country, and her husband has retired. She is learning to play golf and is still active in social groups. Annabelle is now experiencing some of the "insults of aging" and lists them in her self-descriptions: "lots more wrinkles," "some eye problems," "a bit shaky" (on her feet), and "difficulty in remembering the right words." Still, Annabelle is essentially quite positive in her statements: "fairly attractive," "a seamstress," "gardener," "reader," "knitter," "sympathetic," "considerate," and "honest."

These alternates were not all as fortunate as The Four, at least insofar as their status at the final interview is concerned. Winston is quite hostile throughout the last interview. He has recently recovered from a mild heart attack and, under doctor's orders, has added various exercises to his other activities. His car accident still haunts him, and he frequently broods about death. Irma's husband has died several months before our last contact with her. She keeps herself busy with her many handicraft activities, but one of her daughters remains so depressed over her father's death that Irma finds it difficult to be with her "because depression is catching." Cyrus, now seventy-six, has had some serious eye problems but still enjoys travel and visits with good friends. Annabelle's favorite activity is travel, as well, but her husband has painful arthritis so she stays home and tends her garden instead.

Summing Up

This chapter has revealed dimensions of self-views that greatly expand our knowledge of what people in our sample think of themselves. As well, it provides a useful counterfoil to the descriptions of rated selves found in Chapter Two. In particular, it gives us a sense of how the perceived self often accords with the life stage and circumstances in which people find themselves. It also constitutes a logical transition to the next chapter, which focuses on behavioral preferences that frequently hinge on the perceived self.

4

Being Flexible Versus Rigid

With this chapter we shift from formal analyses of the described self to the related issue of flexibility versus rigidity in personality. As noted earlier, there is a great deal of overlap between concepts of personality and those of the self-concept. One of the major distinctions is that studies of personality are more likely to collect objective data that are broad in scope, while studies of the self may focus on the individuals' attempt to construct or describe him- or herself. (See, for example, Riegel, 1959; Bengtson, Reedy, and Gordon, 1985.) Perhaps the key distinction depends on whether the investigators consider themselves to be studying personality or the self.

The Concepts

In studies of personality, an important component is often the flexibility or rigidity of the individual. Probably because of the problem-oriented approach that underlies much of gerontology, the concept of rigidity seems to have a much longer history. Schaie (1958) and Riegel (1959) were among the first to raise the issue of rigidity as central to studies of the older adult, while in the early 1960s several investigators were assessing personality variables that dealt with free-ranging ideation versus a more restrictive mode (Neugarten, Crotty, and Tobin, 1964; Kroeber, 1963). Why this interest? For one reason, earlier investigators wanted to know whether older persons become more rigid in their thinking. For another, rigidity in thinking has been suggested as a possible barrier to problem solving, leading to lower scores in intelligence tests and possibly to poorer adaptation to life's challenges.

After an initial wave of studies, primarily cross-sectional, which suggested that rigidity increases with age, has positive associations with dogmatism and authoritarianism, and has negative associations with intelligence, research on this topic lagged for many years. One reason may be that many of the studies directly or indirectly cast a rather negative light on the aging process, one that by today's terms might seem excessive. Consider, for example, the following statement by Raymond Kuhlen (1959, p. 882), a respected gerontologist: "Evidence from a substantial number of studies of the cross-sectional variety indicates that older adults are more conservative than younger adults. They do not like change; they cling to older ideas and are slower to adopt new ones; in morals, politics and general living they are likely to be 'old-fashioned' rather than modern and liberal; they tend to view themselves as conservative."

Reemerging as a credible area of study in the 1970s and 1980s, rigidity and flexibility are now viewed in terms of general behavioral predispositions, or personality traits, that may be present at any age. The concept of traits, of course, has a heritage going back to Gordon Allport's (1939) view that traits are the building blocks of personality and hence yield evidence of continuity. Long held in discredit, the study of traits has recently experienced a resurgence owing primarily to the work of an energetic team of personality researchers, Paul Costa and Robert McCrae. For years Costa and McCrae have been looking at the issue of continuity and discontinuity in three basic personality traits: neuroticism, extroversion, and (especially relevant to this chapter) openness to experience. They have found that personality is one of the more stable of the personal constructs studied by social scientists.

Costa and McCrae (1976) in their Experience Survey developed sixty statements that refer to the self. Respondents circle whether they strongly agree, agree, cannot decide (or feel neutral), disagree, or strongly disagree. (In the analyses to follow we combine strongly agree and agree and strongly disagree and disagree.) Although Costa and McCrae found evidence for six different facets of openness (and our own factor analyses suggest that up to ten facets may in fact exist), items indicative of rigidity and flexibility are dispersed throughout all facets. For this reason, we have selected fourteen items: seven that represent stagnation or rigidity and seven that reflect growth, open-mindedness, and flexibility. The Experience Survey, introduced at the final contact, covers dimensions quite different from the Adjective Rating List and Twenty Statements Test. Rigidity and flexibility, for example, bear little relation to the concepts of expansion and contraction introduced in the previous chapter. The aptness of the fourteen items can best be judged if we write them out:

Flexible	*Rigid*
Without strong emotions life would be uninteresting.	I'm pretty set in my ways.
The different ideas of right and wrong that people in other societies have may be valid for them.	Letting students hear controversial issues can only confuse and mislead them.
I enjoy surprises even when they mean I have to change my plans.	I feel no need for further learning.
My experiences have sometimes made it necessary for me to reexamine my values.	I like to follow a strict routine in my work.
Most of the time I'm willing to try a new way of doing an old job.	I seldom read anything unless it is useful in my work.
I like to listen to a wide variety of opinions on a subject before I make up my mind.	I prefer to spend my time in familiar surroundings.
I have a wide range of intellectual interests.	On a vacation, I prefer going back to a tried-and-true spot.

The objectives of this chapter are, overall, to examine the ways in which flexibility and rigidity become meaningful terms in the study of adult lives. We begin by describing differences between life-stage groups and between men and women that, in some instances, are surprising; we then characterize those people who fall in the middle, more or less, on the dual concepts of flexibility and rigidity. Life histories of four rigid and four flexible people help to explain how they come to have these preferences, as do stances of the four people we follow through the book. The focus is on how they have coped over the years of the study and their plans for the future. The chapter concludes with an exploration of a challenging question: What is the comparative significance of personality versus life circumstances in accounting for flexible and rigid preferences?

Variations

In general, our data ran contrary to the decades-old notion that older people are more rigid and less flexible. To be sure, there does seem to be a trend among women to lose flexibility; women also were significantly more flexible than men at all stages. For men, on the other hand, the former newlyweds and the pre-retirees scored highest on flexibility, followed by the youngest group and the second oldest.

Looking at our findings for rigidity, the results again run counter to expectations based on analyses of the past. Moreover, the results are opposite to those for flexibility in terms of the presence of age trends. Among males, for example, there is a clear decline in rigidity scores with each successive age group, but this is not the case among women. Among the men, the former high school seniors score highest, followed by newlyweds, empty nesters, and retirees. Among the women, the newlyweds score highest in rigidity, followed by the former empty nesters, the high school students, and the retirement group. Women are generally lower on rigidity than men, save among the second youngest group.

Neutrals. Inasmuch as the statements we chose were simple and explicit, one might assume that people who cannot make up their minds about a statement are either rigid or diffuse in their thinking processes. If rigid, they could be expected, to the extent that they agree with anything, to agree with rigid statements. Support for this thesis, however, is found only among the middle-aged men. They rank highest of all subgroups on neutral flexible, lowest on neutral rigid, next to highest on agree rigid, and next to lowest on agree flexible. Second-oldest-group member Edmund Morain, for example, reports himself at our fifth interview to be neutral on seven statements and to agree with three rigid and four flexible ones. A review of his protocols yields support for the hypothesis that high scores in the neutral category indicate an undifferentiated self. For example, it usually takes Ed some time to make a decision about anything, and after doing so he invariably asks himself whether it was the right one; in some instances the uncertainty can go on for years.

When we first meet him Ed is very proud of his son's athletic accomplishments but worried about his lack of motivation at school. By the next contact the son has been arrested and convicted of public intoxication (a misdemeanor), receiving six months' probation. More than a year after the fact Ed is still castigating himself for not pulling strings to get his son off the hook. At the third interview he reports that several months ago he and his wife had planned a month-long vacation trip, but he canceled it because he was afraid to leave his son by himself. In discussing this decision he now thinks it was wrong: he should have put his wife's interests first. Only at the final interview has he finally decided that his son's problems are his son's problems. (The young man is now in his early thirties.) By this time Ed is nearly sixty-five and speculates about his own life choices: it had been a mistake to be a "federal civil servant." He could have made more money and been happier if he had gone into the hotel business on his own. He also reports himself as having become "very set in my ways." He himself acknowledges rigidity, and his life over the past twelve years, as well as his neutral scores, suggests he is undifferentiated as well.

The Opposite of Neutral. The newlywed women generally ranked lowest on neutrality, so, to provide contrast to Edmund Morain, we selected one low scorer at random to trace what might account for their decisiveness on matters of flexibility and rigidity. Abbey

Knowles proved to be very enlightening but also a bit more than we bargained for. As we get to know her, it becomes clear that had the flexible/rigid statements been introduced at an earlier time, the picture would have been very different. She would probably have circled many more neutrals or else sought her husband's advice. Abbey has an advanced degree in social work, has occasionally worked part time in her field, and, being very attractive, is also in demand as a model.

When we become acquainted, she is married to a well-to-do psychiatrist many years older than she and is trying hard to live up to his upper-class expectations. She has learned to sculpt and to ski and is taking lessons in racketball. By the next interview she has been skiing in the Alps, has moved to a much larger house with full-time domestic help, and has had a baby. By the third interview she has had a second child and the Knowleses have acquired a large condominium at a luxurious ski resort in Lake Tahoe. She has also become as good a racketball player as her demanding husband.

Later the relationship begins to change, and Abbey persuades her husband to join her in seeing several psychiatrists. Soon after the fourth interview the couple separates. She reports a great feeling of relief by the final interview. At this point, the time of the flexible/rigid test, she is well along in law school yet stays close to her growing children. She has dates now and then, but so far has not found the right man. Now much more concerned about the problems of other people and social and political issues, she feels that she has become her "real self." Abbey circles eleven agree flexible and disagree rigid statements, and on the remaining three she is neutral. Her recent emancipation from the lap of luxury to the world of living her own life underscores the best of being flexible, just as Edmund Morain dramatizes the drawbacks of not being able to make up one's mind, on the one hand, and being rigid, on the other.

Generally one would expect people who agree with many flexible experiences to disagree with rigid ones and vice versa. Yet some people, twelve altogether, scored high on both rigidity and flexibility. At first one might think they are all slightly schizoid, but a brief check of their protocols shows them to be both intelligent

and complex, indicating a tolerance for ambiguity, which some
scholars consider to be proof of maturity.

From a broad perspective, we find that those who agree with
flexible and disagree with rigid statements include about four-fifths
of the youngest women, of the newlyweds of both sexes, of the
middle-aged women, and of the oldest women—thus accounting for
five of the eight subgroups. Only two-thirds of the middle-aged and
oldest men are on the flexible side, while the youngest men fall in
between the two groups. Overall, well over three-quarters of them
primarily agree with the flexible side, leaving fewer than a fourth
on the rigid one. It seems quite remarkable that a notable majority
of these mainstream Americans, conservative in many ways, are
flexible people.

Biographical Sketches

For this section we have selected one person in each subgroup to exemplify the range from very flexible to very rigid. Our
objectives are to demonstrate how life circumstances and personal
characteristics interact and to try to account for their preferences.

Flexible People. When asked, Marilyn Mitchell agrees with all
seven of the flexible statements and disagrees with all but one of the
rigid ones. One of the best examples of the flexible type, she proves
to be one of the most interesting people in the sample. Her principal objective as a high school senior is to go to college and earn
a teaching credential. Nominally Catholic, Marilyn is the youngest
of three children; her father is a construction foreman, her mother
a housewife. At first acquaintance she is excessively dependent on
her mother, a symbiotic relationship that, thanks to her mother's
insight, will change.

By the next interview she is in her third year at college and
working as a teacher's aide as well. Marilyn's mother has consulted
a psychiatrist about her daughter's dependence on her. He suggests
that Marilyn visit another psychiatrist, just to keep her from feeling
controlled, and this is done. After several sessions Marilyn begins
to feel more independent and believes she has grown up a lot. At
college she makes some good friends, including a steady boyfriend.

Marilyn notes that she feels very close to him but can be her independent self as well. Somewhere along the line they stop seeing each other—for two years—but by the third interview they are married. When she first knew him he was very liberal, possibly radical, but he no longer seems to be—in fact, he is now general manager of a large construction firm. This was a great disappointment to Marilyn because she once thought "he would make changes in the world and we would be always on the go but, realistically, [life is] not exciting at all." She says she has learned that you have to work at it to make life exciting. In general, she is now very comfortable with herself, more assertive and less sensitive. Working hard for an advanced degree, she specializes in education for the deaf and hard of hearing. The couple has decided not to have children. She plans to spend more time with her family, especially her mother, now that she is "emancipated."

The fourth interview finds Marilyn "very happy." She is now divorced: "probably the best thing that ever happened because there was not enough sharing, we lived totally different lives." At first she feels guilty about not trying harder to make the marriage work, partly because of her Irish Catholic upbringing, but her parents take it well and she feels she has learned and grown from the experience. Her life has broadened considerably, including trips to Europe and a safari in South Africa. Here at home she goes often to opera, ballet, theater, and museums. She attributes her self-reliance and growth to the changing role of women, which gives her a sense of support: "Without it I wouldn't even have been able to *think* about divorce."

Our last conversation with Marilyn clearly documents her flexibility. She has stopped going to church "because it is full of hypocrites" and feels better about other people "because if I am not a sinner any more, they aren't either." Her mother has had a mastectomy, followed by her father leaving home, "which was probably better for both of them." Marilyn took her mother to Ireland to visit relatives and later to the Bahamas "just for the fun of it." Asked about changes in herself over the past ten years, she summarizes: "more secure, more content with myself and my life, and more understanding of others as I grow older." (She is now twenty-seven.) Work is one of her greatest satisfactions; she works in a ghetto

school, where she does a lot of "parenting" and is involved in her
students' families as well. Her roommate is her best friend and they
are "closer than most sisters." Summing up, she says that her mother's illness and parents' separation were most stressful and changed
her understanding of life. "It can change so drastically. In a very
short time one can be upset and torn apart, so you shouldn't really
count on anything or worry about it in advance. You get some
pretty weird cards and you've got to take it as it comes. Everything
can be remedied except death." This coming from a formerly dependent and protected child, we conclude, suggests a genuine
growth of flexibility and maturity as well.

Our second most flexible participant is newlywed Gail Ramsey. Gail is a fairly late bloomer. She is twenty-four when we first
meet her, and so is her husband. Both have had five years of college
and both are sales managers. Her goal is to work for about a year,
save some money, and then have a baby; she plans on having two
more plus a fourth one that will be adopted (for reasons unspecified). Gail's father was an oil salesman; he is not well, and neither
is her mother. Catholic though they are, they separated about the
time of Gail's marriage but it was not connected with that event.
Her feelings about her father have always alternated between indifference and hatred, and her mother is "too dominating, an anti-role
model."

By the next interview her mother is bedridden and has a
caretaker; the parental divorce is almost final. Gail, as planned, now
has a child, a boy, and "all of my days seem to blend into one taking
care of him." Her husband used to "clam up a lot," but now they
talk things over and she feels closer to him and to her mother now
that the child has arrived. She also sees the good friends she made
at her former teaching job.

Three years later the Ramseys have moved a few hundred
miles away because her husband was offered a much better teaching
job. "They" have decided not to have any more children, but it is
unclear whether the conclusion was his, hers, or mutual. Gail's
mother, about whom she had negative feelings, has died and Gail
was acutely depressed for months. As Peter Marris (1975, p. 36) has
noted: "The intensity of grief is often greater when the feeling for
the dead person was mixed." Evenings and weekends, when her

husband can be with the child, she works in a department store; she does not like it much, but the money helps. Rating herself "pretty happy," she feels closest to her husband and looks forward to making new friends in the area. She says that her major task now is to accept herself as she is and to decide what she wants to do with the rest of her life.

Thus far it would be difficult to predict where Gail would stand on the flexibility/rigidity paradigm, though it is clear that she has adapted well to her changing circumstances and has grown in the sense that she is now concerned about national and international issues. Nothing much changes by the fourth contact. By now the Ramseys have bought a house and are fixing it up. Gail still feels in a transitional state, has not decided what to do with her life, and feels "behind time" in that regard. On a scale of one to ten she rates the present year a four because of uncertainty.

At the final interview the current year is rated an eight because she is back to teaching part time, her husband is a department head, and she has taken on considerable responsibility in three community organizations, which has enabled her to make some good friends. At peace with herself, she lives in the present, does not worry, and has learned to "roll with the punches," another way of phrasing flexibility. Gail agrees with all the flexible statements and disagrees with all but one of the rigid ones; the exception is circled neutral.

At the last interview, Gail says that her major social concern is the increase in mental illness. This same concern is expressed by Fay Price, the third most flexible person on the list. We meet Fay for the first time when she is fifty-one and has been a widow for about a year. During the three years before her husband's death (in a car accident) he had been hospitalized eight times for depression and a "persecution complex." Fay's life has been anything but easy. She has two adopted children, a son and daughter, works part time in a nearby university, and is studying for an advanced degree at another school. Her rated self is very positive. A devout Catholic, she feels strengthened by her faith. Some day Fay hopes to marry a person who shares her beliefs.

By the next contact she has done so: she is now the wife of a widowed professor she has known for years. His children are grown up and have their own households. Fay has inherited some money, and before she remarried she took her children on several trips, including one to Europe. To their mother's dismay, both children soon dropped out of school, John to work for an oil company and Susie for a law firm. Fay herself, having joined the life of couplehood again, decides to give up the idea of an advanced degree, which no longer seems very important. Still enjoying her work, she plans to retire in a few years when the departmental chair for whom she works does so.

The couple buys a new home to accommodate her two children. She is not pleased, for "it is time for them to be responsible for themselves." It helps that Fay now has a housekeeper. She feels very relaxed and comfortable with her new husband, his children, and new friends. By the third interview Fay has stopped working, and so has her husband. They now do a lot of traveling, both in this country and abroad, yet on a morale scale she notes that she is sometimes both bored and uneasy. That her greatest satisfaction is volunteer work at a hospital suggests that she misses the involvement and responsibilities of work. Hedonism clashes with her self-image. On the Adjective Rating List she circles both idealism and sincerity, indicating that she feels less idealistic and sincere and does not like it.

At the fourth interview she tells a sad story of her daughter's being raped and beaten; although her daughter had left home, Fay has brought Susie back to live with them until she recovers from shock. By the last encounter Fay, now sixty-three, has assumed more responsibility in her volunteer work, her son has divorced and remarried, and her daughter lives in her own home, which Fay helped her to buy. Although Fay's marriage is satisfying, she notes that it does not involve the spontaneity, humor, and fun that her first one did. Although she is not quite as complex or philosophical as the two younger women, her flexibility has stood her in good stead as she copes with her personal crises and transitions. She agrees with five flexible statements (circling neutral on the other two) and disagrees with all the rigid ones.

Newlywed Lance Shannon is a step down from Fay on the dimensions of flexibility and rigidity; in fact, he falls on the border between the two. Lance agrees with six out of seven items on the flexible side and disagrees with one; conversely, he agrees with one rigid item and disagrees with six. Despite the "flexible" nature of these self-descriptions, through most of the interviews uncertainty describes him best. At first acquaintance we learn that he has had one year of college, is a process server for a law firm (a job he dislikes), and is married to a teacher with two years of college; both are twenty-three. The Shannons are expecting a child very soon. Lance says he will finish college "sometime" and "maybe major in international law or else become a photographer and maybe emigrate to Australia." (His interviewer notes that Lance seems to feel he is being "psyched out" by the questions and seems, consequently, to feel uncomfortable.) After the child arrives the couple buys a house in the suburbs. At the second interview Lance now thinks that, despite his eye problems, he definitely would like to be a photographer but is stuck with his job and that accounts for his "emotional problems." He has some new acquaintances and is closer to certain friends, but relations with his father, a business executive, have deteriorated because Lance is "now going his own way."

Five years into the study finds Lance still confused and ambivalent about his goals, but "I'm more or less stuck with earning a living." Still at the same job, he has "a feeling that I have got to get myself together pretty quick or there won't be any going back." He rates the year a low four on a scale of one to ten because of "indecision." What may be psychosomatic ailments plague him: hyperventilation, chest pressure, and migraine. Despite these problems he enjoys photography, painting, dancing, and museums.

By the next to last interview the Shannons have another child. Lance, now close to thirty, has been promoted at the law firm but still "suffers emotionally from job frustration" and is less idealistic and more cynical than before. Nevertheless he is "pretty happy" and says his marriage has improved. Only at the last interview is he "fairly satisfied" with his work. The most important event reported at this twelve-year contact is a love affair that resulted in harassing phone calls at home and, of course, problems with his wife. Six months of psychoanalysis help him to "mellow out." His most important goal now is a close relationship with his wife. Not satisfied with his current pattern of activities, he rates this year, too, a four. In answer to how he thinks he has changed in the past ten years he says "hardening of the spirit." This admission prompts another: in his view he is now an alcoholic. We are not surprised, recalling that his Twenty Statements Test includes "I would like to be helped" and "I am sometimes ashamed of myself." Ever since our first contact with Lance, he has suffered from a crisis of identity. Another statement on the Twenty Statements Test is "I would like to know myself better." All along he has had problems knowing who he is.

All in all, those we have presented here as flexible people are intelligent, well educated, and autonomous. They know who they are, they like themselves, and probably they will continue to grow; these are also very responsible and outgoing people. Lance is somewhat of an exception, a man whose flexibility results in indecisiveness. His rigidity in some areas may block his creativity and basic openness. He longs for the artistic life but at the same time searches for secure employment; he values wife and family life but somewhat clumsily indulges in an extramarital affair.

Rigid People. We now move to the other side of the paradigm and meet four people who differ in many ways from the flexible ones we have just reviewed. Each of the next four cases is more and more oriented toward stability and predictability and less and less oriented toward flexible options. Bobby Caldwell, a high school senior when we meet, is the youngest son of a salesman and is unique among the younger groups of the sample in that he has five older brothers and sisters. (The family is Catholic.) A handsome young man, he is by no means brilliant. His father is very authoritarian, and Bobby's goals reflect his father's: there are no signs of adolescent rebellion. He would like a good job, preferably as a printer, and now does part-time work in a printshop. He plans eventually to marry, to have a family and a house of his own, and to make his parents happy with travel and "buying stuff" for them. He has a steady girlfriend, disapproves of many of his classmates ("too busy with sex and dope"), and is unusually self-satisfied for his age.

As we trace the course of his life over twelve years, we begin to see why Bobby has chosen an even balance between rigid and flexible aspects of selfhood. Two and a half years after the first interview Bobby and his girlfriend are officially engaged. He has tried a junior college for a year but dropped out because he "isn't learning anything." Now an apprentice printer, he also works at a gas station at night, a situation his fiancée does not like because they have so little time together. Bobby's long-range plan is to become either a fireman or a policeman. Always the moralist, he says a highlight of this period is a big fight with a close friend who refuses to marry his pregnant girlfriend. During this same period Bobby has joined the Knights of Columbus, a fraternal, benevolent organization of Roman Catholic men.

By the third interview, Bobby and his fiancée have married. Feeling more responsibility, he wants the marriage to work and to "make a good life for her." He is a printer in his father-in-law's business. Having failed the exam for policemen, he plans to take a two-year course in police science at a local community college. He and his wife, Trudy, live in a small apartment in an older building; she works as a clerk in an insurance office. During this period Bobby has a clandestine love affair; when his wife finds out, she leaves him—but only for ten days. He seeks advice from a family friend, a priest, and that helps. Nevertheless he checks several items on the symptoms list, including a drinking problem. On his Twenty Statements Test he checks only three: "*trying* to make the best of life," "*trying* to get ahead," and "*trying* to help others."

By the fourth interview the couple has separated. She is living with their three-month-old daughter and is "bitching and complaining all the time," according to Bobby, who also reports they have "sex problems." Having finally passed the police exam, he is now a policeman as well as a printer. Throughout this interview he drinks bourbon mixed with a soft drink, at the same time telling the interviewer he has cut down on alcohol. Now sharing an apartment with a girlfriend who helps with the rent, he concludes the interview by saying it has helped him to figure out whether he wants to stay single or raise a family.

Twenty-eight by the final contact, Bobby has divorced and then reconciled; his wife has stopped working and is pregnant again. Before the reconciliation he had been hospitalized for acute alcoholism; he then went, voluntarily, to a live-in care unit for two months and has not had a drink since. The problems that led him to quit were severe: he had gained nearly fifty pounds, had been

paralyzed from the waist down on two occasions, and "was spending a hundred and fifty dollars a week on booze." Ironically, shortly
after going on the wagon Bobby had a car accident: a fellow officer
had spiked his orange juice with vodka. He blacked out, hit a tele-
graph pole, and was arrested for drunk driving and put in jail. At
his hearing he brought a letter from his doctor and the charges were
dropped. All of his personal relationships have improved, including those with his parents. His goal is to have a business of his own
soon. One can readily speculate that Bobby's adolescent rebellion
came late, but now that he is back in the fold, some rigidity might
even be appropriate for the kind of person he was raised to become.

Retiree Bertha Wilson has had eight years of schooling and
was a child in the Great Depression. Her father, a longshoreman,
had been laid off and she went to work cleaning other people's
houses when she was fourteen. Fifty years old when we meet her,
she seems over the years that follow to be a paragon of resiliency.
Why she agrees with four rigid characteristics (six are flexible, four
neutral) is not quite clear. Her choices may, however, reflect a growing desire for a quiet and orderly life, something she has had pre-
cious little experience with. They may also reflect an underlying
complexity that has led Bertha to cope adaptively and creatively
with the many adversities in her life.

At first contact, Bertha's husband works as a body and fender
man. They have one child, a son, who is assistant manager in a
furniture store; he has two small children. Bertha describes her husband with considerable warmth, is close to her son and his wife, and
"adores" her grandchildren. She calls herself a "homebody." Just
before the second interview, the Wilsons move (her husband has
retired) and Bertha writes to the interviewer giving their new address. A house is being built for them, she announces proudly, and
her husband is doing some of the work. (At his retirement party he
received a chainsaw.) Two weeks later another letter arrives: her
husband has died of a heart attack. "You can see this changes my
life completely; I don't know what the future holds for me." She
adds that she does not know who she is or where she is going and
"is trying to find out." Her son has been promoted and now he and
his family live a thousand miles away and she thinks she may never
see them again.

At the third contact, however, we find that "homebody" Bertha has learned to drive and has taken her parents on several long trips, including one to visit her son and their great-grandchildren. She has also learned to play golf and, in general, feels far more mature and independent than ever before. A boarder in her house is now her closest friend, a gentleman "who helps pay for things." She does worry about her parents, however. Her life is seemingly wrapped up in her many obligations and the roles she plays, as well as her own continuing uncertainties about widowhood. This outlook is reflected in her responses to the Twenty Statements Test, where Bertha has listed only four: "mother," "grandmother," "homemaker," and "a woman alone."

By the next to last interview Bertha's parents are living with her and her mother has cancer. By the final contact her father has died and her mother is bedridden, but Bertha has the satisfaction, at age sixty-two, of feeling sure that she will cope well. In the course of the study she goes from highest to lowest in her subgroup on self-concern (a rating that deals with self-protectiveness as a basic value).

Retirement-stage participant Luke Weaver resembles Bertha except that he circles neutral on more statements and agrees with one fewer of the rigid ones. A good-looking man with a healthy ego, he lives a circumscribed life. At the first meeting he is sixty-one and working at a nearby hospital in the medical records department. Luke has had nine years of schooling; his wife, a seamstress, went only as far as the fourth grade. The Weavers have no children, by choice, and they live in a small apartment in a poorly kept building. A major and consuming goal is to buy a trailer and move into it. They are "very excited about that." Luke likes his work and the doctors he works with, but he is beginning to worry about his retirement pay. His somewhat senile mother lives in a retirement home.

Retired by the second interview, the Weavers have moved south in their newly acquired trailer and Luke notes that they are very lucky to be in good health with enough money to live on. His mother has recently died, as has his only sibling, a sister. Neighbors in the motor home park are now friends, and Luke enjoys fixing up the property and beginning a garden. They had saved money for this kind of retirement, which has proved to be even better than they hoped. They both feel more relaxed and enjoy short trips, fishing, and a few community activities.

Despite these enjoyments, the third interview form has to be mailed to Oklahoma, and the Weavers say they are very happy to be back home. Luke now grows most of their food and sells a lot more. Catching a lot of fish as well, they are very self-sufficient. They have found new friends, and their marriage continues to be rewarding even though Luke reports that sex is less frequent. (He is now in his late sixties.)

By the final contact Luke has had prostate surgery but is fully recovered. He continues to make money from his vegetable garden, has stopped smoking and drinking, and reports that he is "doing better than ever before." They have completely refurbished their trailer. Politically conservative, he thinks that "the refugees" (not specified) are the major social problem in this country. Overall he is a man with modest aspirations, content to live quietly and with minimum disturbance, a homebody to the core. Retirement, he says, "fits me just fine."

By Arnold Erikson's own standards, and those of his (often dismayed) family as well, this former empty nester's best years, occupationally, were in the distant past. One of the more fully expressed examples of the rigid style, he agrees with all seven of the rigid statements. Fifty-five at the first interview, he is working as a stevedore at the docks. His wife is six years younger than he; she works as a part-time research interviewer and enjoys it, but he does not understand why. The couple has four children, all of whom are or will be college graduates.

One of the themes in Arnold's life is a resentment for things past—for example, he still blames his parents for letting him drop out of college after a year. By his senior year in high school he had become a star athlete and was "president of everything, it seems." In the course of World War II he was in Guam and Okinawa, Japan, and Germany. A colonel in the Seabees, he supervised construction and maintenance crews of five hundred men and more. In comparison, his current job is a tremendous letdown and he would like to change it.

This desire to improve himself occupationally is a theme that continues through the next eight years. (He has retired by the last interview.) By the second interview he is anticipating the empty nest; with all of his children gone, he thinks he may "fall prey to excessive drinking." His wife now works full time as a professional caterer, and he cannot understand why she likes that either. Arnold has declined a small promotion because he would have had to "deal with blacks," which reminds us that his first statement on the Twenty Statements Test is "a white person." Another is "a loner at times," which is surprising because he claims to have many friends and to be very close to his wife, children, and mother. At the beginning of the third interview he announces that since he has been pessimistic in the first two interviews he might as well continue in that vein and proceeds with a diatribe about how things are falling apart in this country. Calling himself "not too happy," he explains that he has more physical symptoms, is depressed about the death of his dog, and is "drinking more" and not improving on his job. On the psychological symptoms list he checks seven that apply to him. "Rampant permissiveness" is the subject of yet another diatribe.

The next to last interview finds Arnold "very happy" (up from "not too happy"), but he does not say why. His health has improved, but he had a "fainting spell" at work and was ambulanced to a hospital, where doctors found nothing serious. Sixty-seven years old and retired for two years at the final interview, he is not in good shape. "Scary dreams" keep waking him up and he reports nine psychological symptoms. "My life is ruined," he says, "not on the rocks but just waning, the spark of life is waning." Arnold's family continues to disagree with him about "increasing social decadence," which in turn makes him more agitated. The interviewer notes that Arnold would answer only those questions that offered a springboard for a tirade: on moral decay, absence of discipline, and the total corruption of society. Trapped in his own rigid prison of thought, he is the polar opposite of Marilyn Miller.

In sum, then, three of the rigid types have had very little education; the fourth, Arnold Erikson, as we have just noted, had a year of college and blames his parents for letting him drop out. Bobby Caldwell and Luke Weaver are not very intelligent, at least as judged by the results of the Wechsler Adult Intelligence Scale, administered at the first interview. Although Bertha Wilson went only through grade school, she is innately intelligent and has continued to grow, confronting the new circumstances of her life with grace. The rigid statements she agrees with are suitable: she does not have a wide range of intellectual interests and likes familiar surroundings and routines. Essentially, she has had enough challenge and excitement for one lifetime.

The Four. As it turns out, The Four represent a cross section of rigid and flexible possibilities. Olav Olavsen, who ranks consistently low on self-concern, agrees with six flexible and six rigid self-descriptions, a split suggesting greater complexity as a person than we had suspected. Hazel Sutter, no longer preoccupied with herself, is by far the most flexible in the group. Max Schindler confirms our image of him thus far: he agrees with four rigid and disagrees with four flexible statements. As a sidenote, it may not be entirely a coincidence that many of our more right-wing and conservative participants endorse qualities reflective of rigidity. Adelaide Stone, still not well, manages to respond to half of the fourteen items. Agreeing with five flexible ones and neutral on two, she reinforces our admiration of her stamina and openmindedness.

Personality, Circumstances, or Both?

We next explore the difficult question of "why" and the reasonable thesis that interaction between the two domains is the most helpful explanation. Marilyn Mitchell's profile suggests that it was her mother's success in persuading her to see a psychiatrist (a life circumstance) that was crucial. As a result she becomes an autonomous and flexible person who is able to get a divorce, leave the church, and expand her horizons. Her mother's insight was the trigger, and in finding her real self she continues, on her own, to grow (a personal characteristic). Late bloomer Gail Ramsey did not have an insightful parent (a life circumstance). Indeed, she may well have married and planned to have several children just to prove to herself and her parents that family life is rich and rewarding. If so, it was a passing fancy. Eventually Gail asks questions of herself and decides what she wants to make of her life; finally discovering who she is and what is important to her (self-insight), she goes back to teaching.

Fay Price is very flexible despite difficult years of living with a deranged husband and then widowhood. She has always refused to feel sorry for herself. A "gutsy" woman (a personal characteristic), she has overcome by herself. A need to keep growing and generosity of the spirit best characterize her. Many others would have felt defeated by circumstances that to her were a challenge. Lance Shannon's life, on the other hand, is full of maybes. The person he portrays in his Twenty Statements Test may well be an ideal self. In real life, his erratic states of mind, psychosomatic (or genuinely schizoid) symptoms, and finally alcoholism prevent him from making firm decisions in his own best interest and those of his family. He creates his circumstances and then blames them for his problems—a case of circularity (personality).

In brief, for Marilyn circumstance came first and personal independence followed. Gail's circumstances were negative; she at first took the wrong route, but asking herself the right questions led to insight. Fay's circumstances were extremely difficult, but her personal strength of mind enabled her to transcend them. Lance, on the other hand, records an ideal self that bears no relationship to his life.

Turning to the rigid side of the paradigm, Bobby Caldwell's father was very strict (a life circumstance), and it takes him several years to drop him as a role model. Soon after that Bobby nearly drowns himself in alcohol until the midpoint of the study, when we find him in serious trouble and frightened. By the last contact he has been cured (on his own initiative). His preference for certain rigid statements, such as following a strict routine, is suitable for a former alcoholic.

The concept of relative deprivation is helpful in understanding Bertha Wilson's preference for a few rigid statements combined with an ability, when circumstances assail her, to rise to the occasion. After all, when she was a child she had cleaned houses to feed her siblings and parents. Her life was happy and comfortable until her husband's sudden death. At that point she seems to have realized that the same inner resources (a personal characteristic) that stood her in good stead at fourteen could do so fifty years later when she created a new life for herself. Her rigid statements are common to many aging housewives, a kind of holdover from her past.

Luke Weaver's high score on rigidity fits his circumscribed life, a matter of his and his wife's choice (a personal preference), including having no children and living in a trailer. Though they move around quite a bit, their schedule and activities stay the same. (In addition, some rigidity is necessary to be a good farmer.)

Arnold Erikson, most rigid of them all, was in his late sixties when he made his choices. Though he professes great warmth—in family and other personal relationships—he seems more than a bit hypocritical (a personal characteristic). In his heyday as a colonel with hundreds of soldiers under his command, some rigidity may have been helpful, but it was later applied to political disgust and bigotry. Feeling degraded in his later life's work, he typifies the wrong side of what another Erikson (1982) has called the dichotomy of integrity versus despair.

In sum, life circumstances were crucial for Bobby but he found enough willpower to survive. Negative life circumstances triggered Bertha's innate autonomy, and in the broadest sense she became flexible. Luke created, of his own free choice, a tautly circumscribed life, while Arnold's personality helped shape his life circumstances. Here we can see the relevance of theories that suggest an interaction between personality and the environment (see, for example, Lazarus and Folkman, 1984) and help to clarify the whys and wherefores of flexible and rigid choices.

Summing Up

Other chapters in this book deal, for the most part, with inner thoughts and feelings. The focus of this chapter, in contrast, has been on perceptions of the self that reflect behavioral preferences. Very little introspection was required of our participants as they filled out the Experience Survey created by Costa and McCrae. The results suggest that one cherished stereotype—that older persons are invariably less flexible and more rigid—is probably more myth than truth. Perhaps more important, we found that by looking separately at data specific to flexibility and rigidity, we could begin to group people in meaningful ways. McCrae and Costa

(1984) have created a sophisticated scaling system for their survey, but their approach makes it hard to consider the salience of each concept separately as well as in relation to each other (Whitbourne, 1986).

One intriguing theme in our review of cases is that the relative balance of flexibility and rigidity, within each person, may be critical. Those who are clearly flexible, or clearly rigid, may find it easy to carve out a life-style that accords with their behavioral preferences. An emphasis on rigidity, for example, may be linked to a circumscribed life in which stability is the desired norm. For a person like Lance Shannon, however, one with considerable flexibility but also elements of rigidity, one gets the feeling that the two opposing forces get in the way of each other. Lance yearns for the artist's life, settles for the practical and mundane, and is chronically dissatisfied. Those who are more balanced in the flexible and rigid dimensions of selfhood may be involved in a chronic and potentially disastrous battle between competing desires or, rising above this battle, use the opposing perspective as a means of energizing creativity and new outlooks.

This chapter, therefore, provides a thread to be woven in with some of the succeeding ones. In the next chapter, for example, we find that differences between rigid and flexible preferences are associated with awareness and concern with social changes. We also find support for the reasonable assumption that the rigid are indifferent and the flexible involved. And, anticipating Chapter Nine on inner and outer resources, we will report circumstances under which one or the other of these two behavioral styles is help or hindrance. In this context we will be introducing the concept of ego boundaries, which suggests that, for some personality types, rigid behavior is indeed a resource.

5

Reactions to Social Change

The initial chapters in this volume have focused on various manifestations, both direct and indirect, of the self. In the last chapter, for example, we found that the concepts of rigidity and flexibility are related to self-image. We now consider yet another manifestation of the self: how people react to the outer world. After reviewing some pertinent demographic characteristics of the sample, we summarize reactions to social changes during the early years of the study and then present a detailed report on the impact of social change between the fourth and fifth contacts. People who report strong reactions are compared with those who did not change or even declined in concern. Examining a few individuals in each category will help us to understand why some care about what goes on out there and others do not. The chapter concludes with an exploration of the relationship between awareness of social change and changes in the self.

The Sample Revisited

Here we will not be concerned with reviewing the basic characteristics of the sample, as this information has already been presented in Chapter One. Rather, we want to indicate where most of our participants placed in the socioeconomic scheme of things. As

public opinion polls regularly inform us, how people react to political and social issues is closely related to their age, sex, education,
and knowledge of the issues in question. In order to keep some of
these key indicators in mind while we explore the reactions of our
participants, we turn now to a brief recapitulation of pertinent
characteristics of our sample at the first contact.

For the most part, people in the two older groups belong to
the lower-middle-class and blue-collar segments of society. Most of
them reached their occupational peak, if they were employed, in
early middle age. For many, job boredom soon set in. Their principal concern is the family. Few, if any, are interested in doing
something about civic problems. The older men worry about money. Some of their female counterparts, most of whom work part
time, think they ought to be better informed, and a few of the oldest
women become more autonomous and independent in their thinking. Among them a handful have gone so far as to take action by
writing to a city supervisor or state legislator. While many of the
young people are better educated than their parents, by the time
they marry and have children their horizons begin to narrow. Civic
issues are of interest only if they have a bearing on the family. There
is not a would-be politician among them at our first visit. But, as
social conditions changed, so did their reactions.

The Impact of Social Change: The Early Years

The first interviews took place during 1968 and 1969, years
of marked sociopolitical unrest: escalation of antiwar protests, civil
rights demonstrations, and racial conflict. Many people, especially
those in the two older groups, felt that the pace of change was
unprecedented and not especially desirable. Parents of high school
seniors were distressed about the changing values and behavior of
the young, including their own children. The older people worried
about crime on the streets. As for solutions, women pointed to the
need for personal change: people should become more responsible
and more knowledgeable about social problems and, through community organizations, take action. Men were most likely to place
responsibility squarely on the federal government, which should
enforce "law and order."

A few years later, in 1974 and 1975, more than half of the people studied were somewhat more concerned with social issues. This change was especially notable among middle-aged men. Women in the oldest group were far more concerned than the men. Now in their mid-twenties and mid-thirties, the younger groups were also more aware and concerned than formerly. Exceptions were the newlywed men, most of whom now had children and were engrossed in supporting their families. As the pace of change accelerated during the last years of the study, only people isolated in their own cocoons could be indifferent.

Change Between the Last Two Contacts

At all contact points the data were procured by means of a social change checklist that originally included ten items. Five were former events and five current. In analyzing data from the last two contacts we elected to focus only on items dealing with current issues because these were most likely to be fresh in our subjects' minds and not recollections of things past. The list is as follows:

- New ways of doing things at work
- Changing roles of women
- Changes in rights of minorities
- Crime in the streets
- Changes in the economy and employment

For each item, respondents circled whether it had no (1), little (2), moderate (3), or strong (4) effect on them. At the last session three new items were added:

- The international situation
- Dangers at nuclear plants
- New life-styles

Stronger Impact. We first looked at the items that seemed to be of greatest concern to participants or increased in impact from the fourth to fifth contacts. At the fourth contact, issues of most concern to the four younger groups vary in both nature and degree. Somewhat less than a third of the youngest men cite changes in rights of minorities, and about the same proportion are concerned about new roles for women. Since most of these young men have only recently entered the labor market, they may feel threatened by potential competition. The youngest women are equally concerned about new roles and crime in the streets. The newlywed men worry about new ways at work and changes in the economy. Their female counterparts cite changing roles of women as well as the economy. The four older groups are unanimous: crime in the streets is the big problem, and the proportion singling out that item ranges from two-fifths of the oldest women to two-thirds of the middle-aged men.

By the last interview, changes in the economy and employment are foremost in the minds of the young, ranging from a third or more of the youngest people to well over half of the newlyweds of both sexes. All of the four oldest groups have become even more worried about crime. Two-fifths of the oldest women cite crime at the fourth interview, for example, but more than four-fifths of them do so at the last one. In fact, most of these women have become more worried about everything.

Less Impact. Not all areas of social change are of strong concern or increased in impact. The concerns of the youngest men, for example, have either increased or stayed about the same by the last contact. And as though women's roles are now settled for them, the youngest women are no longer concerned with this issue. (They are in sharp contrast to the oldest women, whose interest in this category increases considerably.) Among the newlywed women only a handful are concerned with crime in the streets whereas the great majority in most of the other subgroups have become more fearful. One can only speculate about the reasons for this decline. It may be worth noting that the neighborhood is adjacent to a large park that now has more police officers assigned to it. One often observes two or more young mothers walking together in the park pushing strollers or with infants strapped to their backs. Street crime is more likely to be "downtown." All subgroups except the oldest women maintain about the same degree of concern with regard to two or three items, primarily new ways at work, women's roles, and minority rights.

The New Social Concerns. Change in any of the five original issues could influence the mundane routines of day-to-day living; the three items dealt with here require more of a sociopolitical stance on matters of worldwide importance. We are, in a sense, asking our respondents to forget their personal peeves and think like statesmen about the international situation, nuclear dangers, and new lifestyles. This last item is minor compared to the two others, but it is of interest because new ways of living, especially those adopted by the young in this country, have a way of spreading to others with astonishing speed.

The data were processed and analyzed in two ways: the first combined moderate and strong, on the one hand, and small or none, on the other; the second separated the four categories. The latter method seemed most appropriate for this section. Scores on the three global items were combined, therefore, and the following results are based on the average ratings. Only if they scored 4 (indicating "strong effect") were individuals classified as being in the strong impact group.

None of the youngest men, now averaging age thirty, are strongly concerned about these situations, and fewer than one-fourth are moderately so. This outlook seems rather shortsighted since they are the only people in the sample who might become directly involved should the international situation escalate (that is, they would be at greater risk of being drafted). In contrast, about a sixth of the youngest women are strongly concerned with these problems and more than a fourth report moderate impact. Only one man in the newlywed group reports strong impact; about a fifth of them are moderates. As in the youngest group, some of their female counterparts are strongly concerned and more than a fourth are moderately so.

Differences between the sexes are somewhat more dramatic among the two older groups. Among the late-middle-aged men, only two are strongly concerned and three are moderates. A few more women in the same life stage experience strong impact, and about a third of them are in the moderate category. More interesting is the oldest group: only two of the men report moderate impact, and they are the *least* concerned of all subgroups. In vivid contrast, over half of the women experience strong or moderate impact, and they are the *most* concerned of all subgroups. This is not the only context in which these oldest women have both broader perspectives and a greater willingness to speak out than other groups. One can almost hear them saying "What is there to lose?" A glance at the other end of our spectrum supports their thesis: while nine young people of both sexes and stages experience *small* impact, only two older people do so, and they are not among the oldest women.

Biographical Sketches

To humanize these variations between the sexes and life stages we have selected one representative individual from each group.

Persons Reporting Strong Impact. Former high school senior Susie Cole was born in Detroit. Her father is a machinist, her mother a teacher, and she has a younger brother and sister. Since both parents are working when we first meet this eighteen-year-old, she is responsible for many household chores and for babysitting with her much younger siblings. About two years later Susie is deeply in love with a well-to-do divorced man much older than she. She hopes to marry. In the interim, Susie has worked in the post office, but "the long hours are killing me" and, to the great dismay of her parents, she has quit. She expects to go back to school and eventually work in an advertising agency; meanwhile she describes her life with her friend as hedonistic.

When asked, a bit more than three years later, about important changes in her life, her first response is: "I fell in love with a dog!" She has not only adopted the stray, but the event has prompted her to enroll in a veterinary program. She still lives with her former lover because he has a large and comfortable house, but they are no longer in love. Getting married is a low priority now, but her family and friends are very important to her. Once grossly overweight, she has slimmed down a lot and is quite healthy.

Another three years find Susie's accomplishments impressive. She is working for a college degree and specializing in psychology and women's studies. She has also experimented with lesbian relationships. Her current friend, she says, has introduced her to new worlds of literature and opera, bringing out an intelligence she did not know she had. Working part time as a postal clerk, Susie also enjoys just staying home and reading. Rating herself as "very happy," she looks forward to a satisfying future.

Susie's future, it emerges at the final interview, is anything but rosy. The interviewer quotes her as saying "I am willing to pragmatically consider suicide or going to Europe as a reasonable response to our social problems." Why these are reasonable considerations is by no means clear, but for the first time she reports that her private life is very stressful. The lesbian relationships have gone from bad to worse because of deaths, illness, and alcoholism. Susie has reevaluated her career plans and is now working toward a degree in developmental psychology. Considering her stresses, her new objectives and strong convictions about social change seem to be welcome antidotes.

Equally strong concern is also reported by the middle-aged women, among them Esther Nash. On first acquaintance we learn that she is fifty-two, has a high school education, is a paralegal secretary, and has two daughters. Her husband, a college graduate, is manager of an aquarium. Esther is very sick at this time, recovering from a stroke that has left her with residual paralysis. Weak and in great pain, she finds that she must curtail most of her former activities but does not think this is a permanent change. Being an optimistic person, Esther hopes for improvement. Her marriage is excellent and her husband very supportive. Esther misses her work but is happy to be alive, "just living from day to day." Two years later she is feeling a little better and pleased that both of her children are in college, albeit some distance from home. Now able to walk out of doors, she does so shortly before her husband returns from work so that he can help her up the stairs. She finds that her illness has made her more tolerant with her family and the friends who visit.

By the third interview, Esther has changed doctors, with positive consequences. Her activities now include driving, keeping house, and working in her garden. The wheelchair is now put away in the basement. Masterminding her oldest daughter's wedding reception and then visiting the newlyweds in Oregon are highlights of this period. Daily life includes serious reading and developing coin and stamp collections. She has none of the psychological symptoms on our long list and rates herself as "very happy." Esther's social concerns at this time include the poor quality of teaching in the city's public schools and the mass media in general. At the fourth interview she is strongly concerned about four social-change items and moderately so about four others. Travel to other countries has broadened her social horizons.

The final interview finds Esther healthier, and though she still tires easily she has resumed her membership in several civic organizations and attends meetings at least once a month. Strongly concerned about foreign policy, the presidency, local politics, the judicial system, and other issues, she is one of the few people in the sample who write to legislators.

Esther's age and life-style are very different from Susie's but the two women share a broad perspective and concern for the world they live in, both are intelligent and well read, and both continue to grow. Their sensitivity to social problems has probably added to the lives of these two women.

Persons Reporting Moderate Impact. Andy Bush is the only son of a Unitarian minister, and his two siblings are much younger. He is the only high school senior who describes the content of his courses. Good grades and high intelligence helped to win him a one-month trip to Germany, during which he began to learn the language. His parents hope he will become a teacher, but that is not to be his path. At the first interview Andy checks yes for nearly all the psychological symptoms; he also has very poor eyesight, later corrected with contact lenses. He does not like sports of any kind and thus far does not like girls either. Even at eighteen, however, he is quite liberal and concerned about racial discrimination and other issues.

By the second interview Andy is in college and expecting to graduate before long. He has spent a very hedonistic year with some thirty-five friends, though he did hold a part-time job as waiter at a retirement home. When he is about twenty-three Andy has a conversion experience and then decides to become a rabbi. At this time he still lives with his parents and works part time as a desk clerk at the YMCA. Prayers and meditation are part of his daily routine. His major social concern is corruption in the federal government.

By the next-to-last interview Andy is on a leave of absence from his college, where he has been working toward an advanced degree in divinity. Short of money, he works full time at the YMCA and also holds a part-time job as a stock clerk. He shares an apartment with a younger man and has become a confirmed homosexual. Not sure that he wants to be a priest, he studies in preparation for the army officers' training test and later scores well but decides not to sign up. The last encounter finds Andy very happy in his niche. He has his advanced degree in divinity and is a rabbi. His work has top priority in his life, and he says he has become "people-centered." He lives a pleasant and peaceful domestic life with his young male friend and says he is very comfortable with himself and his way of life.

Though only forty-five, Forrest Cohen is very bored with his job as an automobile salesman when we first meet. Money is very important to him and he is quite affluent. Several times throughout the interviews he says he wishes he had become a doctor. As it is, his education stopped with high school. His wife, a few years younger than he, has had two years of college. The Cohens have two daughters: the older, a political activist, has his very strong disapproval; the younger, a high school senior, is acceptable.

By the second contact things are looking better to Forrest. He has left his boring real estate job and invested in a franchised electronics shop. His older daughter has married and become more acceptable now that she is "getting establishment." The younger is at an arts and crafts school, which is all right with him. His wife helps in the shop, without salary, and they have occasional part-time help, but he has to work much harder than before and has no time for golf, nearly the only thing he is not negative about. He does not mind working hard so long as the shop gets "squared away" pretty soon. Meanwhile, as a good shop owner, he has joined the Chamber of Commerce, but he still regrets not being a doctor and not having gone to college. (That, by the way, was his own decision: his father was a successful realtor and certainly could have afforded it.) Forrest dislikes most people, hates his mother (describing her in unquotable terms), and is working hard but "not getting anywhere because of taxes."

Three years later Forrest is sarcastic, cynical, and angry throughout the interview; his vocabulary is strewn with curses. We are not surprised that he reports high blood pressure. To several questions he responds only with impertinent and irrelevant expletives. By the next to last interview he has sold the electronics shop and become, at age fifty-three, an officer with a local bank. He has stopped voting because politics disgust him. He is rude and condescending to the interviewer and his answers tend to be superficial. At our last encounter Forrest is back in the real estate business and making more money. He continues to hate people and rather proudly considers himself more intolerant than ever. Forrest seems to enjoy playing Scrooge. His major social concerns are minorities, crime, the economy, and the international situation.

Gloria Brooks, at age fifty-three, is a rather young member of the oldest group. Her husband is ten years older and will retire in a few years. The Brooks family includes five children, rather unusual for this sample. Gloria, who had two years of nursing school training, went back to work when she was in her late forties as buyer and sales clerk in a department store. She loves her work and also manages to keep house and cook for her husband and three of their grown children as well. She is proud of her oldest son but considers him (and her husband) bigoted. The youngest son has speech and reading problems and is very dependent on her; two other sons have had serious problems with the law. Her daughter is twenty and they are devoted to each other, sharing many social concerns.

Although her husband has had only two years of high school, he works as an accountant in a bank. By the second interview he is not well and requires extensive medication. He does not take care of the things he used to do, and Gloria is now head of the household. The problem son gets into many scrapes, and recently she had to have him arrested for forging checks to buy drugs. She does not pursue the case, and the fact that he still lives at home off and on is very upsetting to the other three children. Her work continues to be satisfying: Gloria has considerably more responsibility and an appropriate increase in salary. She is not as close to her husband as she would like, and her principal goal now is to help him find a solution to his problems, which includes their marriage.

The most important change at the penultimate interview is that their youngest son has bought them a new house in a much better neighborhood. Reading good books is her favorite means of relaxing. The final interview finds Gloria "very happy" even though her husband has cancer and drinks far too much. Her work continues to be challenging, and she is pleased to have two grandchildren. In answer to a question about changes in herself over the past decade or so, she feels that she is more tolerant, not so quick to criticize, and kinder than she used to be. Gloria's greatest stress continues to be her husband's health and his heavy drinking. She has many social concerns, rating all items moderate to strong in impact except for the economy. Her reasons for concern are very different from those of Forrest Cohen, who is basically angry at the world and its freeloaders.

Like those who feel a strong impact from social changes, those who have moderate reactions are intelligent and socially concerned. Turning now to people who evince little or no concern about sociopolitical events, we will detect some interesting differences.

Persons Reporting Little or No Impact. Age thirty-eight when we first meet him, Erik Kress is quite old for a newlywed; his wife is twenty-five. He calls himself a craftsman, has a small shop, is taking some college courses, but is quite vague about what he wants to do with the rest of his life. Earlier he had spent a few years in the navy, where his life was structured for him. He liked it. His wife went to college for a year or so and now works full time as a business machine operator. Erik is quite clear about two things, however: he does not want to have any children because the world is already overpopulated, and he loves sailboats, especially racing boats.

Nothing much has changed in his life a year and a half later except for the worse. His Volkswagen "blew its engine and that put me in a financial bind." He certainly will not be buying a racing boat for some time. The only encouraging event he notes is that his wife has a new, well-paying job as a market representative for a retail company. He is not sure he wants to continue with college courses. He is trying to do too much, he says, gets very tired, and feels scattered.

More than three years later, when he is about forty-three, Erik decides to become a photographer. He likes it because he can arrange his schedule to suit himself. Serving on the race committee of a local yacht club gives him vicarious satisfaction. Another three years (at the fourth interview) find him more settled. He runs his own photographic studio, has a fairly good salary, and the couple now has a house of their own. He notes at this contact, as in all other sessions, that he is "completely different" from other people his age. Nearly twelve years after the first interview Erik, close to fifty, seems to have decided who he is. His chosen title is designer/ photographer. He has been so busy finding himself that he never seems to find time to be interested in the world outside his own ego.

Anita Swenson, also a newlywed when we first meet, is, like Erik, not at all concerned with social problems. She is a secretary and her husband is a plumber. Both have had about two years of college and are in their mid-twenties. She likes her work, but other than keeping house her major "activity" is watching television. About two years later, in answer to a question about whether she had changed, she observes that she has become more mature and realistic. Among the new realities of her life is her new job: she works nights in the communications center of the police department answering phone calls and dispatching patrol cars. Like Erik and his wife, the Swensons have decided not to have children; they both see such a dismal side of life, they say, that they would have trouble bringing them up. In any case, her husband does not seem interested in making love any more. In fact, with her night work they do not even have much time to talk. One thing she does enjoy very much is volunteer work in a charity organization.

Three years later (at the third interview) Anita has consulted a marriage counselor and in consequence not only have relations with her husband improved but she understands herself better and feels more mature. Her work has not changed, and she enjoys it because she helps people. Nothing much changes in her life during the next three years, but three and a half years later (at the final contact) she reports events both good and bad. Her husband became an alcoholic, but eventually he sought treatment and is now recov-

ered. She has a new and better-paid job as a postal clerk. What she
wants most is to quit work, get a house with a garden, "take it easy,"
and have fun. The only social issue that concerns her at all is the
economy.

Retirement participant Angelo Martini is rare in reporting
no social concerns at all. Born in Italy, he came to this country with
his parents when he was seven. Now in his mid-fifties, he works as
a health code inspector for the city. His education includes two
years of high school and a year in a trade school. Angelo's wife
finished high school; she does not work. The Martinis have two
sons and a daughter; all of them work and only the daughter lives
at home. Although he had two heart attacks in his late forties,
Angelo now feels quite well but would prefer to work part time. He
is an outgoing, cheerful, and self-reliant man and has many good
friends. Instead of cutting down on work, a year and a half later (at
the second interview) he has an even busier schedule inspecting
older houses for the federal government to determine whether they
should be upgraded. He still has some angina pain but enjoys life
more than ever because with the children grown up and on their
own he and his wife can "play our lives by ear."

About three years later (at the third interview), we find Angelo retired because he has had another heart attack. For a year or
so his activities are so constricted that he feels useless and in limbo.
As time goes on he starts taking some real estate courses and is even
able to play a little golf. Very little has changed by the fourth contact except that he has bought an organ and playing it is a joy for
him. He does not see much of his friends and still feels in limbo.
Much more cheerful at the final contact (he is now sixty-five), he
has been to Hawaii and Alaska, rides a bike, hikes, and works in
his garden. All along he has enjoyed reading books and now sees
old friends occasionally. A coronary bypass is next on his agenda,
and he will take it in stride; getting and staying well is his main
goal. Under the circumstances Angelo's lack of social concern is
understandable. But as we will see in the concluding section of this
chapter, some people who are not well still manage to maintain
broad horizons and are interested in the world outside their own
boundaries.

In conclusion, then, all three of these unconcerned people are quite self-centered: Erik with his identity problems, Anita with her material comforts, Angelo with his health.

The Four

One might assume that people who are very self-concerned have little interest in sociopolitical issues and, conversely, the less self-concern, the more energy left over for other problems. This assumption is only partially supported by the four people we trace through the book. Olav Olavsen is the least self-preoccupied of The Four, but just as he surprised us by being quite rigid, he does so again in regard to his social horizons. Only crime, Watergate, and the international situation have had a strong impact on him and four issues moderately so (the Depression, Vietnam, new roles for women, and energy problems). The rest he views with little or no concern.

Hazel Sutter, who ranks highest in her subgroup on self-concern at the outset and lowest nearly twelve years later, is rather similar to Olav in regard to social issues except that she is a bit less concerned than he. Max Schindler's reactions are once again predictable: he is moderately influenced by only one issue, World War II; the remaining social issues have little or no impact. Adelaide Stone supports the idea that people who are ill or impaired may be very knowledgeable about sociopolitical affairs and have strong opinions about them. Adelaide is still recovering from her stroke, but ten situations have a strong impact on her and two have a moderate impact. These last two people, from the oldest groups, are dramatically representative. As noted early in this chapter, more than half of the pre-retirement women report moderate or strong impact and are the most concerned of all eight subgroups, while their male counterparts are the least so.

The Consequences of Social Change

As noted in Chapter Two, among humanists and social scientists alike there is increasing interest in the dynamics of the social-personal change equation. Kenneth Burke (1977) has noted that social change results in an "unsettling" of the individual. Psychologist Aaron Antonovsky (1987) writes of a disruption in the sense of personal coherence as a result of an unstable social context. And we might add here that Erik Erikson (1982), for psychological as well as philosophical reasons, finds that social problems accentuate personal problems. For all three of these consequences we find some support. In this section of the chapter we have chosen two personal characteristics to examine as possible "consequences" of the impact of social change: self-concept and psychological symptoms. People who report strong or moderate impact will be compared with those experiencing little or none.

Derogatory Self-Concept. More than three-fourths of the people who report strong impact checked many negative characteristics on the Adjective Rating List. This is in contrast to people who are moderately concerned, more than half of whom have a negative image of themselves. Only one person who reports little or no social concern has a derogatory self-view. Does this mean that the stronger the impact, the more negative the self-image? Or does it mean the more derogatory the self-concept, the stronger the impact? This is not only a matter of semantics. Although it is inappropriate to force the data into a cause-and-effect paradigm, it is legitimate to examine life-stage and gender differences and draw tentative conclusions.

Thus far we have found that differences between the sexes are usually quite marked and those between life stages somewhat less so. The relationship between self-image and social concern has a pattern of its own. Within each of the eight subgroups, strong or moderate concern is associated with negative self-image by half or more of the people. The youngest and next youngest women have the poorest opinion of themselves, and the second youngest men and the middle-aged women tie for third place. The youngest men and middle-aged men place about in the middle, while the oldest men and women are least negative about themselves. As previously noted, among those who experience little or no impact only one person, a man in the second youngest group, has a negative self-image.

Symptoms. Psychological symptoms no doubt provide a more objective way to assess the impact of social change. A bird's-eye view

of the eight subgroups combined reveals a direct relationship between strength of impact and symptoms: four-fifths of the people
reporting a strong impact rank high on symptoms whereas only a
little more than half of those reporting a moderate impact do so.
The subgroups differ considerably, however. Only one of the
youngest men is strongly affected, and he ranks low on symptoms,
whereas all five of the youngest women reporting a strong impact
rank high. Among older people the consequences for the two sexes
are reversed: older men reporting a strong impact tend to have many
symptoms, but older women who do so report few.

People who report a moderate impact are more numerous
and tell a rather different story. There are as many young men as
young women in this category, but fewer than half of the men rank
high on symptoms, compared with two-thirds of the women.
Among the older people, reporting even a moderate impact helped
to highlight gender differences. First, there are nearly three times as
many women as men in this group; second, surprisingly, more men
than women rank high on symptoms. Most significant is the fact
that so many of both young and old rank high whereas only one-
fifth of the people reporting little or no impact do so.

Summing Up

In general, the findings of this chapter strongly support Erikson's (1982) thesis that social problems exacerbate personal ones and
Burke's (1977) contention that social change is unsettling for the
individual. Verification of Lifton's premise (the generation gap) is
equivocal in the findings reported here. Our exploration of generational differences in Chapter Eight, based on several domains of
life, will provide another perspective, and we will see in Chapter
Seven that sensitivity to social change may in the long run create
additional stress for the individual.

Part Two
How Stress Affects Development and Adaptability

6

Effects
of Childhood Deprivation
on Adult Adaptability

One way or another we are all haunted by ghosts of the distant past: the paths not taken, the friends unmet, the punishing father. In this chapter we examine these stressors of the past. After reviewing various approaches to the problem, both theoretical and applied, we summarize the data in our own study. Some of the consequences, both negative and positive, of severe deprivation are next assessed by information drawn from the third and fifth interviews, and we briefly explore how respondents visualize the future as well as their current feelings about parents (often pivotal figures in the occurrence of childhood stress). We conclude the chapter as usual: Where do The Four fit into the paradigm?

Theoretical Considerations

Despite decades of clinical inquiry, the influence of earlier experiences on adult adaptation remains an unresolved issue. A basic but unproven tenet of psychiatric literature, for example, is that childhood stress has a powerful and lasting influence on subsequent development (Kagan, 1980; Freud, 1969). Erikson (1982) presents a more refined version of this hypothesis, postulating with his epigenetic model of development, for example, that experiences of earlier stages are significant in the resolution of later stages. More

115

recently, the traditional view that childhood stress may have a detrimental effect on adult experiences has been challenged (Kagan, 1980; Freud, 1969). Indeed, some studies suggest that childhood stress can actually result in reduced vulnerability in adulthood. (See, for example, Persson, 1980; Bornstein and others, 1973.)

In this section we will examine evidence for and against the negative impact of childhood stresses on adult functioning. Studies of childhood events are generally based on retrospective accounts. Sometimes these studies focus on a single major event such as the death of a parent; others consider the cumulative effects of multiple events. In one of the few studies to look at the complexities of emotional impact, Rutter (1977) examined six family variables associated with childhood psychiatric disorder: marital conflict, low socioeconomic status, large families and overcrowding, father a criminal, mother suffering from a psychiatric disorder, and appointment of a legal guardian. Children from families that had only one risk factor or an isolated stress were no more likely to develop childhood psychiatric disorders than were children from families with no risk factors. The presence of two or more risk factors, however, caused the rate of psychiatric disorder to increase exponentially. Rutter concludes that it is not single stressful events that predispose one to problems but rather the persistent conditions of childhood deprivation.

Research dealing with the hospitalization of children tends to support the idea that the single stressful event has no lasting consequences. Generally there is little long-term effect from a single admission, but multiple admissions are associated with a heightened risk of psychiatric disorder in later childhood. According to Rutter (1981), multiple hospital admissions are more likely to cause emotional disturbance when associated with severe psychosocial adversity than in more favored family circumstances.

On the basis of clinical inference rather than empirical examination, Bowlby (1977, pp. 206–207) has related certain patterns of parenting to the development of anxious and insecure adults: "one or both parents being persistently unresponsive to the child's care-eliciting behavior and/or actively disparaging and rejecting; discontinuities of parenting, occurring more or less frequently, including periods in hospital or institution; persistent threats by parents not to love a child, used as a means of controlling him; threats by parents to abandon the family, used either as a method of disciplining the child or as a way of coercing a spouse; threats by one parent either to desert or even to kill the other or else to commit suicide."

Moreover, there is empirical support for the impact of childhood experiences. In a prospective study based on longitudinal data from the UC Berkeley Institute of Human Development, Glen Elder (1981) has clearly demonstrated that exposure to the Great Depression created a lasting, and negative, effect on mental health and behavior in adulthood. An inventory of childhood events very similar to the one used here also produced evidence of an association with greater psychological symptomatology in adulthood (Chiriboga, Catron, and Weiler, 1987).

Childhood stress not only affects adult adaptation and psychological functioning directly but may exert indirect effects as well. Attachments are an example; changes in attachments or social bonds may then influence adult adaptation. Bowlby (1977), for example, delineates three maladaptive patterns of social support during adulthood that derive from disruptions of attachment in childhood. He calls these maladaptive patterns compulsive self-reliance, compulsive caregiving, and compulsive support seeking.

The compulsively self-reliant person consciously or unconsciously attempts to avoid attachments in adulthood because of parental rejection of his or her efforts to form a secure attachment. The compulsive caregiver forms many close relationships but is always in the role of providing rather than receiving care. As a child, the compulsive caregiver may have had a disabled or depressed mother who was unable to take care of the child but instead created a context in which the child took care of her (Bowlby, 1977). Finally, like the compulsive caregiver, the compulsive support seeker develops many relationships but is in constant need of support.

Further evidence for the hypothesized relationship of childhood stress to adult attachments comes from a thirty-five-year prospective study of ninety-five men who were first interviewed as college sophomores (Vaillant, 1978). Findings suggest that a poor childhood environment paves the way for poor object relations in adulthood but not the quality of marital relations. In fact, Vaillant

(p. 657) concludes that "in many men marriage served as a means of mastering unhappy childhoods."

Findings from Our Study

The idea that childhood experiences affect adult life is compelling. Accordingly, despite the reservations often expressed in the literature about the use of retrospective instruments, we decided to include a measure of childhood stress in our research protocol, based on the perhaps quixotic axiom: nothing ventured, nothing gained. Drawing on the advice of those who have attempted to study childhood experiences, we also decided to focus on relatively concrete and substantial negative experiences that participants presumably would be more likely to recall.

Procedures. Our data on childhood deprivation are based primarily on a Life Events Inventory that includes questions about situations that occurred before respondents had reached the age of fifteen. The inventory comprises twenty items ranging from death of one or both parents to problems at school. Here we will consider only the occurrence of events, although for each item the participants were also asked "How did you feel about the event then?" and "How often do you think about it now?" Before presenting information based on this inventory, a basic question must be addressed: Does the inventory contain reliable information?

Reliability is of major importance for most assessments of childhood stress exposure since these assessments are generally based on retrospective reporting. We were able to compare reports of the same life events over a three-year period. We looked at the percentage of agreement over time for the occurrence of individual events. Agreement was surprisingly high, ranging from 77 to 94 percent. To give some idea of the variability, there was 94 percent agreement as to whether a brother or sister had died and whether parents had separated, 93 percent agreement concerning whether a parent had remarried, 88 percent agreement concerning whether a parent had died, 87 percent agreement over whether the respondent had been subjected to severe and unusual punishment, 84 percent agreement over whether the mother or father had been absent frequently, and 77 percent agreement over whether parents had had intense arguments. Overall, then, we were satisfied with the levels of agreement over a three-year period. In other words, the childhood events inventory seems to be a reasonably reliable instrument.

Preliminary analyses began with all items on the list, and not surprisingly we found that everyone checked at least one. After reviewing various clinical studies of childhood deprivation, especially the work of Rutter (1981), we concluded that a reasonable indicator of deprivation would be the occurrence of childhood stressors reflecting persistent conditions as opposed to conditions that while stressful were rare and infrequent. To operationalize childhood deprivation, therefore, we used the reporting of one or more of the following stressors:

- Death of father
- Death of mother
- Frequent or long absences of mother
- Frequent or long absences of father
- Severe or unusual punishments
- Death of a sibling

Basic Findings. Using the presence of one or more of these childhood stressors as a yardstick, we found that life-stage and gender differences are statistically significant. For example, about a third of the youngest people of both sexes report conditions suggesting deprivation; in the second youngest group, two-thirds of the men but only one-third of the women are in that category. The second oldest people are a kind of mirror image of the newlyweds: far more women than men were deprived. About half of the oldest men provide evidence of having experienced childhood deprivation, but only a third of the women. Altogether two-fifths of the sample were deprived as children. Clearly neither stage nor gender explains the logic of this distribution. One purpose of this chapter is to determine whether the distribution makes sense or is simply a matter of chance. The fact that respondents are asked to recollect the distant past makes it inevitable that today's mood influences today's memories. Past circumstances might be reported, for example, as better or

worse simply on the basis of whether things are going well at the
time of the interview.

The Consequences of Childhood Deprivation

One way to examine the continuing effect of childhood deprivation in adulthood is to determine whether deprivation was associated with changes that took place between the third and fifth
interviews, a period of about six years. To simplify the method of
analysis and the situations being examined, we considered changes
in only two instruments: the Adjective Rating List described in
Chapter Two and a 138-item Life Events Inventory (Chiriboga,
1984) that tallied both positive and negative events. The assumption
is that people have some control over their personal characteristics
but little or none over life events. First we will summarize changes
in deprived people and then see how the nondeprived differ from
them.

Changes Among the Deprived. Men and women in the youngest
group strongly resemble each other: both have become less positive
about themselves. At the same time, they report an increase in the
positive events of life and a decrease in the negative, as compared
to six years earlier. The second youngest group of deprived men
have a poorer image of themselves and report an upswing in negative events, while their female counterparts think better of themselves and report an increase in positive events. The second oldest
men and women report that more of their life events have been
agreeable, but changes in their self-image differ: men think better
of themselves; women have changed a bit for the worse but are in
fact quite consistent with their earlier selves. The oldest deprived
people of both sexes have much more positive self-images; life
events improve for men, but the oldest women rank worst of all in
terms of negative life events. Knowing how empathic these women
become as they grow older, one is not surprised: even if they themselves are not experiencing a negative event, they experience the
problems of loved ones as if they were their own.

Except for the second youngest women, then, the young deprived people think less well of themselves than they did six years

earlier. As to life events, the youngest people of both sexes have become more positive. The second youngest women also think better of themselves, but deprived men in the same stage do not. Overall, older people are better off than younger except for the oldest women.

Changes Among the Nondeprived. Nondeprived people have ups and downs, too, but they have many more changes for the better. The youngest men and women become more positive about themselves and their life circumstances as well. Both men and women in the second youngest group improve their self-images, but events in the interim are not satisfactory. Like the deprived, both men and women in the second oldest group report improvement in terms of the Life Events Inventory; but unlike them, women express positive self-images. Women continue to rank very high on the Adjective Rating List. The oldest men and women increase their positive assets on the checklist, but only the men have become more positive about themselves.

Anticipation of the Future. By comparing how respondents rank the present and the future, one can distinguish between people who think their lives will become better, the same, or worse. This approach reveals an unanticipated distinction between life-stage and gender groups: optimists versus pessimists. Since there has been little research on this topic, it is worthy of report. Responses of men and women in the youngest group are almost identical. Among the deprived only one man and one woman are optimistic, while all of the youngest nondeprived people have cheerful views of their future. There is a bit less agreement in the second youngest group: deprived men are more pessimistic than women, but all nondeprived people of both sexes predict that the future will be better than the present.

The two older groups have a different tale to tell. Deprived second oldest women are more optimistic than their male counterparts, whereas the oldest deprived men are much more optimistic than the oldest women. The most interesting finding is that deprived younger people are twice as likely to be pessimistic as the two older deprived groups. In contrast we find that among those not deprived there are four times more young people than old in the optimistic camp.

Feelings About Parents Now. Do people who describe themselves as having had a deprived childhood ever feel close to their mothers, fathers, or both? How do they differ from the nondeprived in this respect? The two older groups do not have living parents, of course, so the focus here is on young people. The possibilities are: less close or closer to their mothers, fathers, or both. As to fathers, the youngest deprived men are more likely to feel close to them than are their nondeprived counterparts—not the outcome one might expect. The youngest women are different: the deprived are less close to their fathers than are the nondeprived women—the expected outcome. The second youngest deprived men resemble the youngest women, but their female counterparts report the opposite: more of the nondeprived are less close to their fathers than holds for the deprived. People closer to their mothers include six nondeprived and only two deprived people. It is as though these deprived young people harbor a feeling of revenge against their parents.

Symptoms. Another way to assess the consequences of childhood loss is to compare the psychological symptoms of deprived and nondeprived people. Logically one might assume that the former rank lower in mental health status and would not change much over the six years between the third and fifth interviews. As noted earlier, however, the reactions of our respondents are not necessarily logical. The youngest men are as expected at first: the deprived have more symptoms. By the final interview, however, they have not only had fewer psychological problems but are at the same level as the youngest men who are not deprived. The second youngest men have a very different configuration: they have had fewer psychological problems than nondeprived men in the same life stage at first, but six years later they have had more than twice as many. The next to oldest men reveal a similar pattern, though not quite so dramatic. The oldest deprived men resemble their nondeprived counterparts at the third contact, but by the fifth they have had many more symptoms. Combined, the two younger groups of deprived men resemble the nondeprived at first, but only the youngest do so at the fifth and last contact. The two older groups of deprived men have about the same number of symptoms as the nondeprived at first, but six years later they have many more. When we check the women's symptoms, we will learn whether gender differences are greater than those of the life stage.

The youngest deprived women at both time periods have many more symptoms than the nondeprived. The second youngest deprived women, however, have almost the same scores as the nondeprived. The second oldest women are even more surprising: they have one third *fewer* symptoms than the nondeprived at the third contact and six years later only about half as many. The oldest deprived women resemble the youngest ones: they have more signs of poor mental health both times. In short, it seems clear that gender differences are greater than those of age or life stage.

Perceived Change in Self. Still another way of examining the effect of childhood deprivation is to consider the extent to which our respondents are aware of change in their inner selves and, if so, whether they appraise them as positive, neutral, or negative. Within the context of this chapter we want to know how those who report deprivation in childhood differ from people who do not. The youngest deprived and nondeprived men and women do have quite a bit in common. Both feel they have changed for the better, the nondeprived having only a slight advantage over the deprived. One nondeprived man, however, did say he has changed for the worse. Very few felt neutral about changes in themselves.

The second youngest men and women are dramatically different from each other: both deprived and nondeprived females are the most positive of all the eight subgroups, but their male counterparts, especially the deprived men, are most likely to feel neutral about self-changes. Among the second oldest people more men than women report positive changes. There are few differences in the oldest deprived group, but the oldest nondeprived women feel much better about how they have changed than men do; they are twice as likely as the men to believe they have become better. Many of these oldest and nondeprived women feel in their prime, but the men, regardless of their level of childhood deprivation, tend to brood over when and how they are going to die.

Repercussions of Current Life Circumstances

Why did several deprived people who ranked high on positive life events at the third contact reverse to negative at the last interview? As many young people as old are, unexpectedly, in this group. Not unexpectedly, in light of what we have learned here, there are many more women than men. The range of current life circumstances accounting for adversity is illustrated by one man and one woman from each life-stage group. Some of these people have been introduced earlier, others not; all are in the deprived category.

A bright, well-educated, and self-confident high school senior when we first get to know him, Frederick Eilers plans to become a rabbi. At the third interview he is in graduate school, where he has good friends and is deeply in love with a young woman he plans to marry in the near future. Then life intervenes. When last we see him, Frederick, though by now an ordained rabbi, has no job, is suffering from stomach pains, and, worst of all, has lost his girlfriend.

Former high school senior Louise Garcia is as sharp a contrast to Frederick as could be imagined. High school is the end of her education. Once cited for the use of illegal drugs, she has a lifestyle that might best be called peripatetic. About twenty-three at the third interview, she is "settling in," as she puts it. Now married and with a child of two, she expects another in a few weeks. Her intention is to spend two years on "child raising" and then go back to school and have a career; in this connection she lists nine possibilities, but at the end she says: "Maybe I'll just wind up being a mother and grandmother." Her husband is a great help with the children and a good cook as well. Louise's circumstances are very different at our last contact with her. She is divorced, her daughter lives with her ex-mother-in-law, her son with her grandmother, and she lives with a lesbian friend, works part time at a gay bar, and reports eighteen psychological problems.

Newlywed Karl Koster, a field surveyor who is also a senior in college when we first meet, is married to a physical therapist. At the third encounter he has an advanced degree and a son and is engrossed in music, his first love. At that time working in his own musical instrument repair shop, with some carpentry and house painting on the side, he will soon be teaching music, a job he loves. But life proves by no means as joyous as he had expected. Six years later, at the final interview, we find his wife has divorced him and has taken their son to another state, more than a thousand miles away. Karl has given up his teaching job and for some inexplicable reason has become a cab driver, a job he finds very boring. He also has lost a woman friend with whom he has lived for four years.

We learned a great deal about Karl's counterpart, former newlywed Abbey Knowles, in Chapter Four. When we first meet she is married to a wealthy psychiatrist and trying to live up to his expectations. At the third contact she considers herself fairly happy. By the last one she is divorced and creating a new life for herself and the children. It is hard work and she is upset and depressed.

In sum, then, Frederick has had bad luck but will no doubt overcome it. Louise is confused and probably mentally ill. Karl is responsible for his own undoing. Abbey is striving to fashion a good life for herself and the children after a divorce but is depressed. That the four of them are on the deprived side of the paradigm may seem unrelated to outcome, but the literature on the relationship of childhood loss to adult problems with attachments seems very relevant here.

Turning to deprived older people whose lives have changed for the worse between the third and the last interviews, we start with another familiar character, Arnold Erikson. He is still working as a stevedore at the third contact and has retired by the fifth. His children rarely agree with his strident conservatism, but he takes pride in them. At the third interview he is in fairly good health, enjoys outdoor activities, and looks forward to a trip to Australia after retirement. Between the fourth and fifth contacts he has gone to Europe with his wife despite not feeling well. Shortly after his return his physical and mental health has deteriorated. He has nightmares and anticipates death. Arnold's preoccupation with death is not common among the deprived members of our sample, and one gets the sense that his zealous stance on political issues is a way of keeping people from getting too close.

Arnold's female counterpart, Mira Levitz, is his polar opposite politically and in several other respects. Liberal and concerned about community, national, and international affairs, she keeps well informed through newspapers and news programs. Her part-time work is taking care of young children while their parents are working; she feels that she contributes to their development. Her husband has ups and downs in mood, but he is still working and she tries her best to soothe him when he comes home. Several un-pleasant events have influenced Mira's life by the time of the final interview. As the reader will recall, she cares for her ailing aunt, who dies shortly before the last interview. Moreover, one of her daughters has committed suicide and Mira blames herself, thinking it might have been avoided if she had not been paying so much attention to her aunt. One senses that her feelings of guilt are mis-placed, but this loss may have reopened old wounds.

Gus Bradford and Martha Zimmer, in the oldest group, have little in common except that they are far less well adapted at the last encounter than they had been six years earlier. Gus is the not very well educated cab driver who is a devout Baptist. He has emphy-sema that is quite well controlled by medication. His wife has a college degree and works as a clerk. The Bradfords have three chil-dren, all of whom will eventually become college graduates. Gus has retired by the third contact and, with his wife, moved to a small country town he enjoys very much. Under no time pressures, he goes to church more often, reads biblical literature, and goes to ball games. He is very sick when last we see him and does little more than eat and sleep, completely dependent on his wife's loving care. Well into his seventies and on the brink of death, he says, "every-thing is as good as I can expect." Sick and near death, he still enjoys receiving the ministrations of his good woman.

Martha Zimmer is quite unique for someone in our retire-ment group: her marriage was annulled for reasons not specified. She is a trained nurse and worked as a navy officer in World War II. When we meet she is teaching music and art in an elementary school. Then sixty-one, she worries about her mother, who is eighty-two and living alone one thousand miles away. Her brother and sister-in-law, who live near her, do nothing for the ailing old woman. By the third interview Martha has retired, rearranged her house, and fetched her mother from New England. Her nursing skills now stand her in good stead and she is gratified to report that her mother feels much better. Martha's favorite activities at this time include sailing on a friend's boat, helping another friend in the mail order business, cooking, reading, and working in her flower garden. She is satisfied with her life and feels very close to her mother. By the time of the last interview a variety of negative life events beyond her control have put her on what she calls a very low plateau. On a scale of one to ten she rates the present year a three. Not only has she had to cope with her mother's death by herself, but she has had complicated foot surgery and is still in great pain. Now about seventy, she is waiting for a space to open up in a retirement home in the southern part of the state. Meanwhile she feels in never-never land. Her only goal now is to preserve her health and safety. To the extent that she may have been a compulsive caregiver, the death of her parent as well as retirement from the caregiving profession of nursing have robbed Martha of the mainstays of her existence.

Unlike the young people, three of the four older ones have very poor health. The fourth, Mira Levitz, takes the blame for her daughter's suicide. These results suggest there may be generational differences in the impact of childhood deprivation.

Growth from Challenge

During our initial research with older persons that prompted the present study, we found that some people can be characterized as being prone to stress while others seem resilient (Lowenthal, Berkman, and Associates, 1967). We have also been struck by clinical evidence, going back as far as Carl Jung, suggesting that under certain circumstances stress may lead to growth and development instead of deterioration. In this section we discuss the lives of two people who, subjected early in life to considerable duress, differ substantially in how they survive and develop. For ease of comparison we have selected a man and a woman from the same stage group, the former newlyweds.

Bret Warner: A New Spirit. When we first talk to Bret Warner he is a twenty-three-year-old of Italian descent, born on the West Coast. No longer a practicing Catholic, he has a part-time job as a grocery clerk and is enrolled full time in college. (This is his second time around, for his studies were interrupted by the Vietnam War.) His father, a white-collar worker, is still living. Bret's recent bride, Becky, works in a paramedical job.

As we look at Bret's childhood, we are struck by the sustained theme of loss. His mother died when Bret was less than a year old, reportedly of injuries suffered during a violent fight with his father (both were extremely drunk). The father immediately left home and was a fugitive for several years before returning and being acquitted of the crime. His father subsequently married a woman Bret firmly believes to have been a prostitute. In the meantime Bret was taken into the household of relatives and for some time thought the man of the house was his father. This man planned to adopt Bret, but before the legal proceedings could be completed he died suddenly of a heart attack. At this point Bret's father returned to the city and, after some conflict with both Bret and his surrogate mother, took Bret home to live with him and his new wife. Bret was now twelve years old.

Bret recalls the next seven years as the most difficult of his entire life. His father was frequently drunk and always became violent in that state. Bret has vivid memories of his father trying to kill him. Bret feels that, drunk or sober, neither his father nor stepmother was capable of any affection and that their main interests were materialistic. He left home at eighteen and went to college for two years, assuming several leadership roles there (as in fact he had while in high school). He was then drafted and spent two years in Vietnam in the front lines.

At the time of his first interview, Bret has been married less than a year and discusses his new wife with great warmth and devotion. He sees her as an interesting person and is concerned with her growth as much as his own. Their effort to work out a mutually congenial life-style involves considerable communication with each other and shared domestic and cultural activities, as well as considerable interaction with friends and acquaintances.

Bret has spent some time working with children through various poverty programs and enjoys it greatly. Even so, he has decided that at college he will take courses designed to help him become an accountant, hopefully in a bank. This kind of work, he says, will give him both security and an opportunity for growth on the job. He hopes to continue working with children and young people on a voluntary basis. During this time of his life, all of Bret's plans and those of his wife center on their most cherished goal: to have children as soon as they can afford to buy a big old house that he will remodel in his spare time. The theme of having children runs throughout the three sessions that make up the first contact (eight hours altogether), and he frequently speaks of giving his own children the love and understanding he lacked as a child.

As we follow Bret through the years of the study, he does in fact accomplish his most cherished goal: he and his wife have had two little girls by the final contact. He has completed his schooling, although this was a much more exhausting task than he had anticipated, and now has a well-paying job with a bank. They did buy their big old house, sold it to buy another, and now have a summer house in a resort area as well. Naturally the family has a dog.

At the final interview he feels "pretty happy" but rates the present year an eight (indicating his life is pretty close to absolute tops) on our Life Evaluation Chart. The reason for such a high score, he says, is that so many positive things have happened. He thinks of the future, feels he has been successful in fulfilling his wants, and expects this pattern to continue. He is very concerned about social issues, especially the acts of the new president. On the dark side, he still has vivid and frightening memories of his troubled early life.

Andrea Knox: Still Trying. Andrea Knox, age thirty-two when we first meet this newlywed, was born in the Midwest. Her father, still alive at the first interview, is a foreman in a large corporation and very religious. She herself has maintained strong church affiliations (Congregational) since childhood and is involved in local church activities. Andrea is a social worker and, like her machinist husband, works nights.

Andrea's mother was only fifteen when she married and sixteen when Andrea was born. The parents fought violently during their marriage, and her father deserted them when Andrea was only two. She went to live with an aunt for two years, at which point her mother remarried and Andrea was sent to join the new household.

Her mother subsequently divorced and remarried four times. Andrea recalls much quarreling and violence throughout the successive stages of her family life. The last marriage was more enduring, but Andrea reports this stepfather molested her on many occasions and finally seduced her at age twelve. She does not dwell upon this episode at length and later in the same interview speaks rather positively about both her mother and stepfather.

When she was about eight, Andrea went to live with her biological father and a stepmother; by this time the two had started a family of their own. Though life was considerably more comfortable there, at least from a material standpoint, Andrea soon opted to return to her mother. A few years later her mother died of a stroke that may have been linked to an alcoholic addiction. At that point Andrea returned to her father's home and says she gave him and her stepmother a rough time during her adolescence.

As a teenager Andrea had hoped to become a teacher but had serious problems at school; her only access to higher education was in social work, an access made available through her father. She found the experience of living in a dormitory and sharing her life with other girls very rewarding and apparently showed leadership potential at this time. After graduation she worked with two doctors, whom she describes as great men, before moving on to a community clinic, where she eventually had a supervisory role.

Having proved her competence in work, she became restless, and, with the help of a pastor who had provided counseling throughout much of her childhood, she went to Brazil as a missionary. Just before leaving she had brief affairs with two professional men in succession, both of whom she describes with much warmth and admiration. In Brazil she had a position of considerable responsibility and did a lot of teaching, finding that she enjoyed it as much as she had thought she would as a teenager. She also had a serious affair with a local community organizer. Reluctantly the two decided that the cultural differences were too great and Andrea returned to America. With long-standing interests in human rights, Andrea became quite active in the civil rights movement upon her return. She did a lot of traveling and on one trip she met her future husband. It was a case of "love at first sight," she reports with a grin. They lived together off and on for a year before finally getting married.

At present Andrea is wavering back and forth about returning to voluntary political work, about changing jobs since she hates the clinic where she now works, about loathing and loving her domestic chores, and especially about whether to have a child. In the second of the three sessions that make up first contact, she says she thinks she will "get pregnant tonight," but later she says she is too old and too impaired to have a child. (She has diabetes and is substantially overweight.) Her husband has a child by a prior marriage and he himself is conflicted about having further children. Andrea also has reservations about her husband, frequently referring to him as excessively dependent on her.

By the second contact, Andrea's life has changed for the worse. She reports that she has attempted suicide. This happened after her husband left her to return to his ex-wife. Institutionalized briefly, she is now under outpatient care and her recovery seems impaired by the fact that her husband has not actually left the city. They meet nearly every week and invariably end up drinking and fighting. Right now she feels that she is in limbo, floating in space, and has given herself six months to deal with the marriage one way or another. In fact, she finds she cannot think more than six months ahead and is desperately unsure of the future. She wants to get out of social work, and she never wants to be married again. Her father died shortly after the initial interview we had with her two years ago.

There are other problems as well. In fact, Andrea reports a level of negative stressors far above the norm for her life stage and gender. Her diabetes has led to a secondary condition that required hospitalization, and peripheral vascular impairment threatens her health. When asked about her goals, she replies that what she needs is to find a goal. She does not know what she intends to do. In terms of relationships, her relation with her stepmother has dissolved since her father's death but she also feels she is now closer to her friends. And, most especially, she has a steady boyfriend and is satisfied with her sex life.

Between the second and third interviews, Andrea gets divorced but sends an interesting note to her interviewer:

Dear Tom:

Just a note to thank you for your holiday greetings and to
share some glad tidings with you. Perhaps you would be kind
enough to change the name on my record from Andrea Knox
to Mrs. Andrea Mathews. Yes, despite our outspoken stand
against the institution, color us copouts! Due to *very* poor
health, I've worked only three months this past year. Damn
near died and found out how badly I wanted to live! We're as
happy as if we were in our right minds. Hurry up with your
next interview—you could get a great tan, I'm so radiant. . . .

The third interview is not so radiant. Andrea rates her marriage as somewhat better than most; there are few ups and downs,
the satisfaction is constant, but her sex life is no longer fulfilling.
The most important thing now is that her diabetic condition has
worsened and she has been forced to resign her job. She misses social
work and does not like being so dependent on her new husband.
Shortly after leaving work she makes a suicide attempt and is now
being treated for depression. Overall she thinks she has adjusted
reasonably well to being financially dependent but is dissatisfied
with her lack of productivity in other areas. She also feels she is
becoming more conservative both politically and socially.

Twelve years into the study, we find Andrea simply maintaining. She no longer feels the need "to be part of the spiritual
community" but continues to miss social work a great deal. Although she feels a growing reluctance to be involved, she continues
her interest in social issues and is actually serving on health advi-
sory boards at both the local and state levels. Upon reflection she
feels she has become more accepting but has less energy and places
greater importance on money. Despite business reverses in her husband's gas station, the couple has just bought their first house
(which she dislikes intensely). "Fairly satisfied" with her current
pattern of activities, she says her most important goals are maintaining her health and greater financial security. She is, she reports,
reconciled to the fact that her health problems will prevent her from
ever having children.

Two Lives, Two Stories. The two life stories we have described show that circumstances such as childhood stress do not necessarily lead to the same conclusions. We can only speculate about the reasons why Bret seems to be doing so well. Recalling Bowlby's (1977) point that some men seek redress for childhood wrongs in marriage, one might ask if Bret is perhaps doing too well. He looks the picture-perfect father and husband, but this may be a somewhat forced image. In his defense one must note that life has not really been that easy for Bret, even recently, and yet he has maintained self-esteem and personal happiness while at the same time giving to others. Andrea's problems may be exacerbated by her chronic ill health. At the same time, she seems to suffer from a history of problems with attachments (her weight may itself be a means of coping with attachment) and mourns for a lost past while still trying to live the present as best as she can.

The Four

Olav Olavsen was certainly not deprived as a child in Sweden. He talks at length about his childhood and adolescence: loving parents and siblings, lots of fun, learning, and devout churchgoing, which has become a major resource for him as an adult. His warm memories help him through the loss of his wife and his move north to be near his children and finally a grandchild, his pride and joy. He had a "very happy" life until his bereavement but after the loss became only "pretty happy." Throughout the study he indicates virtually no psychological symptoms. At the last contact (by mail) he reports that the most important change in himself is that he has become more sensitive about the needs of other people. It appears that an exceptionally happy childhood can be a resource throughout life.

Olav's female counterpart in the empty nest stage did not have many inner resources: Hazel Sutter reports she had an excessively deprived childhood without loving parents or siblings. She has divorced her husband (whom she never really loved but felt security with) long before we meet her, and only by the final interview does she learn how to really love someone. Hazel's achievement is mitigated somewhat by her insistence on being the boss in her new relationship.

Max Schindler, right-wing conservative though he may be, is fearless and hopeful. He suffered no deprivation in childhood; on the contrary, it was a reasonably happy time for him. At the final interview he reports almost no psychological symptoms and considers himself "pretty happy" despite the fact that he has just had a heart blockage, has a catheter, and will have bypass surgery within a few days. We do not know the outcome of his operation, but he certainly is one of the great optimists in the sample, perhaps because he had a happy childhood.

Although Adelaide Stone did not complete the checklist of childhood deprivations (she was in the hospital with a serious stroke), we find in other parts of our interviews that Adelaide had a very troubled childhood: "The Depression was horrible. . . . It was the death of my mother. My mother died due to stress, she got a stroke and died. My father was an alcoholic. He worked for the electric company—it was a good job but he lost it and turned to booze. He lasted about six years at home and died when I was sixteen." Adelaide's illness is the main theme of the final interview, and it brings with it memories of her mother's own stroke and the suffering that ensued while the young Adelaide tried to cope with bereavement and the family's difficult times. She comments that things are different now: she has resources she lacked as a child, including friendship with her former husband, women friends, and learning how to paint. She continues to grow.

Summing Up

In retrospect, childhood deprivation does appear to make a big difference, especially in regard to optimism and pessimism about the future. A majority of deprived people are pessimists, but all of the nondeprived ones are optimists. Young deprived people are twice as likely to be pessimistic as older ones. Most deprived young people also dislike their parents, as though seeking revenge. On the other hand, the second youngest deprived women have about the same number of psychological symptoms as nondeprived women. There is a similar finding among the second oldest women:

they report fewer symptoms than the nondeprived at the third interview, and six years later even fewer. In this respect, as in other instances, gender differences exceed those of life stage.

The great majority of people, deprived and not, say they are happy or very happy. Is this because a confession of unhappiness is self-degrading? Though happiness is explored in another chapter, this question is not answered. As for changes in the self, all men and women in the youngest group, deprived or not, say they have changed for the better. The second youngest women, whether deprived or not, all change positively—much more so than all the other subgroups. Many of the oldest women feel in their prime, but the oldest men begin to brood about how they are going to die and when. We do not know why this is so. Perhaps they have read the statistics that women tend to live longer.

7

Impact of Life Stress:
Crisis or Challenge?

Young adulthood is often portrayed in the media as a time of excitement and challenge, while middle and especially old age are cast as boring times with no major challenges and few defeats except perhaps for aging itself. In this chapter we discuss the problems as well as some of the opportunities faced by our respondents as they experience life in its different stages. If this chapter seems somewhat more technical than the others, it is because it represents the crux of the book and presents more of the background work that led up to our conclusion that social stress plays a major role in adult development.

We begin by considering the idea that since behavioral characteristics and personality are generally very stable, it is the situations in which people find themselves that make a difference. Next on the agenda is stress—one kind of situation that most researchers agree may disturb people's functioning. Most of our findings suggest that while the tempo of life may appear to slow with age, this is in large part an illusion created by the growing complexity of life during the middle and later years. By complexity we mean that each new relationship and experience is more likely to be embedded in a matrix of similar as well as dissimilar experiences, and all relationships and experiences are more likely to have longer and more complex histories. The notion of a social "convoy," advanced by Robert Kahn and Toni Antonnuci (1980), illustrates this point.

Our analyses also make clear that the traditional means of studying stress, the "life events" approach, often fails to capture the kinds of experiences that create problems for older people. In the first section we outline three levels of stress that have been presented in the literature and for which we included instruments in our study. In the following two sections, our objective is not only to illustrate the importance of stressful experiences at any life stage but to address the myriad ways in which stressful conditions may shape the course of current and future behavior. For as Bernice Neugarten (1977) and others have pointed out, how one lives out one's life is determined in large part by life events and other stressful situations. We conclude, as before, with a discussion of the The Four.

Change and Continuity in Adult Life

As a means of understanding the potential role of stress in adulthood, we first consider how theories of adult development handle the question of stability versus change in personal functioning generally. We then explore how the addition of stress concepts enhances our understanding of stability and change.

Three Ways of Looking at Development. Until recently, studies of development have ignored the developmental implications of seemingly random encounters with life events and other stressors. Studies of development in later life have generally followed one of two underlying models. As described by Gergen (1975), the earliest and most widely used is the "stability template" model. Therapists and others who use this model are committed to the principle of stability in adult life; change is thought to occur primarily as a reflection of the continued development of characteristics established early in life. The work of Freud and his colleagues representing the classic psychoanalytic perspective serves as a good illustration of this model, since most of them believed that the trajectory of personal development becomes fixed by the age of five or six. For these theorists, the oedipal period is regarded as "the last great transforming epoch in child development" (Michels, 1984, p. 295).

To the extent that the stability model is valid, health professionals would clearly profit from examining people's early years if they wish to comprehend their later years. During the past fifteen to twenty years, however, a number of longitudinal studies have compiled evidence that no single stage of life assumes primacy and that personal development continues throughout life. Development is now often portrayed as a progression of orderly transformations over time (Gergen, 1975). Theories reflecting this "orderly change" model are usually stage theories, one of the most popular ways of conceptualizing personal development. The works of Piaget, Loevinger, and Kohlberg present stage theories of childhood and adolescent development that are well accepted among developmental psychologists. Common to all these approaches is the assumption that the individual is grounded in the past but interacting with the present and possible futures.

The most recent models of development emphasize the role of chance, or what some would call fate, in our lives. Sometimes called models of random change or nonnormative events, their central thesis is that after the initial push of biological development tapers off in late adolescence, chance factors, such as exposure to major stress, become more important as shapers of personality (Gergen, 1975). Support for this model can be found in the research of such developmental scientists as Klaus Riegel, Werner Schaie, Paul Baltes, and Bernice Neugarten. From the mainstream of psychology, the research of Walter Mischel and C. Murray Parkes also emphasizes the importance of the situational context in determining quality and stability in personal functioning.

Although the three models of change really do not conflict with one another, they are often treated that way by their proponents—as if only one model could hold true and all contrary evidence should be dismissed or reinterpreted. By way of contrast, we found evidence supportive of all three models. In Chapter Six, for example, we found that early childhood deprivation may set the stage for adaptation during the later adult years. Here our results support the stability template model. Yet the same findings could also be advanced as supporting the orderly change model: people change from childhood to middle age, but in orderly or predictable ways. And since childhood stressors are often portrayed as being random events, their effect might also be seen as fitting the random change model.

Stress: The Case for Stability. Because continuities and discontinuities in stress exposure over the life course are rarely considered, we decided to include some relevant findings. Thus we correlated measures of positive and negative life events available at four of the five contacts: the first, third, fourth, and fifth interviews. In other words, we were looking at continuity in stress exposure over a period of twelve years. Overall we found surprisingly high levels of continuity in stress exposure. In fact, the magnitude of the correlations often approximated those reported in personality research. For women, especially, there was evidence that exposure to negative events does not necessarily occur at random and that negative events experienced at one point in time may affect subsequent stress exposures.

For men we found two basic trends. First, positive events correlate at moderately high levels over considerable periods of time, whereas negative events are only minimally correlated. The tally of positive life events at the first contact, for example, correlated at .50 (p = .01) with positive events reported at the third interview and at .33 (p = .01) with positive events reported at the final contact. In contrast, the negative event tally at the first contact was not associated with negative events at either the third or fourth interviews but showed a significant association only at the last contact. Similarly, correlations among positive totals from the Life Events Inventory at the third, fourth, and fifth contacts were in the high .40s to .50s, whereas correlations among the negative totals were in the mid-.20s to mid-.30s. Second, positive and negative event totals were generally uncorrelated with each other. In other words, when men at any of the four stages reported many positive events, this had no bearing on how many negative experiences they reported.

For women we found two basic trends, as well, both of which stood in contrast to the experiences of men. First, negative life events were generally more highly correlated over time than were the positive events, even though the differences were not substantial. Negative events reported at the third and fourth contacts, for example, correlated at the .43 level (p = .01), whereas positive events correlated at .32 (p = .01). Negative events at the fourth contact correlated with the twelve-year data at the .58 level while the positive events correlated at .55. Here we get the impression that while the negative experiences of men tend to be randomly distributed over time, women who experience higher stress burdens at one point in time are more likely to experience them at other times as well. This chaining effect may place women at a seeming disadvantage with respect to stress.

Second, for women there was an intriguing tendency for positive and negative events to be significantly correlated with each other, although the correlations explained only part of the variance. For example, negative events at the third contact correlated .26 (p = .05) with positive events for the same period, .39 (p = .01) with positive events reported at the fourth contact, and .55 (p = .01) with positive events reported at the fifth and final contact. This finding could mean many things. One explanation is that women tend to be consistent in experiencing either lesser or greater amounts of positive and negative events.

A Stress Typology. These findings relate to a stress typology we developed early in the study (see Lowenthal and Chiriboga, 1973). Our examination of cases revealed that some people manifest a life-style characterized by multiple and active involvements and stress, while others seem to drift through life with little exposure to stress of any kind, positive or negative. It was also clear that so-called negative life events were not consistently linked to problems. Depending on the personal makeup of the individual, we found that exposure to stress may represent not only a problem but a challenge. This is certainly not a new idea; we discussed it briefly in Chapter Five when considering the cases of Bret Warner and Andrea Knox.

As a means of examining the possibilities for growth as well as stagnation raised by stress, we distinguished people according to a stress typology that contrasted how many objective life events are reported as compared with how much stress is perceived (Lowenthal and Chiriboga, 1973). Essentially we considered two kinds of information: the number of events tallied by raters on the basis of the lengthy first contact and the degree to which the person appeared to ruminate about these events or to dismiss them as something over and done with. From these two qualities—one dealing with what we called "presumed" stress and the other with "perceived" stress—we developed a fourfold typology of stress: (1) the "overwhelmed," who experience numerous stressful events and dwell on them in great detail; (2) the "self-defeating," who experience few events but talk about them in great detail; (3) the "challenged," who despite many stressful events seem to consider them either as interesting challenges or as resolved; and (4) the "lucky," people who seem to live a charmed life in that they neither experience many events nor dwell on them.

This typology is really a way of describing the relationship between the situation and people's perception of it. Jan Mayakovsky is the kind of person who has experienced above-average levels of negative events but feels stimulated by the challenge. One of the second youngest group of women, she decided early on she preferred to work for herself and subsequently created her own job: she is, or at least considers herself to be, a designer. Dresses are her specialty, and she makes them to order, in a sort of cottage industry, from her own home. Although the first interviews find her struggling to survive, by the final interview she can barely keep up with the demand. She is happy, challenged, and thriving in what many would view as a highly competitive, risky, and stressful life. Like many others who react to stress with a sense of challenge and purpose, she falls at the low end of the self-concern category of commitment. That is, she is not self-protective but rather outgoing and concerned with growth and new possibilities.

In Chapter Nine we will return to the typology and discuss it in greater detail. Suffice it to say, here, that the typology helped us to predict how people handle stress and is also (as in the case of Jan) closely related to self-concern. Moreover, we found that people often are very stable in their basic posture toward stressful situations—even though we also found that stress is often associated with changes in the way people live out their lives.

The Role and Meaning of Stress

As in our study we explored the subject of stability in greater detail, we found evidence that stability and change in one's personal functioning may depend on the stability of the physical and social environment. Specifically we found that exposure to stress can make a big difference in the stability of personality. Before discussing these findings, let us first take a look at what we mean when we refer to stress or stressful situations.

One of the surprising findings to emerge from our longitudinal study concerns how rarely people recognize that they are under stress. Apparently many people accommodate to pressure to such an extent that on the surface at least they pay little attention to it. It was not uncommon to find respondents unable to think of any recent stressors when asked an open-ended question but to report ten or more life events when given a structured inventory. Part of the problem may be that stressors come in many different sizes and shapes. As a means of evaluating these differences, we noted three levels of stress in our research. These consist of the micro, meso, and macro levels (Chiriboga, 1984).

The Micro Level. At what we call the micro level, the focus is on the day-to-day experiences of people: the stressors of everyday life such as running out of toothpaste, getting caught in a traffic jam, or finding your child in the bathroom just when you are in a rush to take a shower. By far the most commonly experienced stressors, they are also the least studied. In one early panel investigation, Holmes and Holmes (1970) reported that such day-to-day problems were associated with minor physical complaints, including the common cold. In a later study, Lazarus and Folkman (1984) found that what they call day-to-day hassles exerted a stronger influence than major life events on the mental health and well-being of middle-aged men and women.

In our study we found that these daily hassles predict mental health and well-being over periods of five to six years (Chiriboga, 1984). The older people are generally frustrated about the same as or less than the two younger groups, with one exception: our oldest people are more frustrated in their relations with parents. This finding underscores the problems faced by aging people as their parents, now in the "oldest old" stage of life, become increasingly dependent on adult children for care. In the next chapter we will return to the issue of daily hassles.

The Meso Level. The most frequently studied of the three types, meso-level stressors deal with situations that are less frequent than micro stressors but generally are more memorable. A marriage, promotion, divorce, or death of a child, for example, can become major markers of the life course; getting stalled in traffic may be disturbing for all of ten minutes (or an hour, perhaps, if you live in the Big City). The life-event approach to research (see, for example, Holmes and Rahe, 1967) covers the category of meso stressors, as do studies of transitions and the more chronic stressors. Meso-level stressors, especially life events, have been found to predict a wide range of physical, mental, and social dysfunction—everything, in fact, from coronary heart disease to general psychiatric symptomatology. One frequently reported finding is that people in middle age and beyond report fewer life events, which may indicate that the risks associated with this type of stressor are reduced.

A central focus of our own work was to revise the original Holmes and Rahe instrument to extend its relevance to the kinds of events that might be experienced by older adults. We also added information tapping the respondents' own assessment of how good or bad the experience was and whether it intruded into their thoughts. In general we found that men and women in the two older groups did report fewer events, both negative and positive, than those in the younger groups. There were exceptions, however, at each contact point. At the fourth contact, for example, the second oldest group reported the most negative events within the family and the oldest group was close behind. And the second oldest group was as high as the two younger groups in the level of positive events reported in their marital and personal lives.

The Macro Level. Stressors at the macro level exert an impact first upon society at large and only secondarily on the individual. The threat of war, bad economic news, a flurry of near-misses in the airlanes, or a spill of radioactive waste not only makes the headlines but can create widespread anxiety and a generally heightened sense of distress (Antonovsky, 1987). In today's world of mass communication and political and social unrest, we know too little about too much. Anyone who reads the newspaper or watches television is exquisitely aware of each new crisis and confrontation. Current estimates say that approximately 62 percent of American viewers watch the evening network news on television (Will, 1987), and this proportion rises to nearly 90 percent when news of special importance is being aired. Clearly a large proportion of Americans are being exposed to macro-level stressors day in and day out.

Perhaps the earliest investigation of macro-level events was serendipitous. Norman Bradburn and his colleague David Caplovitz were testing a new morale measure in a series of national probability studies conducted before and after the assassination of President John Kennedy. They found a national increase in negative emotions in the wake of the murder (Bradburn and Caplovitz, 1965). Recently Harvey Brenner (1985), a sociologist at Johns Hopkins University, reported a strong link between downturns in the U.S. economy and upturns in admission rates to mental institutions. This link was replicated in a study conducted by Richard Suzman (1977) using data from our study of transitions. Our own data have also shown, as noted in Chapter Five, that people vary markedly in how they are affected by societal events. In fact, the entire content of Chapter Five, "Reactions to Social Change," represents a discussion of macro stressors.

The Role of Stress in Development

One reason why stress may influence the course of development lies in its ability to disrupt not only the day-to-day routine but social relationships and social expectations. The role of social stability and stable expectations for the life course has long been recognized as salient for mental well-being. After a series of studies established that there are behavioral expectations for each broad age category of life, Neugarten and Datan (1973, p. 60) concluded that such expectations constitute "a frame of reference by which the experiences of adult life are perceived as orderly and rhythmical." In Chapter Five we scrutinized the ways in which life's events interact with individual characteristics. Clearly these macro-level experiences have a direct impact on personal well-being for people at all stages of life, as do those at the micro and meso levels as well.

As witnessed by the work of Gergen on random change, students of the life course are beginning to recognize the developmental implications of stress experiences. As another example, Baltes and Baltes (1980) have identified three major sources of change during the life course: the normative age-graded changes, which include such factors as biological maturation and early socialization practices; the normative history-graded changes, which include events that help establish cohort differences, such as the Great Depression, World War II, and fads of various kinds; and nonnormative changes, which include unscheduled stresses such as divorce, unemployment, unexpected illness, and the death of a child, a close friend, or spouse.

Markers of the Life Course. The argument for stress as a life force dynamic is being advanced not only in theories but in basic and applied research as well. One research team has gone so far as to suggest that "at the most basic level, the life course can be defined as the major life events and transitions an individual experiences between birth and death" (Schulz and Rau, 1985, p. 130). Although this notion of defining the life course on the basis of life events and transitions may seem radical, the underlying idea has been around for some time. More than twelve years ago Bernice Neugarten (1977) suggested that life events represent markers of passage through the life course. Going to college, starting one's first job, marriage, and the birth of a first child, for example, are more likely to occur in the early stages of young adulthood whereas the departure of the last child from the family home, retirement of a husband from work, and the birth of the first grandchild are more likely to come during the middle and later years.

Neugarten's speculations were subjected to empirical examination. As we met with our younger and older subjects, we asked them to chart the ups and downs of their whole past and expected future lives and then asked them to explain what prompted the turning points. Basically we found that respondents tend to invoke stressors as initiators of change in their life-course trajectory. Perhaps of greater importance, life events are not the only stressors they mention. Transitions, nonevents (such as not getting married), stresses affecting one's children and family, anticipated stresses, and being behind schedule for important transitions are all reported with considerable frequency.

The Role of Transitions. Life-span scientists often emphasize the interactive nature of development. Development is portrayed as codetermined by the internal structure and external sociocultural circumstances; changes in either create the conditions for developmental change. Some theorists suggest that people move from periods of relative equilibrium, through periods of turmoil and change, toward new or restored equilibrium. Certain of these periods of change may reflect normative transitions that fall at predictable points of the life course, such as those that surround a "timely" marriage or retirement. Nonnormative transitions may reflect the impact of chance, as when a person is widowed in early middle age or paralyzed as a result of some accident. But whether normative or nonnormative, transtions challenge a person's habitual ways of living.

The challenge, however, varies in intensity. Some research indicates that normative transitions, possibly because they can be expected and occur gradually over a long period of time, exert less of an impact than nonnormative transitions. In one comparison of persons experiencing either the normative transitions investigated in this study or divorce, for example, it was found that the divorcing persons were more likely to experience both positive and negative changes in nearly all areas of life, not simply the marital (Fiske and Chiriboga, 1985).

In both this study and the study of divorce, one factor emerged repeatedly as a signal of potential change: the piling up of life events and other stressors. When participants report an unusually strong reaction to some stress, it often turns out that it is occurring in the context of a generally heightened level of what might be called background stress. After some deliberation we termed this condition the "camel's back syndrome" because, as it seemed to us, we were essentially dealing with a priming effect: the piling up of stressors leads to a condition where almost any new stress will precipitate a potentiated reaction. This syndrome may also explain why people in the real world outside of stress research do odd things like strolling into fast food stores with Uzi submachine guns and opening fire or killing someone after a trivial traffic accident. Among our participants the results are not nearly so dramatic, but fights with children and with spouses often occur in the context of increased background stress.

Stressors as Developmental Markers. Although life events were not the only stressors that affected the lives of respondents, together with indices from the micro and macro level they helped us to chart the life-course trajectory of respondents. Consider the case of Daphne Randall from Chapter Two. A child during the turmoil afflicting Europe in the late 1930s, Daphne fled Nazi Germany with her family for France and subsequently South America. Because of the numerous moves she experienced early in life, Daphne was eighteen when she entered high school and graduated later than would be expected of her birth cohort. Living in a strange land restricted her work opportunities, and she also had to care for ailing parents. She married late for her age, at thirty-five, and to a man twenty-five years her senior. Three years after her arrival in the United States at age thirty-eight, her first and only child was born. Her husband died when she was fifty-five, and her son left home when Daphne was in her early sixties. At sixty-five, the time of her last interview, she was eagerly awaiting the birth of her first grandchild.

By way of contrast, consider the life trajectory laid out for a hypothetical (but all too plausible) teenage girl who becomes pregnant and gives birth at age fourteen, becomes a grandmother herself at twenty-eight, and becomes a great-grandmother at forty-two. Clearly the life-course trajectories of both women would be affected by the timing of each marker event or transition.

Stress and Challenge in the Course of Life

Up to this point in the chapter we have been examining certain basic concepts and findings related to stressors and adult development, focusing on some of the alternatives to life events that warrant consideration. It was only in the later stages of the study, however, as we began to recognize the limitations of the event methodology, that we expanded our field of interest and included additional measures. In this section we examine the findings on life events, since data were available from all contact points.

Life Events over the Life Course. During the six to eight hours we spent on the average with respondents during the first interview (usually broken up into two or three sessions), there was time to ask questions about the events they had found most distressing in their lives thus far. To acquire a broad perspective, we first compared men and women without regard for their life stage. Nearly three-fourths of the women mentioned education, and half or more had also been distressed by family, health (theirs or others'), and dating or marriage problems. There were only two categories that half or more of the men found stressful: experiences related to education (for over two-thirds) and work (exactly half).

Analysis of events and circumstances found stressful over the year preceding the first interview yielded sharp differences between both sex and life-stage groups. Most surprising was the fact that the two youngest groups reported nearly two and a half times as many life events as the two oldest groups (among whom more than one-fourth mentioned none at all). Differences between the sexes were even greater, as women consistently reported more stressors than men.

The sex differences in the two older groups were of particular interest, since stress experiences are often more difficult to detect in older samples. For the second oldest group of men, work is a major source of distress. Aside from work, there is no aspect of life that even a fifth of these older men agree was stressful. In comparison, only a fifth of the second oldest women report work-related stressors, even though a majority of them work. Health is at the top of these women's stress lists, generally not their own health but that of close others. Some of these women also find a variety of family relationships stressful.

Finances are of prime concern to the second oldest group of men, as they contemplate visions of the retirement years. The first interview in fact finds the oldest men so preoccupied with financial concerns that they tend to evaluate earlier periods of their lives mainly in economic terms. Many recall their adolescence and young adulthood as traumatized by the Great Depression, and its influence has been felt ever since. Interestingly, the University of California, Berkeley, studies report similar preoccupations for older men despite their rather more privileged status. (See, for example, Elder, 1981.)

As we analyzed life events and other stressors during the successive interviews, we became increasingly interested in the quality and quantity of life-stage differences. We have already reported that generally the two oldest groups report fewer life events. In a more intensive analysis, we looked at whether older people are more or less likely to experience a variety of stressors than younger people. Although some life-course studies report that middle-aged and older adults experience fewer life events, our results suggest they primarily report different kinds of stressors than do younger people—particularly stressors relating to health and economic problems (Chiriboga and Cutler, 1980; Fiske and Chiriboga, 1985). Moreover, evaluations of such stresses may vary widely from person to person. Two middle-agers suffering from painful and chronic arthritis have opposite reactions, for example, one considering herself lucky in comparison with her mother, who at the same age was completely crippled, the other feeling depressed and defeated because she feels singled out for some cruel joke.

Stress and Continuity. The longitudinal nature of our research allowed us to assess the extent to which stress exposure influences stability of personal functioning. We hypothesized that life events affect several aspects of personal functioning, including morale, mental and physical health, and self-concept. To test this hypothesis, we combined data from subjects at all stages of life in order to increase statistical power. The first step was to take negative life-event scores from data collected at interviews three, four, and five and add them together. After dividing the sample into those who scored higher and lower on stress exposure, we computed correlations for three measures often used in studies of adult development: those assessing morale, those assessing health status, and those assessing self-concept. For each measure we compared baseline status with status at all subsequent contacts. We did this separately for each of the two basic groups: those higher and lower on stress.

Overall we found that the more stress the person reports, the less the stability in personal functioning. Let us just consider the correlations between data from our first interview and our last. In other words, we are looking at the question of stability over approximately a twelve-year period. (See Chiriboga, 1989, for more detail.) Regarding what Bradburn (1969) has called "affect balance," defined in terms of the ratio of positive to negative emotions experienced over the past week, we find that the correlation is -.03 (not significant) for persons with histories of high stress exposure and .35 (p = .01) for those with histories of low stress exposure. With our forty-two-item California Symptoms Checklist, correlation for the high-stress group is higher at .39 (p = .01), but for the low-stress group it is higher still (r = .51, p = .01).

When we turn to our measures of self-concept taken from the rating list, we find that the twelve-year correlations are generally higher than for any other type of measure; all are significant at probabilities far below the 0.01 level. For negative self-image the correlation for high-stress subjects is .35 and for low it is .63. For positive self the high-stress correlation equals .44 and the low stress is .59. Assertiveness correlates for high-stress participants at .34 and .69 for low. Scores for the hostility component of the self-concept correlate at .44 for high-stress participants and at .66 for the low-stressed.

Apart from providing a convincing argument that stress exposure is linked to reduced stability, these data also suggest there are whole classes of self-related measures that vary systematically in their stability over time. For example, the morale measures show a basically lower level than measures of physical or mental health, which in turn demonstrate lower stability than measures of self-concept. This is an interesting finding that we have not seen discussed in the literature before.

Stress and Growth. We have shown, then, that stress is associated with the stability of psychological and even physical status over fairly extensive periods of time. Another question is the direction in which stress may lead those exposed to it. One's usual inclination is to associate stress exposure with increased problems in living. There is, however, some evidence, from both the clinical and the empirical literature, that in the long run stress may be associated with positive outcomes. In one study based on data from the third and fourth contacts, we found that negative events (as defined by the subjects themselves) were as likely to predict positive as negative changes in a variety of indicators of well-being. Among the second oldest men, for example, greater work stress was associated with improvement in overall happiness, a decline in psychological symptomatology, improvement in self-reported health, and an increase in the scope of activities in which the person participated. Marital stress was generally associated with greater problems, however, for both middle-aged men and women.

Clearly stress is not necessarily a detriment to our health and well-being. In the short run what seems to make a difference is whether the readjustment demands imposed by stressors fall within an individual's ability to cope. Regardless of how the individual fares in the short run, however, stress may in the long run be associated with growth. In fact, there is some suggestion that the experience of stress may be a precondition to the development of a mature personality (Chiriboga, 1984; Vaillant, 1978). Consider the case of Henri Fontenot, one of the group of youngest men. Henri is a waiter in a first-class restaurant when we first interview him. A high school senior, he greets guests with seeming aplomb, menu in hand and the proper napkin folded on his arm. Knowing that the head waiter might be watching makes him nervous and he often obsesses about the fit of his tuxedo and the shine of his shoes. A well-kept secret Henri cherishes is his dream of owning a restaurant of his own some day. By the fifth interview he not only has the restaurant but also the self-assurance and poise we often noted in respondents who had met major challenges.

Stress Among The Four

In each chapter we have presented bits and pieces of the lives of the four intensive cases—important bits and pieces but nevertheless fragments that do not provide much of an overview. In this section we demonstrate the utility of the stress paradigm as a way

of fitting all these pieces together to form a coherent image of each
case.

Olav Olavsen: Challenged and Liking It. Olav Olavsen, a member
of the second oldest group, is consistently low in the self-concern
category of commitment throughout our interview contacts. For
Olav this tendency toward outward expression reflects not only a
strong and positive sense of self but also the self-confidence that
makes change a source of interest and challenge and not defeat and
despair. Why this is so is open to conjecture, of course, but one
source of his strength may lie in the fact that he had a happy childhood. Another source may be a capacity for intimacy that is reflected
in his happy marriage and strong ties with his children; still other
sources may be his strong religious convictions and generally high
morale.

Olav seems to be the kind of person who walks with the sun
shining over his head while it is raining on others. As we first look
at the sixty-one-year-old Olav, we find a very busy man. He gets up
at the crack of dawn, works hard all day, and then spends time with
his wife and the two children who remain at home. Of his activities
he says, "I enjoy working, and I enjoy coming home and being with
my family. And I also enjoy meeting my friends in church." One
of the highest scorers on a checklist of thirty-three common activities, he does not have the time to do everything he would like but
does not feel this is a problem. His one regret in life seems to be his
lack of education, but this is not a major regret. His response to the
"how happy are you these days?" question, however, reveals a person who is more complex than might initially be imagined: "Very
happy insofar that I am very happy with my family life but I'm not
happy with the world today."

At this first interview, Olav definitely is not the kind of person who is preoccupied with stress of any kind. With respect to past
losses, we find that his strong religious background may mitigate
some stresses of life. Regarding his parents' deaths, for example, he
says that "I know that I'm going to meet them again and that takes
the sting out of everything." His reaction to the departure of the two
oldest children shows another side of Olav: his ability to take different perspectives as situations change. "It seem when they were

here I still looked at them as children. Now they are gone and I look upon them as grown-up men." He reports no life events of note. The next important thing he expects to happen in his life is retirement, which he plans to take within five years.

At the second interview Olav is now sixty-three years old. His youngest child has recently left for college and Olav as usual puts this in perspective: "We miss her, but as you grow older you want more quiet so we like it." He is beginning to feel his age and now thinks he definitely works too hard, so he will retire as soon as he is sixty-five or even before. Olav reports the birth of one grandchild, but much is the same as before. He still reports himself to be very happy, reports no symptoms on our forty-two-item checklist, evaluates the present years as "absolute tops," the highest possible rating on our Life Evaluation Chart, and thinks his health is very good. He reports that his wife has high blood pressure, however, which gives him some concern. His most important goal is to make his wife happy and better.

At the third interview Olav's positive life-event score is higher than average and his negative life-event score is significantly below average, even though a former business partner and friend died suddenly the week before the interview. When asked about changes since the last interview he says, "We took a trip to visit folks in Sweden. My daughter graduated from university and got a job as an accountant. I have a lot to be thankful for. I have a wonderful wife, home, and children. I got over my sickness—I feel very healthy." With prompting we find that Olav has retired and now has "a new life— I have the freedom I never before experienced. I try to do some things I never had time to do before. And I really enjoy it." These new things include taking courses at a community college. The best thing that could happen to him "would be to continue to have a happy home life and keep my wife and be thankful for every day." For the first time, though, Olav reports experiencing some of the symptoms on our symptoms checklist: he feels he is more forgetful, loses things, is worried, his feelings get hurt, he is nervous, and sudden movements tend to startle him. On questioning we find that he is somewhat worried about his wife's health.

At the fourth interview, Olav has been retired for about five years. At this point he is experiencing probably the most distressing period of his entire life. When we first attempt to contact him, we have to postpone the interview. Here are the research assistant's notes:

> I contacted Olav Olavsen this afternoon by phone. He said he did not feel up to an interview at this time because his wife is in the hospital in a coma due to recent brain surgery. He said we could call him later; however, when I told him this round of interviews would conclude at the end of May he said this probably would be too soon for him. When I asked if we could send him a questionnaire by mail he agreed to try to fill it out. His voice sounded quite distressed and tired on the phone, but my sense was that the intensity of the situation rather than any enmity toward the research leads him to refuse at this time.

Olav's commitment to our project was such that within a week he returned the sections of the interview guide that we sent. Enclosed was a note: "Since my wife has been in the hospital now for about six weeks, I really haven't been in such a good frame of mind to answer these questions fully. Hope these will help you, though, in some way."

As we read Olav's written responses, we find that he still lives with his wife in the same house they have lived in for the past twenty years. He talks at length about his wife, whom he loves dearly, and how their marriage is now even more satisfying than in the past. His daughter has married, and this was a very positive experience. He also has visited Sweden again and paid several visits to his three grandchildren. Although he perceives little change in himself, on the happiness question Olav says he is "not too happy" and also reports feelings of depression and restlessness. The reason, he notes, is his wife's sickness: he is having trouble coping. When asked how he copes (a general question concerning which stress is causing the most problem), he replies that "I took it to the Lord and put it in His hands." He feels he has no control over the situation, however, and says he feels helpless: "Nothing I can do but pray." When answering a question about stressful situations he anticipates within the next three years, he responds: "My wife's possible death."

He feels he has been "fairly successful" in getting what he has wanted out of life, but, looking ahead, thinks he will be "somewhat unsuccessful" in the future.

At this point Olav is still scoring only about average for negative life events and is on the low side for positive. On the Social Change Checklist he reports very little distress or impact except for a strong and negative reaction to Watergate. He talks about his "disillusionment with government . . . the dishonesty among our nation's leaders."

The fifth contact was conducted by mail, as well, and we did not send the full interview schedule. Olav's wife died less than a month after he returned the final interview. When asked about the most important thing to have happened between contacts, he writes: "The passing away of my wife. I felt the loss of a very dear companion." He completes our Life Events Inventory and we find Olav's negative events score to be close to the highest of any age group, due in part to the death of his wife and a chain of events related to this bereavement. Positive events are significantly lower than average for his age cohort (or for the entire sample, for that matter). Asked what situation during the past year caused him the most stress, he writes, "moving to a new location and being alone." He copes by prayer, feels somewhat in control of the situation, and says that what he is doing is the right thing, though he regrets moving away from old friends.

On the Social Change Checklist, Olav now reports more worry and impact than he has in the past. Crime in the streets, Watergate, the international situation, and new life-styles bother him. He comments that he is troubled by "lawlessness . . . inflation . . . lack of confidence in government . . . breaking down of morality." It seems that the loss of his wife has triggered in Olav a new way of viewing the world. Instead of looking at life from the point of view of a challenged coper, he now views the world with some fear and apprehension.

Despite his problems, Olav provides evidence of recovery. He reports himself overall to be "pretty happy." Although on the twelve-item Bradburn Morale Scale (Bradburn and Caplovitz, 1965) he reports few emotions, two of the three that he does report are positive: he feels "particularly excited or interested in something"

often during the week prior to completing the interview and feels
"pleased" about an accomplishment. He also feels "very lonely"
several times. Olav's health remains good, and he reports that no
emotional problems have interfered with his life. He checks off
eight symptoms on the forty-two-item symptoms checklist, but
none are of the type that suggest severe problems (see Lowenthal,
Thurnher, Chiriboga, and Associates, 1975). On our Life Evaluation Chart he rates the present year as one in which satisfactions
clearly outweigh dissatisfactions, further evidence that Olav is recovering from his loss. When asked once again to rate how successful
he has been in getting the things he wants in life, he puts "very
successful"—the highest possible rating. And whereas at the pre-
ceeding contact he predicted himself to be "somewhat unsuccessful"
in attaining things in the future, he now expects to be "fairly
successful."

     Since his wife's death, Olav has sold his house and moved to
northern Oregon in order to be closer to his favorite daughter. Despite the adversities he has had to deal with, Olav remains among
the most open and un-self-protective of our participants. He feels he
is now "more sensitive to people and things around me" and is also
quite involved in a number of hobbies that he finds quite rewarding.
He has made six new friends since moving away and, looking at the
way he spends his time, he rates himself as "fairly satisfied." His
most important goal in life is "to be a more considerate, warm-
hearted person" and also to travel and visit his sisters and brothers
in Sweden and his children and grandchildren in the United States.
He also mentions that he is getting used to living alone.

Hazel Sutter: Opening Up to Change. Hazel Sutter, a fifty-one-year-
old member of the second oldest group, changed from high to low
self-concern over the course of the twelve-year project. Extremely
concerned with her own well-being and needs at the first interview,
her main concerns are with maintaining the status quo and "plodding along." In fact, when asked what she hopes to accomplish in
life, she says: "Oh, if I can just keep going on like I am now. I'm
not going to do anything outstanding, believe me!" Hazel was divorced about four years before we meet her, but she feels she is now
over the anguish. Currently she reports no life events but several

chronic strains. One such strain concerns a friend who has been ill with cancer for several years and for whom Hazel does many little things.

She sometimes regrets the career restraints her lack of education imposes, but she gains satisfaction from her managerial position in a cafeteria and has a strong social network. Five or six years ago, Hazel's mother moved in with her; the mother is in poor health and needs attention, and the two are not particularly close. Basically, though, Hazel does not seem to expect much from life and steadfastly refuses to let things bother her.

Her overall adaptation is reasonably positive. She is "pretty happy" and reports only positive emotions on the Bradburn Morale Scale. Her rating of the present year of life is "absolute tops," and she expects satisfactions to outweigh dissatisfactions for the rest of her life (which she projects to age ninety). Finally, she rates her health as very good, takes no medications, and reports no emotional problems.

Not much has changed in Hazel's life by the second interview. Her youngest child, a daughter, still lives in the house and is going to a community college. Her sick friend is still alive, and Hazel drove her to another state so she could visit with family. Helping this friend is important to Hazel: "She keeps me going. Not that it is particularly pleasant, but it keeps me going." She expects no major changes in her life or in herself over the next few years. Her mother still lives with her, remains in poor health, but seems determined to survive and at this stage is still not a burden to Hazel. Although worrying about the safety of her son in Vietnam, she now reports herself to be "very happy" and gives the present year a positive rating on the Life Evaluation Chart.

By the third interview, Hazel reports higher than average levels of negative life events on our Life Events Inventory, but her positive event score is also on the high side. Her sick friend has died of cancer and her mother recently died. Reporting her mother's death brings tears to Hazel's eyes and the interview is interrupted for several minutes. Her daughter has graduated from community college and now has a much better job than Hazel ever thought possible. Hazel also reports a new boyfriend she has been seeing almost every day. This new relationship is taking a lot of her time, but she enjoys it and is even beginning to think of marriage. She also is very satisfied with her job, as always, and is quite satisfied with her life in general.

At this time Hazel continues to report high morale, and her level of psychological symptomatology is consistently low throughout the twelve years of study. She rates the present year as both very positive and very negative, explaining that her mother died but her children came to visit and her youngest daughter is well. Her health continues to be very good and she reports no emotional problems.

Three years later, at the fourth contact, Hazel still works for the same company and in the same position. She is now fifty-nine years old. Her income has improved steadily during the course of the research project, and this makes her life a little easier. Hazel's youngest daughter continues to live at home. When asked what important things have happened since the last interview, she mentions a trip with her male friend to Europe and a world fair. Her relationship seems to be satisfying and has become a routine: "We both work and are both pooped after work. We eat dinner, watch a little television. That's the end of the day. We both get up early."

Hazel reports no unexpected events, mentions no expected events that failed to occur, anticipates no stresses. When asked what situation during the past year caused her the most stress, she describes a chronic problem at work that involves the complexity of the organization she works for. She has had many meetings about the problem, feels some control over the situation, and is not really bothered by it. On the Life Events Inventory she reports only two negative events but is above average on positive events. On the Social Change Checklist Hazel comes across as only slightly influenced by stressors in the world at large. The continuing problems in Vietnam do register, although her son has now completed his tour of duty and returned to the United States. Hazel's health continues to be good, and in fact she reports no serious health problems over the past three years. She does rate herself to be only "pretty happy," but the specific emotions she reports on the Bradburn Morale Scale are all positive. She rates the present and immediate past years as all "very good" on the Life Evaluation Chart, feels she has been fairly successful in getting what she wants out of life, and expects to continue being fairly successful.

When we last visit with Hazel, we find that her exposure to negative life events has dropped to a level significantly below average. Still, the events she reports are serious: her sister died of a heart attack last year, and even though the two were not very close, the loss is troubling. Her health is slightly worse than usual: she has visited a doctor four times over the past year due to some problems with arrhythmia that have now been resolved. On the Social Change Checklist she now reports Vietnam, the student movement, and dangers at nuclear plants to be societal stressors that have affected her. She also feels moderately affected by issues like crime in the streets, the changing role of women, the international situation, and the energy crisis.

While negative stressors do exist in her life, her positive events are above average in incidence. Work is still very satisfying on the whole, and she plans to continue working as long as possible. She now reports that she and her boyfriend are "living together," and this provides considerable satisfaction.

Accompanied by her youngest daughter, the two have gone on another trip to Europe; the three get along very well. Overall, Hazel reports that having a secure relationship with her male friend seems to have released something inside her. Meeting him was a turning point in her life, she says, and her renewed commitment to intimacy may be related to her reduced commitment to self-protection as a style of life and possibly to her high rating on flexibility (as reported in Chapter Five).

Max Schindler: Even the Tough Can Change. When we first meet Max Schindler, he is, at age fifty-one, the youngest man in the preretirement group. Selected as an intensive example because he shifts from a strong commitment to self-concern to a low commitment, he is a rough and tough but likable man who works as a factory supervisor for a small company just south of San Francisco. Max had few childhood stressors and like Olav Olavsen describes his early life as very happy. His current life appears relatively stress-free and is run the way Max likes it: "I got no set routine and I hardly even make appointments. I just live life easy. I don't like appointments where you gotta do this and you gotta do that. I hate to be strung out on that stuff, you know."

Behind this self-protective life-style lies an episode with a health stress. Max suffered a heart attack about twelve years ago. Before that he used to be in a rush, but he no longer likes to push himself: "My whole life changed when I had a heart attack. I was pretty set back by that and I had to reshuffle all my cards again. I didn't hunt deer for ten years after that and I figure this was one of the causes, you know, anxiety and tramping around in the mud and drinking booze with a bunch of guys and whooping it up. So I laid off deer hunting although I took up quail about two years later. But I took it easy and I didn't hunt like I used to. But I think I feel better now than I did in my forties before the heart attack. I quit smoking and now I wake up in a better frame of mind."

Aside from the heart attack, Max reports few negative or positive life events, a few hassles at work, but major concerns with social unrest in this country. When asked about social problems, his concerns reveal a curious mix of the ultraconservative and the liberal: "This race stuff and riots and generation gap between hippies and yippies and the older people. We have left-wingers here who are just beating this country to death and we are hung up in inflation so bad that the average young person can't even make it now. . . . The companies that have got the money don't pay adequate wages and these kids are getting bitter. You wait and see, one of these days everything is going to blow up. Not from Red China, but because we are meddling in people's affairs in Vietnam and people are soured on the whole thing."

Max plans to take an early retirement because "I want to get out of this rat race." He evaluates the present and future years as "very good" (the second highest score possible), but perhaps because of his heart problems he does not expect to live past seventy. He rates his health as good but states that he has some minor problems with arthritis in his hands. He and his wife, "a loving person," get along very well on the whole; he feels he gets along reasonably well with his children as well.

At the second interview, Max's youngest daughter has left home, he has just finished paying off his house, and he has been investigating property in southern Washington in preparation for his early retirement. He does not expect any big changes in the next few years, but in retrospect he thinks he has changed as a person: "Kind of cynical, you know, biased."

On our Activities Checklist he has a lower than average score; the things he does report are mostly low-energy activities: visiting and being visited, daydreaming, talking, resting. He reports that he cooks frequently. He is "pretty happy" and rates the present year as "absolute tops" on the Life Evaluation Chart: "It's getting better every year. I'm making progress, I'm not going backward. It's been a hell of a good year." He rates his health as "very good" and his energy as better than average.

By the third interview, Max is closer to his dream of retirement. He has bought a membership in a quail lodge in Oregon since he plans to spend a lot of time hunting and fishing after he retires. He reports experiencing increasing stress at work, due to minority hiring policies that bring in untrained help but also because he feels a generation gap with the people he supervises: "They've got a different way of thinking. There is no pride in their work." Perhaps in consequence, he now gets no satisfaction from work except for picking up his paycheck. On the Life Events Inventory he reports four negative events (a death in the family, divorce of a child, separation from a friend, and trouble with people at work) and five positive events. Social problems bother Max more than before, especially unemployment and inflation and the cost of the Vietnam War. (The year is 1974.) Despite the increase in stress, Max is still "pretty happy." Curiously, he is one of the few older people to rate the present as the best age to be: "Right now and I guess the best is yet to come. I'm having less responsibility. My house is paid for. My kids are all married or all raised. It's just starting toward the golden years." The last sentence may reveal a primary ingredient of Max's life right now: one gets the sense that he is just marking time toward retirement. This impression is reinforced by the fact that although he rates the present year lower than he has in past interviews, he views the future in much more positive terms.

By the fourth interview Max has been retired about a year and a half. Retirement is the single most important thing that has happened to him during the three years since his last interview, but he has also bought a farm in Washington and spends a lot of time there. Currently he is building a house on his new property. The construction has led to problems with the contractors, and he has recently had to hire a lawyer; this situation, he says, has caused him the greatest stress during the past year. Other than this he feels nothing is causing him stress and anticipates no problems for the next three years at least. On the Life Events Inventory he now scores low on negative events and significantly higher than average on positive events. On the Social Change Checklist he reports a moderate influence from World War II, Vietnam, the student movement, the minority rights movement, crime in the streets, and changes in the economy and employment during the past three years. Although he reports that world news interests him the most, Max no longer seems very disturbed about these social stressors. In fact, when probed about the minority rights movement he replies: "A hard bunch to understand. No effect on my life."

Max still lives in the same house in San Francisco together with his wife and a divorced daughter. He is now "very happy" and reports his highest number of positive emotions on the Bradburn Morale Scale. Reporting no serious health problems since the previous interview, he seems to see some personal growth. When asked about changes over the past eight years, he replies: "I have learned a lot about things most people take for granted." He feels himself to have been very successful in getting what he wants out of life and expects to be fairly successful in the future.

The fifth contact, in March 1980, is conducted by mail. Max and his wife now live on their fifteen-acre farm. His income is actually higher than ever because Max is now a part-time farmer and uses his farm income to supplement his pension. Only one negative (health) event is reported on the Life Events Inventory, but positive events abound. His major stress seems to be "too many weeds." He plans never to retire from farming. When asked what he would do if he could do it over again, he replies that he wishes he had retired earlier from his former job: "Why wait till you're too old to do the things you want to do?" On the expanded Social Change Checklist he scores only World War II as having had even a moderate impact on his life. When asked to note specific social problems that give him concern, he writes that he is not really upset with things anymore.

Max reports himself to be pretty happy and reports more positive emotions on the Bradburn Morale Scale than ever before— even though he has had a very stressful health episode: Max was hospitalized last month with a heart blockage that will require four bypasses. (The operation will take place in three months.) He has also had prostrate problems that were "minor" and is experiencing some weight problems as well. When asked to look back over the past twelve years and note the changes he has seen in himself, he lists:

1. Hair got a little white
2. Got a few more wrinkles
3. Not so much sex
4. Money not as important as it seemed to be twelve years ago

Overall, Max is now where he hoped to be all those years ago when we began the project. He reports himself to be "very satisfied" with the way he spends his time, and the way he spends his time in fact sounds quite idyllic in a Daniel Boone kind of way: carpentry, farming, gardening, hunting, and fishing. He not only feels himself to have been very successful in getting the things he wants out of life but expects to be very successful in the future. He describes his relationship to his wife as "very close" and thinks she is "the best." According to Max she is someone he can talk to and be affectionate with, who spends money wisely, an all-around good person. Although in all prior interviews he has reported himself to be "boss" in the family, he now thinks they are equal in their relationship. He also reports having made at least thirty new friends since moving to their new home.

Adelaide Stone: Kicked in the Butt. In Chapter One we learned that Adelaide Stone is consistently low in self-concern until the time of the last interview, when she becomes more self-protective. We also learned of a rather troubled childhood and teenhood. Adelaide's problems did not end with her early years: she has had adult stresses as well. Her first experiences with menopausal symptoms, about three years ago, left her in a deep depression, and two years ago, when Adelaide was nearly fifty, her son separated from his wife and this "nearly killed me."

When we meet Adelaide in the first interview, however, she is basically content with life. She has what she wants and things are progressing at a slow but comfortable rate for her. "I know this may sound stupid," she says, but "I have what I want. I would like my life to just stay status quo and no tragedies to occur." When asked what the next important event in her life will be, she has no idea and implies she hopes there will be none. When asked what she expects for the next few years, she replies: "I will live for my husband and myself. I expect quite a fulfillment in my mellow years. I will have less worries about other people and my family. I think I'll have more fulfillment than before, unless life kicks you in the butt."

By the second interview, Adelaide's hopes for a status-quo life have been dashed. During the interim between interviews she discovers that her son and his wife are both heroin addicts. Adelaide pitches right in and gets them both hospitalized, but "it was hell on earth, I assure you." The children have had to stay with Adelaide and her husband while the parents were repeatedly hospitalized, and now the daughter-in-law has been jailed for theft. Moreover, Adelaide herself had major surgery less than a year ago, and just a few months ago she and her husband surprised a burglar robbing their house. At this point, Adelaide reasons, "things have got to get better, because they can't get worse. I've also changed my philosophy of life. All my life I have been giving to my family, but now I'm going to start living for myself and Mr. Stone." Her morale has slipped from high to moderate between the first and second interviews, but she still has optimism. As an indication of how things stand, however, she refuses to fill out a Life Evaluation Chart for anything but the present year, which she rates as being less than satisfying. Symptom-free at the initial interview, she now reports four psychological and physical symptoms: people annoy her, she is afraid of noises at night, she sometimes feels life is not worth living, and (related to the menopause) she experiences hot spells. She takes medication for hypertension and hormones to control her menopausal symptoms.

When we called to arrange for the third contact, Adelaide put off the interview because of a death in the family. Two months later, when recontacted, she had suffered a massive stroke and was hospitalized for over four months. By the fourth interview, Adelaide is feeling better. Originally paralyzed on the left side and unable to talk, she has regained use of her limbs and her speech is much better. Adelaide is on disability retirement and reports the divorce and severe emotional problems of her son.

More surprising, however, Adelaide herself is now divorced. The couple divorced after her stroke, but the divorce was caused by the husband's difficulties in adjusting to retirement and Adelaide's irritation with having him around the house all day: "All he did was stay around and gripe." She still views her husband positively and says they are now better friends than while married. In consequence of retirement and divorce, her income has taken a sharp drop. On the positive side, she reports the birth of four grandchildren. Her negative life-event score puts her among the highest scorers in the entire sample, and her positive life-event score is quite low. She now reports she is "not too happy." When asked what changes she has seen in herself during the past three years, she says: "I've changed a lot since I've come home [from the hospital]. I've always liked people but now I'm more introverted than extroverted." She sees the stroke as a major turning point in her life and thinks it has changed her for the better. She even hopes to return to work soon.

At this fourth interview, Adelaide fills out the Social Change Checklist for the first time. She scores among the highest in terms of the impact of both past and ongoing events. She reports, for example, that the Great Depression "was the ruination of my family and my childhood." Crime in the streets, changes in the economy, and Watergate have made her more fearful for the future of the world, although she sees the changing role of women and the minority rights movement as positive forces that have affected her.

At the fifth contact, the sixty-three-year-old Adelaide again reports extremely high levels of negative events and low levels of positive events. Many things continue to bother her. She reports, for example, that she would like to be working but "I can't do that now because I get too nervous." When asked to report how happy she is, she says "I'm existing, that's all." She reports feeling bored and vaguely uneasy about things and frequently mentions her stroke and the fact that she sees a doctor at least once a month. One of her brothers has also suffered a stroke and is completely paralyzed, which adds to her distress. Her drug-addicted son stole everything from Adelaide's summer cottage and left the state, and as Adelaide discusses this and the resulting problems with the son's children, tears pour from her face and she runs from the room. She cries intermittently for the rest of the interview.

At this final interview Adelaide responds positively to thirteen of the forty-two symptoms on the California Symptoms Checklist—about twice the average. When asked about expectations for future success in attaining what she wants out of life, she rates herself at the bottom: "not successful." She adds that the problems with her son and his children tend to preoccupy her mind. On the Social Change Checklist, which was expanded at the fifth contact, Adelaide ranks higher than ever on the impact of social issues. Dangers at nuclear plants, the energy crisis, crime in the streets—nearly everything seems strange and frightening. It is no wonder that Adelaide's open and unprotective way of approaching the world has now shifted to an emphasis on self-protection as measured by our commitment scores. It is perhaps not surprising that she is now contemplating voluntary institutionalization: "They say retirement homes are nice." Life, indeed, has kicked Adelaide in the butt.

Summing Up

We have spent considerable time discussing stress in its various guises and effects. Until recently, stress was not viewed as a concept relevant to development. Instead, theorists and researchers have traditionally viewed stress in terms of its relevance for short-term changes in physical and social function. In study after study of bereavement, amputation, relocation, divorce, and other personal traumas, the typical investigation evaluates respondents, at the most, for one or two years after the event. It is only within the last ten years, more or less, that students of adult development and aging have begun to recognize the long-term impact of stress (Chiriboga and Cutler, 1980).

The importance of stress lies not only in its theoretical effect on general stability and change but in its immediate impact on personal functioning. As we have seen, stress exposure seems to have an effect, both positive and negative, on nearly all aspects of life. Whether the focus is on physical health, sexuality, cognitive functioning, social relations, or marital satisfaction, stress seems to make a difference in the life of middle-aged men and women. And one must keep in mind that stressors, whether negative or positive, may be packaged in deceptive ways. What is stressful to one person may be a challenge to another, and the same basic situation may be viewed quite differently in different life stages. A middle-aged and somewhat rundown father may greet his new baby girl with considerably less enthusiasm than a parent in his mid-twenties.

Our objective in this chapter has been to discuss not only the general impact of stress on adult development but also its impact on respondents at all stages of life. For life events and other stressors, although frequently reported to occur with less frequency, continue to play an important role in later life. As we found in developing our stress typology, however, stressors need not always lead to pathology and decline and may in fact signal the beginnings of a period of major growth. More important than the stressors may be the resources the person brings to bear on the problem, the way he or she views the problem, and the social context. Whether stress leads to growth or to decline may rest, ultimately, on whether the experience taxes but does not exceed the person's adaptive resources.

8

Influence of Mythical
and Forgotten Stressors

We have illustrated, in the last chapter, the often critical role that stress may play in shaping the course of human development. There are some stressors whose role may be overstated, however, and others whose role appears to be barely recognized. Here we consider examples of both varieties. Two stressors that may in fact have been overstated in the literature are the generation gap and the midlife crisis, while understated stresses include boredom and hassles.

Generational Chasms and Bridges

Interest in relations across the generations has grown considerably over the past half century as improvements in nutrition and hygiene, coupled with advances in the medical sciences, have combined to extend the life expectancy of most Americans. In both professional and lay circles it is no longer uncommon to read of four living generations in the same family. The notion of five living generations seems almost incredible, but they do occasionally occur.

With the rise in multigenerational families, it is not surprising to find greater concern about intergenerational conflict. Student protests in the 1970s, in particular, seemed to spark intense debate across the generations, whether the focus was on Vietnam, nuclear energy, or toxic waste. But intergenerational conflict is no longer seen as the stressor of the twentieth century. Instead, many are saying that there is a kind of reciprocity: the young pick and choose what they want from the old, and in turn they influence their elders through their choices (Bengtson, Furlong, and Laufer, 1974). Some older people find that the social changes favored by the young are more fulfilling, humane, or simply more enjoyable. In short, it does not appear that a dialectical process, manifest in revolt and protest, necessarily underlies the succession of generations.

One way to examine relations across the generations is to consider residential proximity and number of contacts, which we will do using information obtained from the fifth and final contact. By this time, approximately twelve years after we initiated the study, two of the youngest males still live with their parents, one of the youngest women lives with both parents, and another two live with their mothers only. None of the second youngest or second oldest men and women live with parents but two of the oldest group of men have their mother living with them. Among the oldest women one has a father living with her, and another three have mothers at home. For several of the oldest men and women, then, we can see that the family has come full cycle: they left home early in life but find themselves living with a parent again in later life.

While the oldest men and women are assuming more responsibility for their own parents, ten of the middle-aged parents still have not experienced the empty nest when we interview them for the last time: in each case at least one child still lives at home. The same is true for four of the retirement-age sample. Five of the middle-aged parents have experienced what might be called a "return to the nest": their children have suffered either financial problems or divorce and have returned home to recuperate. The same is true of all four children of our oldest group. In most cases these full-nested parents, of the second oldest and oldest groups, are somewhat discomforted by the experience of suddenly being full-time parents again.

Our next topic is the frequency of cross-generation contact, and here we will only consider contacts where the two generations do not live in the same house. Seventy-two parents of the younger groups live in the same community as their children and fifty-three live outside the community (most within one hundred miles). The youngest men and women still have both parents; the oldest ones offer an interesting and nationally prevalent statistic: nearly twice as many fathers as mothers are dead.

Of the youngest men, all but one see their mothers and fathers at least a few times a month. (Six see them daily or at least once a week.) Only four of their grandmothers are still alive, but they are visited fairly often. Only two grandfathers are alive, one of whom is visited at least once a week, the other a few times a month. The youngest women are more conscientious about maintaining connections across generations: more than half of them see their mothers at least once a week. The mother and daughter bond is closer than the father and daughter relation: fathers are seen or called much less often by their daughters. And the skip-generation bond seems quite weak: only one of these youngest women has a living grandmother and another one a grandfather, both of whom are visited less than monthly.

The second youngest men, who by now have an average age of thirty-five, include several who see their mothers at least once a week and the rest a few times a month. Fathers are not visited quite so often. Only two have grandparents and they are visited a few times a month. The second youngest women are equally divided: half see their mothers at least once a week, the other half a few times a month. Precisely the same ratio holds for visiting with fathers. Two of these women have grandmothers, but they live out of town and are rarely visited.

The second oldest men include only three who have living mothers and two with fathers, all of whom they visit at least a few times a month. With these second oldest people we introduce the concept of generational chasms and bridges as a way of viewing parental relations with sons and daughters who are now grown up and have not lived with their parents for a very long time. Most sons are seen at least a few times a month, while nearly all of the daughters visit or are visited at least once a week. The second oldest women for the most part see their sons a few times a month whereas the majority of them visit with daughters at least once a week. Essentially, women appear to serve as generational bridges.

The oldest men do not fare so well with either sons or daughters, both of whom are seen only a few times a month. Our data, in fact, support the position that it is the women who foster familial cohesion across the generations. Most of the oldest women rarely see their sons daily or weekly, but the majority of them see their daughters at least once a week. All in all, the data to this point suggest that intergenerational relations are positive, although sometimes people adopt a certain "benign neglect" regarding family ties. With one exception, the empirical data, as well as the case materials, definitely did not portray intergenerational relations as a major source of distress to participants in our study. The one exception lay in the case of caring for elderly parents, an obligation that came as an unpleasant surprise to most of our respondents. We will return to this point later in the chapter.

The Proverbial Midlife Crisis

The importance of life events as shapers of the life course has been reinforced by findings from this and many other studies. Certainly no discussion of stress and loss in adult life would be complete without some reference to the midlife crisis. It has become fashionable in the popular press to speak of the "midlife crisis" and other phrases that refer to a time of major personal, social, and physical change during the middle years of life. In reviewing our own findings, as well as the empirical and clinical literature on this phenomenon, we began to see the emergence of three themes: one based on a developmental perspective, another on a more circumstantial or "stress" perspective, and a third on a clinical perspective.

From a developmental perspective, the literature and our own findings suggest that during the middle years people begin to question the values and rules of conduct they have grown up with. A gradual phenomenon, this questioning was first described by Carl Jung, who commented on a time, during the "second half" of life, when people seek to balance their lives. If they happened to place a major emphasis on achievement and instrumental activities earlier on, for example, they might begin paying more attention to the expressive and social side of life. When personal and social change in the lives of our middle-agers did occur, it was often due to situations, mostly loss-related, that created specific demands on them— loss of the role of "all powerful mother" when the children left, for example, or loss of the role of "chief" or "boss" or "head mechanic" when the respondent retired. These conditions seemed to create an identity vacuum that had the potential of leading to a downward spiral of adaptation. In other words, loss of critical roles seemed to precipitate what Kuypers and Bengtson (1973) have referred to as the "social breakdown syndrome."

The departure of children from the family home has often been said to prompt a crisis in the lives of middle-aged men and women. When we looked at our second oldest group of men and women, as they adjusted to the departure of their last child, we found the majority viewed the event with a sense of relief and welcomed the occasion as a time to focus on personal interests and growth (Lowenthal and Chiriboga, 1972). For a minority of about 10 percent—especially among those particularly invested in the parenting role—there emerged a theme of struggle and anxiety that continued for several years. Many of these people were catapulted into the "self-defeating" category of our stress typology, as they mourned the loss of an extremely rewarding and fulfilling role. Surprisingly, it was more likely to be the father than the mother who had trouble letting go (Krystal and Chiriboga, 1979). Certain fathers, for example, seem to experience a marked difficulty in letting a beloved daughter leave home, even when conflict over her departure is creating rifts in the parent-child relationship.

Considering both the developmental and the nondevelopmental perspectives on problems at midlife, we must return to the notion that the personal world and physical status of many of these people were changing and that these changes themselves created a demand for change on the part of the middle-ager. From the third perspective, the clinical orientation, comes the notion that these demands for change may so disrupt the person's life that significant proportions experience what has come to be known as "the midlife crisis." With these perspectives in mind, let us consider some evidence for a midlife crisis in men and in women.

The Male Midlife Crisis. At the most general level, community surveys have produced little evidence for a midlife crisis in males. Although various observers have discussed the occurrence of a "male climacteric" and other issues evolving from purported changes in sexuality or health in general, very few men appear to experience a full-fledged midlife crisis. Thus the continuing portrayal of a male crisis of the midlife period is hard to explain. Perhaps the problems center on the empty nest. Although we are certainly not accustomed to viewing men as family-oriented creatures who cannot bear the thought of children leaving home, we found that during the middle years of our study the men as well as the women in the second oldest group reported the most negative family events.

Among the other problems at midlife, the second oldest group of men expressed a sense of being locked into the same job until retirement, the potential career stagnation faced by these men, and the growing reality of retirement. Few of them expected further promotions, and most men and women in the second oldest group felt they had already reached the peak of their careers. Work generally was becoming a less positive experience, an impression borne out by our Life Events Inventory: significantly fewer positive work events are reported by our two older groups of men and women compared to all but the second youngest group of women. The gradual but progressive loss in physical strength and reaction time, sensory decrements, and an increasing number of health problems are also beginning to signal the occupants of middle-aged bodies that life is not forever.

To gain a sense of the multitude of changes facing men during this period, consider the case of Miles Baker. An automotive mechanic specializing in transmissions, Miles has worked for nearly thirty years for the same automobile dealership. He enjoys his work, especially as the company sells a line of distinguished European road machines in which Miles takes great pride. At the time of our first interview, he rates himself "on top of the world." His three children are getting "fantastic" grades in high school and college, he has just received a substantial increase in pay, and he and his wife are planning a major vacation as soon as their youngest child graduates from high school.

Five years later, Miles presents quite a different picture. A long-term smoker, he has developed symptoms of emphysema and is limited in his activities. He still talks with great nostalgia about the vacation he and his wife took after Junior graduated from high school, but he feels that may have been the last bright spot. When asked to draw his life graph, he rates that year as the all-time high point; the rest he sees as downhill. The kids are now all in college, and while this is a source of pride, it also creates economic anguish for this self-educated blue-collar worker. In fact, the first round of gasoline increases in the mid-1970s has really hurt sales for the company, and there are rumors of layoffs and cutbacks. Miles is now a tired and frightened man, unsure whether his dreams of golden retirement will ever materialize. Social and personal changes have been far more than he ever bargained for.

The Female Midlife Crisis. The general categories that define the stress experiences of men during middle age apply to women, as well, but with certain differences. Perhaps most obviously, the biological clock of women ticks away faster than for men with respect to reproductive capacity. The loss of this capacity may symbolize the beginning of the end for many women, just as the pending loss of the worker role may symbolize an end to productivity and feelings of self-worth among many middle-aged men and women.

At the same time, the negative stereotypes of the postmenopausal period have been known for some time to reflect fantasy rather than fact. For most women in our sample, menopause is not a devastating time of life. In this our results correspond with those of researchers such as Kahana, Kiyak, and Liang (1980), who report that middle-aged women generally rate the menopause as producing very few changes in their lives. We found much the same thing in our sample of second oldest women over the years. Comparing their reports to the retrospective reports of the oldest group of women, this newest generation of menopausal women appears to be having an easier time in midlife. Apparently the newer generation of women entering middle age feels very differently about menopause than their predecessors. This attitude may have something to do with greater use of estrogen therapies and an increased salience of work in their lives compared to their predecessors. On the other hand, the increase in personal choice about life careers seems to have created a precondition for crisis in some women. Those who have chosen the single life or delayed parenthood, for example, may view the closing of the parenthood option with greater distress than has the present cohort (Chiriboga and Fiske, 1987).

Also apparently more a misconception than a reality is the idea that the departure of children from the parental home, the so-called empty nest period, creates great conflict among women—and men, for that matter. For the majority of middle-aged women the departure of children signals a new freedom. Not only are they gaining dens and extra rooms for guests, but many immediately begin making plans for long-awaited vacations. In fact, our middle-agers who have reached this stage of life are more likely to report greater positive experiences in their marriage than any other group in the study (Chiriboga and Cutler, 1980). They also rank lower than any other age group in the number of negative events associated with marriage.

The New Midlife Stress: Caring for Parents. In the lives of our second oldest group of men and women, we found that exposure to life events generally is reduced, but the ratio of positive to negative events begins a gradual shift toward the negative. Moreover, there is evidence that people in the middle and later stages experience more chronic stress and fewer of the sudden but short-lived events. One chronic stressor faced by middle-agers has to do with the slow erosion of power and status at work that many researchers have found to occur toward the end of middle age. Another example is the growing need of their own parents for help with the tasks of day-to-day life. This stressor has only recently received attention but seems to be on the increase; it is linked to the dramatic increases in life expectancy during the twentieth century.

In midlife, people often assume the primary responsibility for family integration and rituals. They also expand their responsibility for providing care to those who are dependent—not only children in the throes of becoming adults but parents as well. Brody (1990) and Hagestad (1986) note that "kin-keepers" are most likely to be women caught in a generational squeeze that can leave them with less and less free time and choice during a period of life usually associated with increasing freedom. As one recently retired woman put it: "I guess it's terribly selfish of me, but in 1963 his mother and father moved out here, and in 1964 my mother and father moved out here. And you're never free. That is the only thing that has depressed our lives at all. For many years we've been building up to the future and now we feel constrained."

At the fourth interview we asked respondents to tell us the two most stressful experiences they had faced since the last interview. Surprisingly, those reporting the greatest stress with parents were not the two oldest groups but the youngest, more than a third of whom found parents to be the greatest source of stress. Next were the second oldest group, with approximately one-quarter reporting their most stressful experience to involve one or both parents. On the other hand, when asked the source of the greatest anticipated stress, one-third of the second oldest group said parents. That this anticipation may have some validity is demonstrated by the fact that while none of the second oldest group had parents living with them, five of the oldest group had a mother (or mother-in-law) and one had a father. Moreover, the oldest group reported being most hassled by parents.

According to our data, the assumption of parent-keeping responsibilities is usually anticipated. And indeed the responsibilities associated with the roles of kin keeper and kin carer are quite compatible with what theories tell us of middle age. Erikson has cast "generativity," or the willingness to devote time and energy to the nurturing of others, as one aspect of the middle years, for example, while Havighurst (1953) says that adjustment to the reality of aging parents is a key developmental task of midlife. The fact that parent keeping becomes a demand at much the same time that people are first facing up to their own personal mortality can only exacerbate existing stresses (Robinson and Thurnher, 1979).

The middle-aged, especially the middle-aged women, have been labeled the "sandwich generation" because they seem to be caught between competing demands of their children, on the one hand, and their parents, on the other. Norma Bates, a middle-aged and married mother of four, exemplifies this dilemma. At the time of the first interview Norma's youngest son is still living at home, and he stays at home through the fourth contact. But Norma's mother lives with her and has done so ever since she was eighty-five (between interviews two and three). Now close to ninety, the mother is alert but somewhat feisty. Rather than feeling caught in the middle, Norma has enjoyed her mother's presence. She likes it most when the two of them can sit down over coffee and talk about "the good old days," which now means World War II to both of them.

Boredom: The "Make or Break" of Later Life?

As we investigated the concept of stress over the duration of our study, we had time to consider a wide range of potentially stressful conditions. We discovered that events which do not occur—such as an anticipated marriage or a child leaving home—distress respondents as much as life events themselves. We also found that people often talk about a basic rhythm to life that suits them: sometimes life seems to be going at a comfortable rate, sometimes it is going too fast, and sometimes it seems to drag on and on. They also speak of being frustrated by little things that did not appear even in our 138-item Life Events Questionnaire. Naturally we listened, and responded by adding the measure to be described next.

What makes for boredom? This issue became of special interest to us since many respondents, especially in the two oldest groups, report boredom to be a stress for them. At the fourth interview we inserted an eighteen-item instrument, developed by our colleague Robert Pierce, entitled the Enough Scale. The intent of this scale was, not surprisingly, to find out if people get enough out of various activities and pursuits of life. Do they, for example, get enough—or more than enough—intellectual challenge or peace and quiet? Or, conversely, do they get not enough or just barely enough? Generally there were few age and sex differences, but those that emerged seemed to defy the stereotypes. Among the men, for example, those in the youngest and the oldest groups feel they get enough physical activity, play, and peace and quiet, while those in the second youngest group feel the most deprived. Among the women, several patterns emerge. The youngest and second youngest feel more deprived than the two older groups in both peace and quiet, on the one extreme, and flamboyance, on the other. For sensuality, however, the second youngest women and the oldest women report equally low satisfaction, while the youngest women feel most satisfied.

With these initial results in mind, we then turned to the

question of whether getting enough of what life has to offer is associated with morale. We examined this issue by creating four groups: those who do not get enough, those who get barely enough, those who do get enough, and those who get more than enough. Our findings suggest that whether one gets enough of life's offerings has very little to do with the morale of the two younger groups but is very important for the two older groups.

The differences between the second oldest men and women are particularly intriguing because they seem to reflect two very different orientations to activities and perhaps to life itself. The men in this group, all of whom are fast approaching retirement at this fourth contact, are very intent on minimizing stimulation. All they seem to want is peace and quiet, with just enough creative activity to keep life from becoming boring. In other words, the men with the highest morale report just barely enough creative activity and so forth while those with none or enough or more than enough are significantly lower in morale. By way of contrast, the middle-aged women cannot get enough novelty, intellectual challenge, excitement, and creativity. There is also a suggestion that these gender differences are associated with critical life experiences. For men, growing awareness of stalled careers and impending retirement is associated with a dissatisfaction with the demands of the workaday world. The second oldest group of women, on the other hand, are involved in the transition accompanying the departure of their youngest child, and this transitional period is associated with a growing recognition of one's potential, especially among those who have, until recently, dedicated their lives to the care of children.

The pattern of needs most associated with morale among the oldest group of respondents sends quite a different message. For these oldest men and women, there may be a fine line between the peace and quiet they seem to value and boredom. Among both sexes we found that some degree of new experiences or creative activity— but not much—is most associated with morale. This finding suggests that these dimensions provide the stimulation necessary to keep tranquillity from becoming boredom, at least for men and women in the oldest group. In other words, too much or too little of a good thing may create stress; the issue is one of balance and individual need.

Daily Hassles: Influential but Soon Forgotten

One of the curiosities we found in studying stress experiences over twelve years was how often our participants could not remember anything eventful when simply asked about events and changes in their lives. When given an inventory of items that behavioral scientists have found to be stressful, however, the same people report stressors galore. Apparently people simply do not dwell on their lives all that much. Many stressors, moreover, such as the day-to-day hassles we discuss here, are not all that spectacular or even upsetting in and of themselves. As mentioned earlier, however, hassles have been associated with both physical and mental health problems. (See, for example, Holmes and Holmes, 1970; Lazarus and Folkman, 1984.)

For the fourth and fifth interviews, we included a rating list of hassles modeled after the Hassles Checklist of Lazarus and Folkman (1984) but including only 11 general items instead of the 115 specific items in the Lazarus version. Interviewers introduced our hassles list as follows: "Now I would like to find out how hassled or pressured you feel in certain areas of your life. That is, I want to know the day-to-day things that really annoy you. For each area please tell me whether you feel hassled all the time, very often, fairly often, once in a while, or never." Respondents were then handed a card listing the situations to evaluate. Altogether, eleven situations are involved: work, spouse, children, parents, friends, relatives, neighbors, health, finances, time pressures, and social situations.

Hassles with People and Work. The fourth interview finds the youngest men, who are now about twenty-five, not very hassled at work—fifteen who are never or rarely annoyed and seven who are. They have fewer hassles at work three years later—the proportions are now seventeen and five. Evidently they have straightened things out with their bosses. Marital disagreements are rare at this time and increase only slightly by the fifth interview. Problems with parents occur "once in a while" at both times except for one man who says he has problems with them "all the time." Since "one inherits a family but selects one's friends," we are not surprised that at both times these young men at the most have disagreements only "once in a while" with a friend; relatives other than those already mentioned are on a par with friends, and none of them mentions having disagreements with them fairly often or very often.

The youngest women tend to report substantially more hassles than the youngest men. To illustrate this gender difference, we look only at the response categories "fairly often" and "very often." The youngest men at the fourth contact include eight who fairly or very often have job hassles; by the fifth contact there are only two. The youngest women echo the men at the fourth contact, but three years later we find them in sharp contrast: only two men have work hassles fairly often, and none have them fairly or very often. At this time nearly half of the women have job hassles, perhaps reflecting a greater demand on women who are creating careers for themselves. Women's disagreements with their spouses are notably more frequent than among their male counterparts at the fourth interview (three times as many), but at the fifth contact only about twice as many have spousal problems. Despite the growing convergence, it is sobering that these youngest women see so many more hassles in their marital relations than do men.

Having long since flown from the nest (by this time their average age is twenty-five), hassles with parents are not very severe among the youngest people. At the fourth contact nearly all of the youngest men are in the "never" or "once in a while" category when it comes to hassles with parents. There is almost no change at the fifth contact. Again, the youngest women are a little more apt to report hassles. At the fourth encounter five of them have problems with their parents, but the figure drops to four by the last interview.

The second youngest men have somewhat fewer parental problems. At the fourth contact nearly all of them are in the "never" or "once in a while" category, and three years later they have changed very little. More women than men never have hassles with their parents at the fourth contact, but three years later there is a drastic change for the worse. Evidently their parents, or at least one parent, are becoming cantankerous—and in our culture it is usually the women who take care of them.

Generational differences are highlighted when it comes to the four older groups. A few of the second oldest men are retired by the fourth contact, and at the last session a few more of them are.

As for the rest of them, work hassles are more frequent at the fourth interview than at the fifth, possibly reflecting an evolving disengagement from work. Hassles with their wives are few at the fifth contact and even fewer at the last encounter. Evidently they are learning to tolerate the idiosyncrasies of the opposite sex. Now in their late fifties at the fourth interview, their children are all grown up, most of them married and working. With three exceptions, hassles with them are rare at both times. Problems with their own parents do not exist at the fourth contact, and three years later only six of them have living parents and they have no disagreements at all. At the fourth contact these next to oldest men never or only once in a while have disagreements with a friend and there is no change at the fifth contact. These men are anything but flighty; they know how to treasure a close friend. Hassles with relatives are rare. At both times nearly all of these men are in the "never" or "once in a while" category.

The second oldest women tend to be more tolerant than their male counterparts on some issues and less so on others. None of them check "never" on work hassles at the fourth interview, and only two do so at the final one. Eight of the men say they never had spouse hassles at the fourth contact, but only one woman does so. The ensuing three years provide time for changes, and they are surprising: all of the men say they never or only once in a while have spouse problems, and all but three women agree with them. Women, perhaps understandably for this more traditional generation, have had more hassles with their now grown children than did men at the fourth contact, and the situation has worsened somewhat. We suspect they have more hassles with sons than with daughters, and a review of cases confirms our impression. At the fourth contact they have had a few more hassles with parents than the men, but three years later they resemble the men: very few of them have living parents and those who do rarely disagree or have hassles with them. Like the men, at both times they say they have never, or only once in a while, had problems with friends (except for one woman who is hassled in every category at both times and may have hypochondria).

The oldest men and women share more differences than they do similarities; we might call them idiosyncratic. At the fourth in-

terview their average age is sixty-seven. Only eleven men are still
working and more than half of them never have work hassles; the
rest have them once in a while. More women are still working, and
they are about equally divided between having no problems and having them only once in a while. Two of these women are very hassled
at the next to last interview. At the final contact, oddly, one more man
is working than at the previous interview—and he "never" has hassles. Thirteen women are still working at the fourth contact, and two
of them are hassled fairly often; both feel that their bosses wish they
would retire. Half of this oldest group of women has never had problems and the others have them only once in a while.

By the last interview one of them has stopped working. Ten
never or only once in a while feel stressed, two fairly often. The
oldest men rarely have disagreements with their wives at the fourth
contact, but two of them have arguments with their wives fairly
often. Three years later they have changed very little, and only one
has spousal disagreements fairly often. The oldest women, as noted
earlier, are more outspoken. Only two of them have never had disagreements with their husbands, and, at the other extreme, two have
had them very often. They have changed very little in the course of
three years except that now only one of them has not had disagreements with her husband.

Since the children of this oldest group are now approaching
middle age, we are not surprised to learn that few have had hassles
with them. At the fourth contact, three-quarters of the oldest men
have never had disagreements with them. At the last encounter,
however, one man reports hassles with children "all the time" and
there are fewer "nevers" and more "once in a whiles." Evidently,
among men, generational differences may become more negative,
even though they remain infrequent. The oldest women also have
mixed feelings about their middle-aged children. At the fourth session a majority of them are in the "never" or "once in a while"
categories but five of them are very annoyed, and nothing has
changed at the final session. There are fewer "nevers" among the
oldest women than the oldest men. Apparently women disagree
with the way in which their offspring are bringing up their own
children.

Given the age of people in the oldest group, not many of

them have living parents. Four of the oldest men have parents: one reports no hassles with his parent, two admit to hassles once in a while, and one is very hassled. At the final interview only two of the oldest men have a parent (or parents); one never has problems, the other once in a while. At the fourth contact, six of the oldest women have parents: two of them never have problems, one has them once in a while, and three have them quite often. Three years later only two have living parents and they represent the extremes: one has had no hassles, the other has them "all the time." (In the latter case there seems to be considerable evidence that the parent may have Alzheimer's disease since the onset was gradual and the confusion has shown no sudden change but has steadily worsened.)

Among the old, as among the young, hassles with friends are few. At the fourth interview, the oldest men have never had any or have them only once in a while. By the final contact there is little change except that one, who is no doubt getting crotchety, has problems all the time. The oldest women are quite benign. At the fourth contact only one has disagreements with a friend, and three years later none of them does. Relatives (other than those already discussed) seldom cause hassles for the oldest men, but three years later two of them feel hassled. Their female counterparts include three who are hassled with relatives at the fourth contact, but three years later they have outgrown them.

Other Hassles. In this section we consider four additional hassles: hassles with neighbors, health, finances, and social activities. At the fourth interview about half of the youngest men have never had difficulties with neighbors and the rest have them only once in a while. Three years later they have become even more patient: all but one have neighbor hassles only once in a while, and the one exception never does so. Money problems are more serious: only six have never had financial problems, and the number drops to four at the last session. Being sociable is not a chore for most of them at the fourth contact, but nearly half of them by the final interview consider it a hassle.

The youngest women are even less likely than men to have problems with neighbors at either the fourth or fifth interview. They are also less concerned than men about their health at the fourth contact, but the men have become less concerned at the final encounter and so the gender gap is nil. At both times women are more worried about money, so much so that many of them have part-time jobs. Contrary to our expectations, they have experienced as many hassles about sociability as men at the fourth contact but have become their normal sociable selves by the final contact. The next to youngest people are like the youngest in terms of gender differences. All of the men have never or only once in a while had hassles with neighbors at the fourth interview, and there is no change at the final encounter. Women in the same stage of life have changed more. At the fourth contact most of them are in the "never" category regarding hassles with neighbors, but at the final contact they are split: half "never," the other half "once in a while." One woman is very hassled by a neighbor who "borrows" things but does not return them.

Most of the second oldest men have never had hassles with neighbors at the fourth contact, but by the final interview there are more in the "once in a while" category. They may be reaching the age when older men begin to get grumpy. Most of the second oldest women are never upset by neighbors at either time. (They have more patience than men.) The oldest men have more hassles with neighbors than younger ones do at both times, but most women are never or rarely upset by neighbors at the fourth contact and though they are a bit more so at the last session they are not as upset as men in the same stage of life. (The average age of the oldest people at the last encounter is seventy.)

Health problems are more serious, especially among the four older groups. The youngest men, who are all healthy, seem to be worried at first: three-quarters of them think about their health rather often at the fourth session, but three years later most have decided they are healthy. All but one of the youngest women never or only once in a while feel hassled by their health at the fourth contact, but three years later we find a few of them more health-conscious. This does not necessarily mean they have been sick, but they think about that possibility. Far more than half of the second youngest men are worried about health once in a while, fairly often, or very often. Their only change by the final interview is that there are even fewer who never worry about their health. As for second youngest women, at both times they brood less about their health than men do, but the differences between them are slight. Most of the second oldest men are no worse off than younger people at the fourth contact, but they drop from sixteen to four on never having been hassled about their health by the final interview. The second oldest women include only five who worry about their health at the fourth interview, and the number increases only to six at the final session. There are unanticipated findings among the men and women in the oldest group: at the fourth interview they are no more concerned about their health than the second oldest people. Three years later only three men and five women are fairly or very hassled about their health—an excellent record for people now in their seventies. And, as we will see, they do not worry much about money either.

With a few exceptions, our respondents are by no means well-to-do. They are, for the most part, blue-collar and white-collar workers with rather modest incomes. Since change is not very likely—promotions do not involve much money—we report on their financial hassles only at the final interview. More than half of the youngest men report that they fairly or very often have money problems, and almost half of the youngest women feel the same way. The second youngest men are probably at their wage-earning peak, but with children still in grade school and probably a wife to support as well (they usually work part time after their children are in high school), it is not surprising that many feel pressed for money. Their female counterparts almost match them except that a few more of them feel very hassled about finances. Whether they blame themselves or their husbands is a moot question.

The second oldest men have evidently come to terms with their economic problems. More than half of them never worry about money issues, and the rest do so only occasionally. Women in the same life stage resemble the men except that there are more of them who feel hassled once in a while. Most of the oldest people are retired and live on a fixed income. They know there is nothing they can do to change it unless they are willing to look for another job. At any rate, all but six of the men never feel hassled by their financial circumstances. The oldest women differ: almost half of them feel hassled by money problems once in a while.

Offhand one might assume that women are more sociable
than men and that they find social events, casual and not so casual,
enjoyable (unless they must go to a party given by someone they do
not like). Since degrees of sociability are often age-related, in this
section we consider both the fourth and fifth interviews. Here, however, we look at the number of people *never* hassled in social situations. Nine of the youngest men but only six of the youngest women
never feel bothered in such situations at the fourth contact, but by
the final interview the situation is reversed: more of the youngest
women are never uncomfortable at a social gathering than is true
of men. The second youngest people are very much alike: only five
of the men and five of the women never feel hassled at the fourth
contact; three years later there are only five men and two women
who do *not* feel uncomfortable at social events. Perhaps they have
simply gone to too many parties.

In contrast, the second oldest men and women are very sociable. At both times they prove to be more sociable than any of the
younger groups. The oldest people are divided in terms of gender.
Men, to our mild surprise, are far more sociable than their spouses
and their female life-stage counterparts in this study. The women,
interestingly, are quite happy to see their husbands meeting with
old friends to play chess or whatever, so long as they do it away from
the house.

The Four

We have seen that the kinds of stress we are considering in
this chapter can play a potentially important role in the well-being
of people at all stages of life. The four intensive examples are all
affected to various degrees by these less-studied stressors, but here we
will primarily focus on hassles and problems between generations.
Adelaide Stone will be discussed in greater detail: she is affected by
nearly all the stressors we have discussed.

Olav Olavsen. When asked at the third interview about his relations
with the children, Olav reports that he disagrees strongly with his
youngest daughter's liberal political stance but adds that he respects
her judgment and they have never had a fight over their political
views. At the final interview he says he is closest to this daughter

and has in fact moved away from San Francisco to live closer to her. About his children he says at the last interview: "I know they all love me and they have turned out to be mature, responsible adults." When the children left home, earlier on, he accepted it as a part of life and even welcomed it. There is no real evidence of a generational conflict for this respondent.

All is not roses, of course. On the Hassles Checklist administered at the third interview, he says he is hassled by his children once in a while and is hassled once in a while by neighbors, his health, his social activities, and time pressures. All in all, however, Olav scores relatively low on hassles at all contacts. He does not feel bored at any of the interviews, and at the last contact he is learning to live alone and enjoy it. His extensive hobbies help keep his life interesting despite the loss of his wife and his separation from many old friends. In short, Olav's open and challenged style of living has helped him cope not only with the kinds of stress discussed in the previous chapter but with the hassles that form the focus of this chapter as well.

Hazel Sutter. During the first three interviews Hazel reports that she and her daughter tend to have fights and episodes of being "nasty" with each other. Hazel does not like her daughter's choice of friends and feels she needs to sort out her goals more clearly. Eventually her annoyance and problems with her daughter straighten themselves out, and by the fourth interview she reports no hassles with children. The only hassles she reports—and they happen only "once in a while"—come from work, friends, and health. Hazel is rarely bored, and when she is she simply goes out and shops or cleans house.

Max Schindler. When we first meet him, Max Schindler reports that he gets into arguments with his two daughters occasionally, but about nothing in particular. "I don't have any problems with my kids. Oh, we might get into a hassle once in a while, but we've never had any delinquency with the children." At the final interview, having grown more tolerant over the course of the twelve-year project, Max sees no problems in his relationship to his son and daughters: "We understand each other."

Max also provides no evidence of a midlife crisis in the usual form, although his heart attack, occurring in his early forties, did prompt some major life-style changes that were described in the last chapter. He never reports himself to be bored at any interview and is generally low on hassles as well. At the fourth interview, for example, he scores moderately low on hassles. None occurs more than once in a while, and those that do occur include hassles with work, parents, relatives, health, and time pressures. He definitely does not feel hassled by his wife or children. By the fifth and final interview, Max reports only two infrequent hassles: with neighbors and with his health. (He recently learned of a heart blockage that will require surgery.)

Adelaide Stone. Living as part of a "reconstituted" family, Adelaide Stone and her husband might be expected to experience more than their share of difficulties with all their children, his and hers. During the first interview, surprisingly, there are few hints of trouble. When Adelaide is asked what activity is most important to her, she replies: "My children, anything that revolves around my children." As we learned in the last chapter, by the second interview Adelaide's son is hooked on heroin and throughout the remainder of the research project a series of fights and encounters leave Adelaide bitter and anguished over both her son and herself. We leave her, at the final interview, disillusioned and anticipating that her forty-year-old son will return home once more to beg forgiveness and steal yet again.

Adelaide also goes through a series of midlife crises, although it is hard to say if any of them is indeed The Midlife Crisis. She has more problems than most with symptoms of menopause. She takes hormones but still reports hot flashes that bother her. She also encounters problems with her husband that lead to a divorce and also suffers a massive stroke that leaves her, at the final interview, grimly contemplating life in a retirement home.

Turning to the less studied stressors, we find Adelaide to be experiencing these as well. At the first interview Adelaide is full of life and activity and certainly is never bored. By the second interview she reports being bored once during the past week. By the fourth interview she reports herself to be often bored; by the last interview she not only is often bored (the highest rating) but says she is bored "all the time."

Adelaide reports a growing experience with hassles as well. At the fourth interview, when the Hassles Checklist is introduced, she curiously reports no hassles with children despite the problems with her addicted son; she is hassled once in a while by her former husband, she says, and all the time with health. She adds that she feels hassled all the time by wanting to do things that her disability prevents her from doing. By the last contact, Adelaide reports being hassled all the time by her son but never by her daughter. She is hassled by her fear of driving a car, her health, and her health-related limitations on social activities. Adelaide has moved, during the twelve years of the study, from a relatively stress-free life characterized by openness to experience to a life fraught with stress of every description.

Summing Up

We can see that the so-called crises of generational relations and the empty nest are often nothing more than popular stereotypes, perhaps mixed in with vintage reports by clinicians whose caseloads ordinarily include only those who have failed at meeting the demands of life. There are, however, new problems emerging on the horizon, especially those that deal with caregiving. Given the ever-increasing life expectancies we enjoy in the United States, caring for parents may well become a normative fixture of both the middle years and early retirement. We have also seen that the steady pitter-patter of everyday stress can begin to erode the quality of life and that solitude, something long sought by the busy middle-ager, may well become the bane of the retirement years. How a person responds to these life conditions depends in large part on how the condition is perceived and the resources the person can bring to bear in coping with the problem.

9

Resources and Deficits: Clues to How Adults Handle Stress

In this chapter we introduce a number of characteristics that may buffer the impact of stressful life circumstances or, conversely, may exacerbate what is already a troublesome situation. Such characteristics, from a general perspective that owes its origin to Hans Selye (1956), can be divided into those that are internal and those that are external. By far the best known and most studied are social supports.

Drawing on the same community study of older persons that gave rise to the present study, Marjorie Fiske and Clayton Haven (1968) considered the role of confidantes. After tallying the number of stressors reported on a simple life events inventory, the number of psychological symptoms reported, and the presence or absence of a confidant, they found a strong association between stress and symptoms in the absence of a confidant. When the older person had a confidant, however, there was no relationship between stress and symptoms.

Naturally the research conducted since the 1960s has become much more sophisticated methodologically, but the same basic finding seems to hold: Social supports apparently help people deal, in some fashion, with the stress in their life. In this chapter we will look at a number of mediators, some related to social supports, that may affect how people progress through a stressful situation. The first section is devoted to change, for better or for worse, in such

190

situations as marriage, work, and goal satisfaction. The second deals with personal assets and liabilities, including creativity and spirituality, on the one hand, and self-centeredness, on the other. The stress types described in Chapter Six, ranging from overwhelmed to lucky, represent characteristic stances toward stress. After summarizing where the participants in the eight subgroups place themselves in the stress typology, we present several case studies to enrich our comprehension of the whys and wherefores. The fourth section focuses on the complex issue of solitude. Being alone at times is a necessity for some people, but a persistent state of solitude is generally distressing. The chapter ends with a brief report on the resources of The Four.

Mediators of Stress and Response

In previous work we have found a number of characteristics, both internal and external, that influence how strongly people respond to negative stress. (See Fiske and Chiriboga, 1985; Chiriboga, 1989.) Here we consider some of these characteristics, starting with one frequently invoked in stress research: psychological symptomatology.

Psychological Symptoms. As noted throughout, at each interview one of our standard instruments was the forty-two-item California Symptoms Checklist (Lowenthal, Thurnher, Chiriboga, and Associates, 1975; see Resource D). As we reviewed findings obtained with this instrument, we noticed that a few remarkable people reported no symptoms at all. First let us examine how they distribute themselves in terms of stages of life and gender. There is no subgroup that does not include at least one person who is symptom-free. In the youngest group no males were free of symptoms at the third interview, but a few had become so by the fifth contact. Women reversed the order: some reported symptoms at the third contact but none did so at the fifth. Older men were more consistent than younger people: just as many reported no symptoms at the fifth contact as did so at the third. The older women do not resemble them at all: at the third contact several reported having no symptoms, but none were symptom-free at the fifth interview. The mental health of people having only one or two symptoms can be assessed as "normal" unless they were undergoing a serious depression and having suicidal thoughts. Only one person in the sample felt that way, and she is not considered in this section. The young males at the third contact included one person with one symptom, but at the fifth contact there were more of them. The younger women were better off: no one at the third contact had symptoms and only two did so at the fifth. The two groups of older men who had one or two symptoms started out with five people having one or two symptoms but by the final interview there were only three of them. Older women were the reverse of older men: instead of showing a decline in one or two symptoms, they showed a slight increase.

Turning to the spectrum provided by the entire sample, we can later compare people who have no or very few symptoms while paying special attention to the relationship between mental health and commitment. Particularly important is the extent to which people having no symptoms or one or two symptoms differ from the mainstream in terms of strength or weakness of commitment. The reader may be surprised at the differences between men and women in this analysis. Twice as many of the youngest men ranked low on symptoms at the third contact and little change was evident at the final contact six years later. Among the changers, exactly as many switched from low to high as from high to low. The youngest women provide a sharp contrast: about half of them ranked high on symptoms at both times.

The second youngest men changed more than any other subgroup. They did not check many symptoms at the third interview, but six years later they averaged more symptoms than any other subgroup. This deviance from the norm is quite normal for them, as we have noted in other chapters. Todd's story offers some enlightenment. At the third contact he is happily married, has a young son about four years old, and would like to have another one. He works as an itinerant salesperson for a Fuller Brush company. He enjoys knocking on doors, meeting new people, and opening his suitcase to display his wares. Six years later he has lost his job because he failed to meet his quota. He soon finds a job as teller in a small local bank and though he likes some of his co-workers, there are few of them and he describes his job as boring.

The second youngest women were more consistent: well over half of them had many symptoms at both times. They are an almost perfect replica of the youngest women. Anamay Martinez is a good example. Shortly after the birth of her first child, a girl, she developed a severe neurosis that involved many symptoms by the third interview, including fear of heights and fear of large groups of people she does not know in supermarkets, museums, and theaters. A therapist might help, but Anamay does not trust strangers. Six years later she had a son, now almost a year old, and Anamay now has only one symptom. In an inverted way she suffered from male chauvinism at the third interview because her first child was not a boy.

We have already said that the second youngest women, like the youngest, have many symptoms and do not change much. Perhaps more important, nearly all of those who did change changed for the worse. Margy Dunlap is a good representative of this group. A victim of rheumatic fever when she was a teenager, she had to stay in bed for almost a year. An only child of devoted parents, she says her mental health status was "officially" (by which she means professionally) diagnosed as neurotic depression shortly after her illness abated. She had nightmares and phobias that sometimes kept her parents awake all night. When we first meet Margy she feels better but is still quite introspective about her physical symptoms. By the third contact she still worries about both of her impairments, but by the fifth interview her physical health is fine and her mental status slightly improved.

The older people in general have quite a lot in common with the younger ones. The women tend to have more symptoms than the men, just as in the younger groups. Some of them, however, report more changes than young people do. The second oldest men are the only ones who do not change. The second oldest women, who reported many symptoms at the third contact, list even more at the fifth. The oldest women were in better shape, reporting far fewer symptoms at the fifth interview. Their male counterparts, the oldest men, averaged more symptoms at the fifth interview than they had at the third. Phil is a good representative for the oldest men. He is about sixty by the third contact, and his wife has recently left him because he did not pay much attention to her. He has what one might call a peripatetic personality by the fifth contact, moving from place to place with no real place to call home. Phil considers himself lucky to be earning a little money by being on call as a clerk in the grocery store where he worked full time before he retired.

Personal Relations. In our discussion of symptoms we focused on an inner resource (or deficit) of people: their psychological well-being. Here we consider how people change in six categories reflecting the external or social world either directly or indirectly:

- Marriage relative to other marriages
- Frequency of seeing closest friend
- Feelings about job
- Satisfaction with present activities
- Change in goal satisfaction
- Success in fulfilling present wants

As we consider how our respondents changed between the fourth and fifth interviews (not all these categories were assessed simultaneously in prior interviews), we find that most people in each subgroup reported no change. These six characteristics, it appears, are not only major influences on the outcome of stress exposure but are themselves relatively stable. In short, one can determine a person's status and reasonably expect that this status will not change much.

Change, of course, did occur. Among changers (about two-fifths of the sample) exactly as many changed for the better as changed for the worse. More women than men reported change for the better in all four stages of life except for the youngest group (and they are close to a tie). About two-thirds of the positive changers are young people. In other words, both gender and life stage make a difference. Charting subgroups by category of change reveals surprisingly little overlap. Among young negative changers only dissatisfaction with present activities was shared, and that involved the youngest and next youngest men. Old negative changers include only the oldest and second oldest men, who, like the younger ones, share dissatisfaction with activities. Only one of the eight subgroups, the next to youngest men, reported significant negative change in feelings about work.

In contrast, among positive changers three subgroups, all of them older people, were unanimous in satisfaction with present wants. But by and large the main finding of this overview is that, among both young and old and positive and negative changers, there is not much of a pattern: changes are scattered across the six categories. The second youngest women (newlyweds at the outset) had much more positive change than anyone else; the second oldest women, youngest men, and oldest women, in that order, come next. The second youngest men report as many negative as positive changes. Most negative change is found among the youngest women, followed by the oldest and second oldest men. As we turn now to assets and liabilities as reported at the fifth and final encounter, some of these widely dispersed findings about change may become more understandable.

Assets and Liabilities. At the fifth interview we expanded the Adjective Rating List to cover characteristics not included in the original one. The new characteristics represent the following inner resources and deficiencies:

Resources	*Deficiencies*
Committed	Anxious
Creative	Possessive
Curious	Restrained
Generative	Self-centered
Spiritual	Self-protective

On the positive side of the scale, we find overall that the four young groups report far more resources than do the four old ones and that men report a few more resources than women. Life stage is therefore far more significant than gender in terms of distribution. But if we pair off the sexes within each subgroup and examine the assets separately, interesting results emerge. The youngest men and women are very similar to each other on the first three assets (committed, creative, and curious) and markedly different on the last two; somewhat surprisingly, more men than women report themselves to be generative and spiritual. The next youngest men and women resemble each other on four characteristics, but men are more likely to report being curious. The next to oldest people, the former empty nesters, have the strongest gender differences: women rank much higher on all assets. In the oldest group men are more curious and women more spiritual.

On the negative side of the scale, the overall view suggests more unanimity in reports. There are no differences between men and women and only a few between young and old. Furthermore, significantly fewer people report liabilities: the ratio is about three to five. None of the eight groups has more liabilities than assets. Except for the second youngest group of women (newlyweds), the young groups have twice as many resources as deficits. The next to oldest men and women have only a few more assets while the oldest women have twice as many resources as deficits. In sum, then, there are no significant differences between men and women or young and old in regard to deficits, but the young of both sexes generally have more resources than the old. If one considers each asset and deficit to constitute either a risk enhancer or risk reducer when exposed to stress, therefore, the younger participants would seem to have the advantage.

To examine the significance of these assets and deficits in greater detail, we selected four people, one from each life stage. Their cases illustrate how two of the assets, commitment and spirituality, and two of the liabilities, self-centeredness and anxiety, may affect people's lives.

We begin with the assets. Former high school senior Jenny Bakov is a highly committed person and an interesting one as well. Her parents came to this country from Russia and she grew up in the Russian Orthodox church. Her parents were divorced when Jenny was about seven, and her father moved to Los Angeles, where he is a social studies teacher. Her mother, with whom she is living when we first meet, is a clerical worker. About two years later, after getting a job as a dental hygienist, Jenny moves to an apartment that she shares with a friend. In addition to work she is also taking some evening courses. By this time she has a steady boyfriend as well as several close friends. Three years later (at the third interview) she is married to her boyfriend, with whom she has been in love for eight years. A medical student, he is about to go to Boston for additional training. She plans to join him as soon as she has worked long enough to pay their bills. Her concerns center on him and his education.

Three years later (at the fourth interview) Jenny has a nine-month-old daughter born in Boston. She lives with her mother and brother, but her husband will return soon and they may then go to southern California for the last part of his medical training. Not working, she misses her colleagues and friends, many of whom now have children and live in the suburbs. When we last visit Jenny we learn that the couple has indeed spent a year in Los Angeles and he has finished his training. His graduation is the most wonderful event of her life up till now, and it is to this end that she has been totally committed. Her personal life is well rounded; she has good friends, another child, the oldest now in the "Terrible Twos," and strong interests in arts, crafts, and serious reading. Jenny also has a great sense of humor, a quality that, unfortunately, was not included in the assets list.

Retirement stager Gus Bradford is a very spiritual man, a devout Baptist who thinks "religion could save us all." Sixty when we first meet him, he has worked as a bus driver for most of his adult life. Gus is married to a former teacher, a college graduate; he himself went only through high school. The Bradfords have three children, one of whom is married and has children of her own. He plans to retire in two years and then would like to move to some "country village." For now he only has time to teach a Sunday school class, something he dearly loves doing.

Two years later his plans have been shattered. He has had an accident that demolished his car, but luckily no one was hurt. Worse still, he drove his bus through a red light and got his only citation in forty years of driving the bus. He was so stunned by this event that he retired the very next day, even though he knew he would greatly miss his regular passengers. The Bradfords have now put their home on the market and plan to move to a southeastern part of the country where he has relatives and there is a college nearby for his youngest child. The new place must be close to a Baptist church where he can "lend a helping hand."

Three years later his dream has been realized. Gus now lives near the Blue Ridge Mountains, goes to church several times a week, and has time to read more religious books. His daughter is in college, and he has made some close friends at church. By the next to last interview the daughter is close to graduation and his two older children have paid for a trip to Hawaii that he and his wife much enjoyed. His marriage, by the way, is consistently rated "much better than most." Attending church functions is his favorite activity; being able to take daily naps, he adds, is one of the greatest advantages of retirement. In his early seventies when we last hear from him, he writes simply that "I have aged three more years." He still rates himself as "very happy," but his emphysema has become more bothersome. Churchgoing continues to be his major resource.

We turn now to the deficits. We do not have many married couples in this sample who remain childless, but one of them told us that not having children makes a couple selfish. Former newlywed Irene Beck, however, is quite self-centered despite having children. College educated, she teaches in a private preschool. Her husband has a degree in administration and works as an office manager in a large corporation. The Becks' income is above average for this second youngest group. She is twenty-two at the first encounter and the interviewer notes that she seems extremely smug and self-righteous and lives in a Pollyannaish world.

Three years later, she now has a son and expects another child before long. Her goal is to be an "ideal mother." She considers herself a "role model" in her volunteer work with a Girl Scout troop. By the next to last session she is one of the leaders in a community organization and says she "basks" in the glory of it all. Like every good mother, she has joined the PTA and plans to be very active in that too. Irene seems to have a profound need to collect all the kudos she can get.

Empty nester Bart Erwin is an anxious man. Fifty-seven years old at first contact, he did not graduate from high school. Experienced as a machinist, he currently works for the county but does not like it because he gets his hands dirty. His wife is a secretary and has a secure, full-time job. The Erwins have a son and a daughter. A third child was born after these two, but she was killed in a hit and run accident when she was three. Bart wept as he told her story, adding that he went from teetotaler to heavy drinker as a result. Later in the interview he says he has had back problems and headaches for twenty years and a few drinks help. He feels that his bosses, whoever they are, are always against him and his wife is too domi- nating, making him feel impotent. At the same time he has great respect for her.

Our efforts to arrange a meeting with him two years later are not very successful. His son tells the interviewer that his father wants to retire but his mother objects. Bart at first refuses the next to last interview, but he agrees to fill it out if we mail it to him. Now sixty-five, he has had a mild stroke and cardiovascular surgery. Re- tired at last, he is somewhat less anxious but feels he has had a tough life and "missed out." Bart Erwin died of cancer just before the last interviews were scheduled. Compared with Irene Beck, he certainly was an unlucky person with few inner resources to carry him through. Alcohol was not a rewarding substitute.

More on the Stress Typology

For years investigators have been interested in whether there may be a "stress-prone" personality style. In Chapter Seven we talked about the fact that life events and other stressors are signif- icantly correlated with subsequent exposure to stress—signifying that life events are not simply random accidents in terms of when and how they occur. When we developed the stress typology, one question of interest was whether people generally remain stable in their typological classification over time. There are four categories in the stress typology, two negative and two positive, labeled over- whelmed, defeated, challenged, and lucky. In this section we first describe people who are very consistent—that is, they are the same type at the last contact as at the first one. We then describe one person who moved through several types and conclude with a dis- cussion of differences among the eight subgroups.

More than forty people were identified as being of the same stress type at the first and last interviews. Classification was based on median splits on variables having to do with the amount of stress they had been exposed to and their perception of how much stress they had experienced. About three-fifths of those who were consis- tent were women. The great majority considered themselves chal-

lenged or lucky. Only three, all women, were overwhelmed, two
from the youngest group and one from the next youngest.

Empty nester Miles Baker is an apt example of being *challenged* throughout his life. In charge of the publications department of a large company, he is happily married and has two
children and an infant grandson. Though not in the pink of condition, he finds it important to keep active in mind and body and
"to accomplish anything that is satisfying." Stress, which he has
plenty of, "makes for fortitude." Agnes Bishop, a retired professional by the second interview, thinks she is very *lucky* because she
is healthy and money is no problem. "Keep on growing" is her
formula. She takes several courses, does a great deal of volunteer
work (she is an usher at the opera house), and travels wherever and
whenever she wants to. "Every day is exciting and worthwhile."

Robbie Collins, in the youngest group, is *overwhelmed*. His
background is low middle class and his vocabulary is extremely
limited. Deciding that he did not want more education after high
school, he works as a full-time bank clerk. He does not like his
mother and says there is a "generation gap" between him and his
father. By the second interview (two years later) he has rented a
small apartment for himself. His responses to most questions are
muddled: he might get a roommate, or another job, or go back to
school, "but I probably won't do any of those things." Three years
later (at the third interview) we find Robbie a confirmed bisexual.
He lives with two roommates and works part time at a gas station.
At this point he reports "lots of ups and downs." He would like to
"get into life more" and "be able to understand things better." The
interviewer describes him as "nice looking, tense, uncomfortable,
slow in answering questions, and not understanding several of
them."

Three years later, at the time of the fourth interview, Robbie
has a new job, a full-time teller at a bank. He has moved back with
his parents because he did not like the apartment (or, perhaps, being
with his age peers). This interview is short since he gives capricious
answers to many questions and is rather inarticulate. At the last
interview Robbie is now unemployed, still living with his parents,
but trying to get in the navy. He has been arrested for drunk driving
and has now cut down on, but not stopped, going to bars and

drinking. If the navy does not accept him he will look for another job. Just living seems to be a chore for Robbie. He does not like being with people and spends most of his time watching television (which, unlike his parents, does not tell him what to do). He seems forlorn.

Empty nester Doris Lauer is one of the relatively few *defeated* people. She is married to the office manager of a large shipping company; they both are high school graduates. The Lauers have two daughters. Doris, an attractive and well-dressed woman, tends to be narcissistic. She is not very fond of her husband, and now that her daughters are no longer pretty and well-dressed little girls she can dominate, she does not much like them either. For about seven years of her life, right after her second child was born, she was partially bedridden with heart problems.

The best thing that happens between the first and second interviews is a cruise, by herself, to the Caribbean. (She received many compliments on her clothes.) Her older daughter married but did not tell her parents that she was pregnant until it became obvious. The new son-in-law is unemployed and they live with his parents. Doris "feels like getting a job" but has not really looked. She is very upset that her other daughter, now unemployed, has moved back home. Three years later, the third interview finds her more dissatisfied than ever. She checks most of the items on the symptoms list and still thinks about a job but does nothing about it. She says, rather coyly, that she has had an extramarital love affair (probably while on a cruise) but it did not seem to cheer her up. The interviewer notes that she seems depressed and "listless."

By the next to last meeting her problems have been exacerbated by her parents' demands on her. They live about fifteen miles away; she visits them occasionally but feels "put upon." Nothing has improved when we last talk with her. She describes her life as dull and herself as stagnating. Her father has died and her mother now lives two blocks away in a guest house with other women. Most frustrating is her marriage. Her husband still works long hours and wants peace, quiet, and television when he gets home. Her daughters are driving her crazy, she says. She sometimes thinks of divorce but, after all, he hands her his substantial paycheck every month. Being a narcissistic person may have made her more self-defeating.

She may well suffer from the chronic depression often associated with growing older and, more important, less attractive.

Former newlywed Tab Bennett, a cheerful contrast to Robbie and Doris, represents the *challenged* type. Thirty when we met him, Tab is a free-lance journalist. He is married to a Finnish woman who went to college for two years and then to "finishing school." Tab himself went through junior college and also spent a year majoring in journalism. His wife, several years younger than he, works in the jewelry department of an elegant department store. Two years later his business is improving, though he is tired of being what he calls "just a starving artist." He has joined two professional journalism associations; he is on several committees and finds it all very stimulating. Tab has had several interesting adventures in the three years before the third interview. His parents and grandmother paid for a one-month trip to Finland to see his wife's grandfather on his eightieth birthday. Most important to him, however, is his increasing success in his work, where he is gaining a reputation for political reporting. Always fascinated with skiing, he has finally taken lessons. He loves his work and gets so absorbed that he forgets to have lunch and sometimes dinner too.

We are rather surprised to learn at the next to last interview that Tab is divorced from, as he puts it, "a very negative wife." As a result he now sees several of his old friends she did not like. The work goes well, he likes himself better, and he often helps other people with their problems. Now an experienced skier, he is trying sailing as well. One can readily conclude that Tab is not only challenged by life but very adventurous as well.

Eva Hirwitz is a fitting representative of *lucky* people. Fifty-one when we meet, she earns a modest income by telephone canvassing but plans on retiring some time in the next five years. She likes the opportunity her job provides of getting acquainted with people. Her husband, a machinist, is nearly ten years older than she. Eva has had a year of college, he only two years of high school. They have four children; the first, a girl, is adopted and mentally retarded. As often happens, shortly after the adoption Eva becomes pregnant and eventually they have three additional children. She thinks they are lucky. Three children are living at home. Eva's mother lives in her own house nearby and seems to be just a bit senile. A very versatile and competent woman, Eva is taking a course in writing, keeps two prizewinning cats, arranges family musicals, creates her own tapestries, collects coins, and tends her flower garden. She also does volunteer work with retarded children.

The two years between the first and second interviews produce both bad and good events. Her mother has become very senile, and her married daughter and husband have been evicted from their rented house. Very upset at first, Eva concludes that those events have made her a stronger person; she has been challenged and, luckily, has handled both situations well. Three years later, at the fourth interview, only the retarded daughter is living at home. Her mother has died ("a blessing for her") and her husband has retired. Now that he has more time, "our marriage is wonderful." Both of them are healthy and feel lucky. On top of that she is taking organ lessons and much enjoying them. At the concluding interview we learn that Eva is happily spending more time with her husband, has been to several social gatherings, and has met new and interesting people. Rating herself as "very happy," despite her need to care for a retarded child, she feels luckier than ever.

Solitude: Resource or Deficit?

In the mysterious land of stress research, social supports have come to be regarded as the sine qua non of effective social resources—despite the protestations of some researchers (such as Gubrium, 1975) that long-term social isolation may in fact be the best buffer in the long run against stress. Gubrium makes the distinction between long-term social isolation and social desolation—the loss of a friend or loved one, which can lead to psychological and physical distress. As we examine our data and review numerous cases, we find that solitude is a welcome respite for some, a mixed blessing for others, and for a few very painful because it bespeaks loneliness. People are lonely for a wide variety of reasons, and the consequences may be temporary or long-lasting.

Although few in our sample profess loneliness, these cases shed light on a problem that has been estimated to affect one-fourth of all Americans at some time in their lives. One set of questions we asked of participants concerned whether they got enough, more than enough, or less than enough in many different areas of life. We will consider this instrument and what it tells us in the next chapter, but here we focus on just one item: solitude. About two-thirds of the sample report that they have enough solitude; a fourth have not enough or barely enough; and the rest, about 12 percent, have more than enough or too much. This does not necessarily mean they are lonely, but some certainly are. Three times as many young people as old ones do not have enough, or have barely enough, time to be alone. A few more young women than young men do not have enough solitude, probably because they have children at home. One might assume that people who live alone feel more solitary than those who do not, but of the twenty-five people who do, only four complain of having more than enough solitude.

Not Enough. People without enough solitude represent a wide range and cannot be readily characterized. One man in the youngest group married a widow his own age and in the process acquired three young stepchildren. A master carpenter who builds houses and works with people all day, he finds that when he gets home he gets little of the peace and quiet that "would be heaven to me." A woman in the youngest group was a clerk in a large insurance company. A few years later she married and her husband happened to inherit a great deal of money. Neither of them is working now, and she sums up her problem as too much togetherness.

Similarly, a production manager for a large shipping company, in the second youngest group, has three young children. He has to work overtime nearly every day and is very active in private clubs, which he considers part of his job. Sundays he spends with his wife and children. Obviously he is seldom, if ever, alone. A woman in the same life stage grew up with four siblings and certainly was not accustomed to being alone. Even when grown up (about twenty-five) she lived with her parents, a sister, and a brother and his wife. Later, married, she became an exercise instructor. In addition, she and her husband have four foster children living with them. Neither at work nor at home can she be alone. Another woman in the same life stage married and had three children within a space of little more than three years. Not yet in school, they keep her very busy. Her husband has his own winery and seems to be drinking much too much of his own product, so she has tried to be with him as much as possible. She has no time at all to herself.

A man in the next oldest group plays second trumpet in the city's symphony orchestra. One of his favorite hobbies is conducting symphonies at public grade schools, high schools, and colleges. He also teaches individual students; working ten or more hours a day, he fears he does not spend enough time with his own three children, though they do attend concerts quite often. He also belongs to a private men's club where he lunches daily with colleagues in the orchestra. As he grows older (he was in his mid-forties when we met), he also conducts the orchestra on tours. By now he wishes he had more time to himself. After a tour to Russia, he has some heart problems and resolves to spend more time at home, preferably alone.

More Than Enough. On the other side of the paradigm are those who have more than enough solitude. They are not nearly so busy as those who do not have enough. There are fewer of them and more are in the older groups. We start with the young.

Vince Page is the son of a policeman. A senior in high school when we first meet, he plans to be a policeman too. By no means a brilliant young man, he has given up the idea of being a lawyer because he knows he could not handle the required set of courses. To earn a little spending money, he works part time as a mail boy. Two years later (at the second interview) he is attending a junior college with a major in fire science, working harder than he had in high school and "not fooling around as much." He has a part-time job in a supermarket that he thoroughly dislikes. He now has a steady girlfriend he hopes to marry when he gets a good job.

Three years later (at the third interview) there have been unexpected changes in his life, the worst being losing the girlfriend. Very self-protective, he does not associate with people who use drugs and avoids anything that would be "harming." He is now a full-time mail clerk in the daytime and is satisfied with his job. He has passed the test for policeman but some new rules about minority groups, which he considers unfair, have hampered his joining the force. Vince says he just wants to be left alone. Financial security is his prime goal.

With the passage of three years, by the fourth interview he finally has his security and is a policeman with a beat of his own. He and his girlfriend have broken up and reconciled twice in the interim. His main recreation is fishing, which he usually does alone. At the final session he reports surgery for an ulcer, feels tense, is easily "touched off" and nervous. Reunited with, but not married to, his original girlfriend, he prefers to live alone. The security of his job and the gratitude people sometimes feel toward policemen are satisfying to him. A new hobby gives him satisfaction: making fishing equipment, which he does by himself. Vince chooses to be alone.

Frederic Eiler's parents are Polish Jews who emigrated to this country; his grandparents were victims of Hitler. His father is a lawyer and business consultant for whom he works part time as a clerk. An intelligent and serious young man, he did not make any close friends in high school. Twenty by the second interview, he first attended a junior college and then transferred to a state university. His courses include philosophy and Jewish history. Recipient of an educational loan, he spends one summer in Israel. He now lives in the college dormitory and has been exposed to drugs, alcohol, and "other people's sexual practices." Upset, he had some helpful talks with a college counselor.

Three years later he sometimes dates girls at the college but is not serious about any of them. He had hoped to become a rabbi, but was not accepted in the local rabbinical school. He then spent a year in New York, at City College of New York, and transferred to a state university in Los Angles for its Jewish studies program. He feels more self-confident now because he understands Judaism better. Working too hard, he has developed an ulcer, for which he takes medication. He still hopes to become a rabbi. The impression of the interviewer is that Frederic is sad and shaken by being turned down and weary from studying so hard. He will soon finish his last course and hopes at long last to have a B.A. degree.

Three years later (at the fourth interview) we find him on the East Coast attending a rabbinical school. When school is out in the summers he teaches at Jewish summer camps. He expects to be ordained soon. By the fifth and final interview he has indeed been ordained, is back home in the West, and is looking for a job. He would like to work as a college chaplain. His girlfriend got married while he was away, and he would like to find a "lifemate." Meanwhile he lives by himself and has "more than enough" solitude.

Christina Davis is also in the youngest group. Daughter of a warehouse foreman, she has one sibling, an older brother who at the time of the first interview is seeing a psychiatrist for a "reading problem." She has had a few sessions with a high school psychiatrist because of her own uncertainties. Questions about her goals in life make her confused and uncomfortable; she simply does not know. The interviewer comments that she seems withdrawn and depressed. The second interview (about two years later) has to be mailed to her: she is living in Chicago with an aunt, uncle, and cousin. Her aspirations are still very vague and scattered. She wants to learn about "different things," get more schooling, and find something "I can always work at." Her present job is part-time waitress in a restaurant. Christina now has a boyfriend but does not think they will get married.

A lapse of three years (third interview) finds Christina back home and living with her parents. Her father has retired and is now an alcoholic, a situation that came as a shock to her and a source of constant worry. She is back in school full time and has a part-time job as a pizza delivery person. This time the interviewer finds her "sweet, sensitive, and rather depressed." By the third interview she is in better shape, a full-time student specializing in recreation with a part-time job as a recreation supervisor. Her father has died and she lives with her mother and brother, to whom she feels closer than ever. A breakup with her boyfriend was stressful, but "things were just not working out."

By the fourth session she has received her B.A. degree in recreation and works as a playground supervisor; she also takes some courses in hope of becoming a medical assistant. Christina marries just a month before the final interview. He is a postal carrier and has a "calming" effect on her. Having changed her professional goals, she is now enrolled full time in a nursing school and expects to be an R.N. within a year. With her full-time courses, part-time work as recreational director, and a new husband, Christina is never alone.

These three people from the youngest group also have other issues in common: all have had problems deciding what work they want to do and then getting the right job or more training in order to do so. Vince wanted to be a policeman, but it took years before he could join the force. Frederic was frustrated in his efforts to become a rabbi. Finally locating a school on the East Coast, he eventually achieved his goal. Christina had trouble making decisions about a career or anything else, eventually went to college, and became a certified recreation supervisor. Not satisfied, she then went through the long training to become an R.N. All three worked very hard to reach their goals. Finding a suitable spouse was also difficult for them. Vince separated and reconciled with his girl three times but preferred living alone to marriage. Frederic's girl married someone else when he was away. Christina was more or less engaged to two men before she finally married the "calming fireman."

Very few of the second youngest group have more than enough solitude. One of them is Joyce Koster. She has an advanced degree in counseling and works full time. Her husband, just her age (twenty-three), is about to finish college and enter graduate school. About two years before we first talk with her, she has had a year of psychotherapy treatment. Joyce has no close friends. Less than two years later the Kosters have moved and she is working only half time. On the side she takes courses on "herbs, weaving, and magic." Three years later, at the third interview, she has a son and has left her husband. She now meditates, keeps track of her dreams, and attends an institute of psychic studies. In addition she attends religious services of various types two or three times a week. Divorced by the fourth interview, she has moved to Nebraska, is very lonely, and is back in psychotherapy. Working for a Ph.D. degree from the university there, she is also a part-time teaching assistant. Her son goes to public school. Very depressed, she has lost her self-confidence and is "just plain miserable." The last interview finds her somewhat more cheerful but there are "ups and downs." Her religion is "Spiritualist Occult." Working part time as a rehabilitative counselor, her progress toward a Ph.D. degree is slow. She is still very lonely and far less "social" than she used to be. Her life centers on her son, and the few professional groups she belongs to seem very peripheral.

Ellen Murphy, a member of the second oldest group, had a very difficult childhood. Her mother died when she was a young child and her father, an alcoholic, was killed in a barroom brawl.

When she was ten an aunt and uncle adopted her. The uncle was erratic and very strict with her, and she was afraid of him. When she grew up and married he did not speak to her for six years because her husband is Catholic. The Murphys have two daughters. The youngest lives at home and the older is married, has a four-year-old son, and lives in Georgia. Ellen's husband is a well-educated investment banker. They are more prosperous than most people in our sample, and Ellen collects antiques. Shortly before the first interview she has had a mastectomy and subsequently experiences acute depression. Seeing a psychiatrist several times does not help her much, nor is her husband supportive.

Less than two years later (at the second interview) she has developed a "thick" feeling in her head resulting in an "inability to think clearly." She connects it with the hostility of her uncle. The psychiatrist has given her some medication that helps, and she sees him less often. Feeling stronger, she flies halfway across the country to visit her new granddaughter, but she has not wanted to see her friends. Her goal is to improve her mental health and become a "useful person."

After a lapse of three years, by the third interview her oldest daughter has moved back to the city and the younger is now a college graduate looking for a job. Ellen's own mother "gets on her nerves" because she always wants to go shopping with her. She is less depressed and is enjoying lessons in oil painting. She sees both a psychiatrist and an internist once a month, and the antidepression medication still helps. Three years later (fourth interview) her husband has retired. Ellen's mother, now ninety, has broken both of her legs (on different occasions) and she spends most of her time taking care of her. A trip to England to celebrate her husband's retirement is the highlight of this period. Her brother is very ill and not expected to live much longer, and she is quite depressed about that. She finds that keeping busy helps. At the last visit, Ellen, now sixty-six, is "pretty happy." Her mother is in a rest home for around-the-clock care. Although her "head feels very heavy," Ellen keeps busy and is rarely alone. Like many retired husbands in the sample, hers gives orders about how to run the household. He is a perfectionist and when they have guests he is a good host. These days Ellen is alone only when he is out or she is painting in another room. It is difficult to explain why she has "more than enough" solitude except that she is not a very independent person and possibly becomes uneasy when alone.

Retirement stager Aaron Lombard is one of the very few people in the sample who have never married. He is an only child, very self-protective, and has lived with his mother all his life. He works as a mechanic. Although he checks "more than enough" solitude, he seems ambivalent about it (as he is about many of his life circumstances). Aaron is a high school graduate and is sixty when we first meet. He would like to travel but is not sure how to go about it and anyway has to take care of his mother, who is not up to it. He has a woman friend, but she does not seem to be an intimate, nor does anyone else. The male "friends" are people he exchanges stock market notes with. While his investments do not always pay off, his average income is very high. Politically very reactionary, his fury about politics seems to sustain him.

Aaron refuses the second interview, explaining that things at work have "blown up" and he is busy trying to hold on to what he has (presumably money). Three years later (at the third interview) Aaron has retired and finds it a "letdown." He has gone to court about a large investment loss involving a partner who "bilked" him. His favorite activities involve his fishing boat, but he does not enjoy it anymore. His mother's health is much worse, and he wishes he had a relative to take care of her. There are problems with his lady friend too, but he refuses to discuss them. He expounds at length about the economy: poor people drain it and income taxes are much too high. Making more money in the stock market is his only goal.

In his late sixties by the fourth interview, Aaron is disgusted. His boat has burned up, his mother is quite sick, he is bored with retirement, he drinks too much. The only good thing is that he is making more money and has reached his financial goal. He takes several vacation trips between the fourth and final interviews but feels they were "humdrum." His mother, crankier than ever, has accused him of stealing her money. He feels "trapped." It is perhaps, via some distortion of logic, because he has to live with his mother and take care of her that he checks "more than enough" solitude. He sees his lady friend often but has no thought of marrying her. Ambivalence about everything but money seems most apt in describing his behavior.

Unlike the youngest people we described earlier, who seemed to share several characteristics in common, the older respondents who report more than enough solitude share only one thing in common: all three have psychological problems. Joyce has been in and out of psychotherapy several times and has wound up adopting a "Spiritualist Occult" religion. Ellen has had treatment for depression and reports a "thick" feeling in her head. Aaron has a lifelong obsession: money.

The Four

Given the importance of solitude, we focus here on how The Four fared on this topic when we talked with them at the final interview. Three of the four have enough solitude. As one might expect, Olav Olavsen reports he has "more than enough." His wife died just after the fourth contact; he has subsequently moved and now lives alone in a small town far from the friends he has known for the past thirty-five years. He is still a creative machinist and hobbyist; indeed, work seems to be his salvation. Hazel Sutter, in love with a neighbor, is alone only when she wants to be. Max Schindler's marriage is ideal and he too pursues solitude only when he feels like it. Adelaide Stone, like Olav, feels she has "more than enough." Still impaired by her stroke, she lives alone and often is very lonely.

Summing Up

Many of the dimensions of life and activity we have considered in this chapter have a direct relevance to stress and coping. We find, for example, that people who seem creative and curious are likely to fall into the challenged category of our stress typology. They seem to thrive on stress. Others, especially those who are anxious and restrained, resemble what Beiser (1971) has called "homoclites," a curious word he coined to refer to people who wear conceptual blinders and prefer to wish away change, denying its existence and striving forever to maintain the status quo.

Also worthy of note is that younger participants by and large have greater resources to help them cope with stress. But since they also are somewhat more likely to encounter stress, this extra edge may indeed be necessary. Moreover, we have found in our work that the disparity in resources generally does not mean that older people will fare worse in a crisis. For one thing, they generally have had more experience with stress and for this reason can make efficient use of what they have. We have also found a tendency for older people in the sample to focus more heavily on social resources. The capacity for intimacy and mutuality becomes of increasing importance for older persons, who may suffer health and economic problems that deprive them of former resources. Friends, we find, are generally available and seem more important as a coping resource than almost anything else.

Part Three
What Matters Most
at the
Four Stages of Adulthood

10

Goals and Values:
Giving Life Meaning

In preceding chapters we have commented on the goals and values of our participants. Here we focus specifically on the topic by relating goals and values to several dimensions of their lives. Why should goals be studied? Goals and values tell us what people think is important to them. Goals and values can also provide a source of continuity in the midst of change. Certainly the need for continuity was suggested, either directly or indirectly, by many of our respondents over the twelve years we studied them. Peter Marris (1975, p. 46), who has studied how people react to change, explains the need for continuity: "Change appears as fulfillment or loss to different people, and to the same person at different times. In either aspect it preserves some common features: the need to reestablish continuity, to work out an interpretation of oneself . . . one which preserves the thread of meaning."

Goals and values have variously been described as reflecting personality, the social environment, or both. Because they can impart a direction to the life course, Lowenthal (1971) has suggested that goals and values may be reinterpreted and reorganized as the need arises. Moreover, maintaining some degree of harmony between goals and behavior is a significant component of the adaptive process in adulthood. In the first section of this chapter we evaluate seven goals that participants rank ordered in terms of personal sali-

215

ence. Using the criteria of change between the first and third contacts and the third and fifth contacts, we compare consistent and changeable people and note the differences between young and old and between men and women.

In the second section we focus on goals as deficit or resource, while the objective of the third section is to test the assumption that the degree of goal satisfaction is related to concepts of the self. One would expect, for example, that people satisfied with their goal achievements have a more positive self-image than those who are not. Lastly we explore the interactions between happiness and goal achievement and, conversely, dissatisfaction and unhappiness. The chapter concludes, as before, with a brief summary of the goals and values of The Four.

The Seven Goals

After reviewing the literature on goals and values, we identified seven that seem to appear in most instruments and theoretical models. To assess the importance of these seven goals for our participants, we developed what, in social science jargon, is called a "card sort." Respondents were handed seven cards printed with the names and descriptions of the seven goals and were asked to rank them from the most important to the least so. The seven goals are:

- Achievement and work (competence; economic rewards; success; social status)
- Good personal relations (love and affection; happy marriage; having good friends; belonging to groups)
- Philosophical and religious (living a spiritual life; doing God's work; having a philosophy of life; seeking the meaning of life; being wise; being morally good)
- Social service (helping others; serving the community; contributing to human welfare or some aspect of it)
- Ease and contentment (freedom from hardship; security; self-maintenance; peace of mind; health; simple comforts)
- Seeking enjoyment (recreation; exciting experiences; entertainment; seeking pleasurable sights, sounds, feelings, and tastes)
- Personal growth (self-improvement; being creative; learning

new things; knowing yourself; meeting and mastering new challenges)

Our list is clearly a mixture of diverse goals and does not derive from any specific model. For the sake of this chapter, goals and values have been grouped as follows:

- Goals: achievement, social service, and growth
- Positive values: philosophical/religious
- Negative values: hedonism
- Neutral values: people; ease and comfort

These are specific goals and values. As we will see, some of our more intelligent and creative respondents have more global objectives.

Change over the Life Course

Naturally the goals and values of people alter considerably as they become nearly twelve years older. At one extreme, the youngest people are about thirty years old when we last interview them, and some of the oldest ones are in their mid-seventies or older. One might assume that such goals as achievement and such values as hedonism decline among old people, but some do and some do not. In this instance, as we will see, gender differences are notable. At the other extreme, one would expect young men and women to give goals of achievement a high priority, but by and large women do and men do not. Human nature is indeed a puzzlement.

Younger People. With eight groups of people, seven goals, and two or three time periods of assessment, presenting the findings in a clear-cut fashion is a problem. One of our principal interests in reviewing the goals and values of our subjects, however, was to determine the extent to which these in fact represent stable components of personal functioning. We therefore start with a discussion of the values and goals that changed the most, followed by those that were rated about the same at each interview. The philosophical/religious category can be omitted for a very simple reason: each subgroup considers this to be the most important value, and there is almost no change among any group. Few are philosophical; a majority are religious. A concern with good personal relations is deleted for the opposite reason: no one considers it significant except for a few of the oldest women; the rest just take it for granted.

The youngest men are very changeable: ranking high on achievement at first (nine people), only two of them did so at the last interview. Social service got the same treatment: ten of them valued it highly at the beginning of the study and only two at the end. Growth was of little importance at any time, whereas several chose hedonism and ease and comfort as their favorite goals at all times. It is taking these men a long time to grow up, and they would probably prefer not to. They bring to mind a sixteen-year-old in the sample. Although this subject is a girl, her attitude captures the feelings many of these youngest men manifest as well: at the first interview she has an extremely active and pleasurable life and asks, "Why can't I stay sixteen forever?" She has what might be called a "Peter Pan" syndrome.

In some ways the goals and values of the youngest women are slightly more mature than those of the men: they consistently rate achievement and social service highly. As is true for the youngest men, they are not interested in growth and even more of them are hedonistic. On a par with the youngest men on ease and comfort at the first interview, only one of them is at the last contact.

The second youngest men and women resemble the youngest in that the women are somewhat more consistent and mature than the men. Like the youngest males, these somewhat older ones lose interest in achievement and social service and even become a bit more hedonistic but less concerned with ease and comfort. Like the youngest women, the second youngest ones rate achievement high on their agenda; social service is rated high, too, but only at the last interview—possibly because the children of most of them are now at school and they can do part-time work, take some courses, or be volunteers. The same reason may account for the fact that at the last interview they rank highest of all eight subgroups on growth, wanting to broaden their horizons and learn more. They move from down to up and back down again on hedonism whereas the youngest women still favor "fun and games." Both the youngest and the second youngest women become less interested in ease and comfort as time goes on.

Older People. The second oldest men, like the younger ones, become less achievement-oriented than previously, but with better reasons. Most of them have worked at the same job for many years and find they look forward to retirement, fixing up their homes, planting a garden. Some even buy an old house and renovate it. Social service becomes less important than in the past, perhaps because, as one participant expressed, "I've paid my debt to society." Their declining interest in growth suggests they know they are unlikely to get another promotion and worry about their retirement income. An interest in growth reappears when they can carry out postretirement plans.

The second oldest women rank achievement much higher than men, and many of them still work part time to supplement the family income, which gives them a gratifying sense of accomplishment. Because they work only part time and their children have grown up and left home, they are also free to do volunteer work, a social service goal that goes up dramatically in the course of twelve years, as does growth. Seeking pleasure (hedonism) is of strong interest to them at the beginning of the study, much less so at the end. These are middle and late middle-aged women, and many are self-generating and enterprising.

The oldest men are strong achievers at the first interview but much less so at the end. As achievement goes down, however, social service goes up. Social service involves a variety of activities for these men. One helps a neighbor who is sick by watering his plants and mowing his lawn; another helps to register voters; a third volunteers to help the police department by patrolling the neighborhood and phoning in if anything looks suspicious. They feel like useful citizens. Growth and hedonism, important to them at first, are not a concern by the end of the study. Interestingly, they do not favor ease and contentment at any time.

The oldest women, following a very familiar pattern, have quite different goals from those of the men. They rate achievement much higher at all interviews, and their low point at the last contact is almost as high as their male counterparts' at the beginning. In-

stead of increased interest in social service like the men in this stage
of life, they drop to almost none. Concern with growth per se seems
to be a matter of semantics. Many of these women read about the
world "out there" and would love to travel. For them it is not
hedonism or self-indulgence but a way of broadening their horizons. Their hopes are not hedonistic, but they are not very realistic
either. For most it is only a fantasy, but the few who can afford it
come home feeling enriched by the experience—a satisfying goal
attained. Neither men nor women in this oldest group are interested
in ease and comfort, hoping to have no boring years in whatever
time is left to them.

In summary, then, the youngest men become more hedonistic and so do the youngest women except that they have consistent
goals of achievement and social service as well. The second youngest men are hedonistic for quite a few years but less so by the final
interview. The second youngest women consistently rate achievement as their top goal, and throughout they outrank all other
groups on growth. The second oldest men rank achievement low,
but the women are achievement-oriented throughout. The oldest
men, no longer ambitious, devote themselves to social service; the
oldest women still value achievement and also growth in their own
terms.

Such an array of findings may seem bewildering, but creating
a meaningful story out of all these data is rather like a jigsaw puzzle:
when properly put together, it does make sense. From our perspective, the data suggest that the younger people are striving toward
a semblance of adulthood, with the women consistently coming out
somewhat ahead of the men. For the older groups, there is some
support for the notions of David Gutmann as well as Carl Jung that
there is a balancing out in the later years: men become more accepting of social and perhaps community and personal issues, while
women become more instrumental and task-oriented.

Goals as Resources and Deficits

Given that there is both stability and change in values and
goals over the life course, we became interested in the implications
of change. We have seen that certain group changes may represent

developmental progression, but individual change may also reflect a lack of inner direction. To examine this question we selected one person from each subgroup to reveal more about the decline or increase in values and goals between the first and fifth interviews.

Younger People. High school senior Dick Youngblood represents a decline in achievement orientation. He has many goals concerned with hard work and success when we first meet, mainly because his father is a successful doctor and encourages them. About two years later Dick's main goal is wealth, and he now seems to think that the only way to achieve it is through outsmarting other people and tricking them out of their money. But three years later he has found a girlfriend he loves very much, and a happy marriage is now his primary goal. Dick's future wife, considerably more mature and responsible than Dick in the interviewer's estimation, knows what her goals are, and her goals complement his. His father continues to pressure him about medical school, but Dick insists on doing things his way. He wants to become an administrator of some sort and studies at a less-than-elite university with that objective in mind.

By the fifth session, despite his father's severe disapproval, Dick is married and has two children, explaining to the interviewer that he is not as ambitious as he used to be. He enjoys his work and his favorite "hobby" is reading about other cultures and people. The interviewer suspects that Dick in fact is a nice young man of no particular aptitude and that his father's incessant demands for high achievement might have led to Dick's undoing had he followed them as slavishly as he did at the first interview.

High school senior Cindy Long is the obverse of Dick in that she shows a growth in achievement goals from the first to last interviews. Born in Hawaii, she is one of the few Oriental persons in the sample. At first her main interests are in going to parties and taking trips, but she soon focuses on getting a good education (achievement-oriented). At the same time she is also distressed that her mother wants a divorce: Cindy's main goal is to get her parents reconciled.

By the third interview Cindy is in college and her primary goal is to get a master's degree in public health. Other goals include all sorts of lessons: dancing, skiing, tennis, cooking. At this time she also checks yes on most of the long list of psychological symptoms and says she sometimes feels suicidal, especially when thinking about her parents' problems. Twenty-six at the next to last session, her life is much more satisfying. Very much in love, she is engaged and plans to marry soon. She enjoys her work as a legal secretary with a law firm. By the last interview she has moved out of town and writes that she is happily married to a doctor. Since Cindy often contradicts herself, it is difficult to fathom which statements are true and which false. Inasmuch as she was not interviewed face to face, her interviewer for the first four contacts notes somewhat pessimistically that with her severe mental health problems she could not have married a doctor unless he was a psychiatrist who thought he might help her. We do not really know what Cindy's goals are at this last contact, but she seems to have had considerably more success than one might have anticipated. She has tried hard to make something of herself despite her considerable personal problems.

Craig Roberts, in the next to youngest group, represents an increase in religious/philosophical orientation, in his case religious. His childhood was sad and reflects the deprivation we discussed in Chapter Six: his father died in Korea before he was born, his stepfather died when he was fourteen, and a few years later he had yet another stepfather. At the first interview Craig is thinking of becoming a minister, but he soon opts for the insurance business instead. Two years later, having been promoted, he and his wife buy a house. His goals now include having children in about three years and meanwhile getting involved in the community (social service). By the third session he has separated from his wife and now has a girlfriend. He soon marries the girlfriend and by the last encounter they have a son. His goals are to maintain their good relationship and to be promoted to training and development consultant. Along with his new wife, his church involvements have increased. Craig's major value, religion, is an important resource for him.

Audrey Cutting, also in the second youngest group, becomes less philosophical or religious. A devout Catholic and graduate of a junior college, she does secretarial work. In part because her husband is a member of the Congregational church, she had several appointments with a psychiatrist before her marriage rather than seeing a priest. Her husband is in college studying for an advanced degree. Her main goal at this time is "to do whatever is necessary for inner peace." Her other goal is to go back to college. A few years later she joins her husband's church. Though she hopes to give up her job and have children, she will postpone any action on these plans until her spouse finishes school. The third interview finds Audrey ecstatic: her goals of not working and of having a child have been achieved. Another child arrives shortly before the fourth interview. Audrey manages, with the help of babysitters, to take a few courses in adult education that she finds very satisfying. At the last contact she describes herself as "an anachronism because right now I am an old-fashioned housewife." Like many in the study who had actually achieved their goals, she finds herself uncertain about plans for the future. When the children are in nursery school, she thinks, she will return to college. Meantime her long-term goals are serving as an inner resource.

These four young people illustrate that a resource may become a deficit if held too long. Whether by chance or design, the goals and values they espouse have changed in conformity with new demands and needs. While Dick's early goals were formulated more in response to his dominating father than to his personal (and at that time quite undefined) desires, he has gradually created less dramatic and achievement-oriented goals that appear more compatible with his abilities. Cindy, psychologically unstable, has problems but has managed to establish herself in a well-paying job and create what appears to be a successful marriage. Craig's spiritual goals are an abiding resource forged during a tragic childhood: his profound religious faith is a source of strength to sustain pursuit of his goal. Audrey is not ambivalent but her academic credentials are an open question. She has demonstrated considerable flexibility in changing and postponing goals, but one wonders whether this flexibility has not been achieved at the cost of her personal development.

Older People. Edith Manning became less interested in social service goals between the first and last interviews. Thirty-nine when we first meet, she is one of the few people who have married for a second time. A high school graduate, she works for a utility company, at first part time but then all five workdays. Her husband is a sales manager and they have two daughters (no children from her first marriage). Their older daughter is chronically ill with a blood disease but functions well. Both girls are teenagers when we first meet Edith. Her goal now is to put them through college. Busy as she is, there is no time for social service. She hopes they will get good jobs and, later, worthy husbands. A few years later her daughters have both left home; one is married and expects a child soon, the other has a career in the arts (acting and dancing). Since her husband's job requires a great deal of travel, an important long-range goal is to join him, but it would mean giving up her work. At the third session we learn that the married daughter (who now has a child) has gotten a divorce. Edith is glad but hopes she finds a new husband soon. She and her husband have bought a house, their major goal for several years, now that they no longer have to support their children. Edith certainly does not suffer from the empty nest syndrome. After doing volunteer work with disabled people of all ages, her goal now is semihedonistic: she plans to cultivate a flower garden. In a way she is substituting a form of modest creativity for social service.

Harry Scrivenor, in the oldest group, declines in growth orientation between the first and last interviews. About sixty-five when we meet, he works for an insurance firm. Although he has only a high school education, he knows four languages and reading them is his favorite spare-time activity. His wife died when she was very young and there are no children. Harry lives in a hotel; he has a close woman friend, a widow, and may move in with her when he retires. As it turns out, Harry retires sooner than expected because of high blood pressure despite medication. Growth, especially through reading serious books in foreign languages, is still important to him, as we learn at the third interview. By the fifth interview, however, he has several illnesses, including diabetes. His main goal is to get better. Now seventy-six, with very poor eyesight, he finds reading, in his terms the only way to grow, impossible. He has lost his major resource for reasons beyond his control, is still trying to make the most of life, and continues to readjust his goals. The alternative, he says, is to "just give up."

Ann Simon, on the other hand, feels that she continues to grow. Graduate of a business college, she is fifty-one at the first contact and still works full time as a secretary. Her husband, much older than she, is a lawyer. They have no children. Her general goals are to be independent, useful to others, a good citizen ("contribute to charity"), and a good Episcopalian. About three years later Ann has retired but still misses work and the people in her office. She and her husband have repainted their house inside and out, sold it, and moved to another state in order to be near her elderly parents. As many other women have found when their husbands retire, hers dominates the household. He does not cook, but he does clean house because "she is not good at it." During the third interview she reports many goals being accomplished: her husband has joined her church of his own accord; they have visited relatives in other states not seen in many years; and, most important, she is taking courses in cooking and sailing.

At the next to last interview Ann is recovering from surgery for a ruptured disk, but she is still able to continue as president of a church group that runs bazaars to raise money for the poor. More goals have been achieved by the final interview: two trips abroad, increased responsibilities in church, and masterminding a family reunion of more than a hundred people. She keeps learning and growing by reading serious books. Ann's growth goals are clearly a resource for her. She does not know what it means to be bored, for she is a spontaneously self-actualizing person.

These three older people encompass a broad spectrum of what we might call psychological types. Edith, though not very well educated, is instinctively a do-gooder: when she decides to cultivate a garden, we are quite sure her neighbors will be given many beautiful bouquets. Harry is essentially a scholar, and even though he winds up almost blind, we can easily imagine him reevaluating many of the books he has read, perhaps with his lady friend reading to him. Ann generates her own steam and is a doer whose enthusiasm is contagious.

Personal Goals: Beyond the Structured Instrument

In our research on goals and values we asked our respondents to think in a different mode—one that they are, for the most part, unaccustomed to. These are practical people not given to introspection. In fact, we vividly remember spending half an hour trying to explain to a participant what was meant by the very word *goal*. We may have been wrong to combine philosophical and religious in one category; very few, as has been noted, favor the former, but a considerable majority consider themselves religious. Because of the skeletal nature of the card sort, we decided to flesh it out with questions covering specific aspects of life:

- Marriage compared with other marriages
- Friendship ("how often do you see your closest friend?")
- Favorite activities (other than work)
- Work
- Satisfaction with attainments

In a broad sense, these questions all deal with values or goals since a change in how one views these aspects is often reflected in one's goals and values.

Marriage Compared with Others. Again we focus on change, but because this question was not asked at previous interviews, the change is between the fourth and fifth contacts. Questioned about how their marriage compares to others, most participants responded "much better" or "somewhat better." Only five people ranked their marriage as "worse" or "more worse" at the last interview; twenty-three rated it "about the same," almost equally divided between the young and old. We have no way of knowing whether "about the same" is good, bad, or indifferent. The youngest men at the fourth and fifth contacts ranked their marriage lower than did any other subgroup. Their average age at the fifth contact is twenty-nine; how many years each of them had been married is not stored in our computer, but it is startling to learn they do not feel like happy newlyweds. The youngest women feel better about their marriages, but not as much as the older people do. It is as though the youngest people sense a letdown after the courtship period is over. The second youngest men and women provide a refreshing contrast to the youngest ones. At the fifth contact men rate their marriage better than any other subgroup, and women rank it almost as high.

The older people are not so extreme as younger ones. The

second oldest men, though not as positive about their marriages as, say, the second youngest men, are quite satisfied at the third contact and continue to be. Women in the same stage of life report improvement. The oldest men change markedly for the worse in judging their marriage, women only a bit less so, contradicting the popular myth that old folks get used to each other. We know from our many case studies that sexual decline in men helps to explain this state of affairs.

Friendship. Here the question is "How often do you see your closest friend?" and it was asked at both the third and fifth contacts—a time span covering approximately six years. Categories are daily, weekly, monthly, and less often than monthly. Having a very close friend, a confidant with whom one can "let off steam" and who can be trusted, is an important resource for most people. Some people, of course, are very close-mouthed by nature and they are more likely to be men than women. In this "mainstream" sample the women put a high priority on gossip, sometimes malignant, sometimes benign. Overall, differences among subgroups are not as notable as on most topics, but there are interesting variations—especially over the six-year interval between the third and fifth encounters, when some groups become more sociable and others less so. The youngest men do not change much; most of them see their closest friend every day, only a few at monthly intervals. Their closest friend may work in the same trade or in the same office.

At the third interview the youngest women see their friends about as often as the men, and in addition they often have many friends whom they see once a month or so. Some of these women do not work, have children not yet in school, and have time to drive or take a bus, along with the kids, to visit friends. Six years later they are less involved with friends. With children now in school they spend more time getting them there and bringing them home. Others move to larger quarters (or their friends do) and distance precludes much visiting. Raising young children is often considered a chore, yet in retrospect many of these women insist these were the best years of their life.

The second youngest men at first see their friends less often than the youngest men and have more friends they see only monthly. The pattern is reversed six years later: more friends are seen daily or weekly, probably because they are now well established in their careers and can afford to have lunch with their friends. Women in the same group change very little: keeping house and seeing that their children do their homework is a full-time job.

At the third contact the second oldest men are like the younger ones and visit with friends quite often; six years later they are considerably less sociable but are not yet retired. Women at the same stage see their closest friend more often at both times than younger women do. Since their children have left home, they can easily manage to do so.

The oldest men see their friends just as often at the third contact as the younger men do, but at the fifth contact they are not very sociable: many are worn out and some are ill. The oldest women see less of their friends at both points in time. Some have husbands who are not as hardy as they used to be, and they have to take care of them. Others are not well themselves, but their best friends do not seem to rise to the occasion and visit them.

Favorite Activities. The uses of leisure time are about as diverse as the people in our study. Data collected at the first interview reveal about forty activities (or nonactivities) people in the sample like to do, and it is clear that one person's leisure is another's chore. Here we simply report whether or not they are satisfied with what they do. In a sense, leisure choices are another kind of goal. There are four responses: very satisfied; fairly satisfied; somewhat dissatisfied; or very dissatisfied. The analysis combines very and fairly satisfied as well as somewhat and very dissatisfied. Few people fall in the latter group. An overview contrasting the four young groups with the four older ones at the third contact yields quite surprising results: few of the young are satisfied, many dissatisfied. There is little change over time, but exceptions are interesting. More of the youngest men than women are satisfied at the third contact, and they change very little. The youngest women are the most dissatisfied at the third contact but not six years later.

The second youngest men have changed a great deal: at the third interview they include twice as many satisfied as dissatisfied people, but at the fifth interview almost as many are displeased as enjoy their spare-time activities. The second youngest women have changed very little and enjoy whatever they do. The second oldest men enjoy their leisure at the third contact, but they are not pleased at the fifth. Most women in this subgroup are very pleased with whatever they do or do not undertake at both times.

Most of the oldest men are satisfied and stay that way. The oldest women start out satisfied, but six years later they seem disgruntled. Since many of these women told us their husbands had become ill or impaired, they may have no leisure at all. For a few of these women there is an alternative explanation: their husbands talk them into doing things they do not enjoy. While there are a few very independent women in our sample, most of them feel duty-bound to cater to their husbands. In short, many wind up doing things that match the goals of their spouse and not necessarily themselves.

Work. Job satisfaction can be defined in many ways: the work itself, money, responsibility, camaraderie, or all of the above. Although we did not ask for details, presumably the more of these attributes the job involves, the more satisfying it is. The youngest men at first (third contact) include five who do not like their work. Six years later (fifth contact) all but one of them do. They may have changed jobs, been given a pay raise, or both. Fewer of the youngest women than men at the third interview dislike their jobs, and by the fifth interview the two youngest groups are very much alike in enjoying their work. There are greater gender differences between the second youngest men and women. Only about half as many women as men find their work agreeable at the third contact, and they are not yet on a par with them at the fifth. Most work only part time to supplement the family income.

The second oldest men like their work at the third interview; very few are unhappy about it. Six years later fewer of them are still working, but all those who do enjoy it. Women in the same life stage are all satisfied with their work at both times, with the exception of only one. Very few people in the oldest group still work, but among those who do all are very satisfied both times. Since few people in the sample do creative (to say nothing of glamorous) work, one suspects it is the camaraderie that appeals to them.

Satisfaction with Attainments. In contrast to these specific questions about roles and satisfaction, we also asked a more global question: "Looking back over your life thus far, how successful have you been in getting what you want out of life?" At the third contact the youngest men and women said they were quite successful, and they continued to be so over the next six years. The second youngest men, as in other instances, are "deviant." At the third contact the majority of them are successful, more so than the other three young groups; by the fifth contact they are the least so. They may feel overwhelmed by financial and other responsibilities of supporting, in both senses of the word, not only a wife but growing children as well. The fact that women in the same life stage are very positive about getting what they want out of life at both times confirms this thesis.

Three of the four older groups, perhaps only because they are growing older, report that they have become less satisfied in regard to achieving what they want. The exception is the oldest men: they do not change for the worse. The oldest women follow the general trend and report themselves very unhappy about not having achieved what they want. As they discuss the reasons, one theme which emerges is that of the lost opportunity—of having compromised personal goals for those of husband and children. Another reflects a perceived loss of attractiveness.

We turn now to highlights of our findings on these five variables. The youngest people rate their marriage lower than people in later stages, and the second youngest ones rate it higher than all subgroups. Differences are minor in regard to friendship: all stay about the same except for the oldest people, who tend to taper off. The second youngest men become very dissatisfied with their leisure time; the oldest women do, too, but considering their age, it is not surprising. As to work, most of the young people enjoy it and so do the few second oldest women who still have jobs. On satisfaction with their attainments, the second youngest men have the highest rating at the third contact and the lowest at the fifth. Volatile seems the right way to describe them.

How these five variables interact with goal satisfaction is worthy of our brief attention. Four of the subgroups rank high in goal satisfaction and four rank low. The highs include the youngest men and women, the next to oldest women, and the oldest men. The "lows" are therefore the second youngest men and women, the second oldest men, and the oldest women. Marriage does not correlate with anything, but each of the four groups ranking high on goal satisfaction see their closest friend often and are very satisfied with the way they use their spare time. Three of the four like their job and believe they are getting what they want out of life. Conversely, two of the four "low" groups see their friends less often, three are not satisfied with their use of leisure time, and three have not been successful in attaining what they want out of life. There is indeed a strong correlation between four of these five characteristics and goal achievement.

An Example of Generativity. A few of the oldest men may be living up to near legendary standards. Philosophy, folklore, and tradition in many cultures tell us that the virtue of old men is "wisdom," which ensures continuity and growth in their societies. *Generativity* is the word that fits them best. One of them is a sampling fluke, but his story is a good way to conclude this section. Phillip Stark is chairman of the social science department at an eminent university. His goal is to "function at the fullest," solve problems, and "be in tune with the universe." He is said to be a perfect role model for his students. A wise and cheerful man, he is sixty-five when we first meet and seventy-seven at the final interview. Phillip's private life is not exactly a bed of roses, but he and his wife are still very much in love. They give each other, as he puts it, "moral support." The Starks have two children. Their daughter is married to a corporate executive and has two grown-up children. The son married a young student who later divorced him; he subsequently made a suicide attempt and wound up in a psychiatric ward for several months.

At the second interview Phillip says he is learning to accept things as they come. Plenty of things do come: he has had a prostectomy and vasectomy and, among other ailments, has tennis elbow and arrhythmia. His son is now an alcoholic and has been hospitalized for jaundice and cirrhosis of the liver. Phillip says he has learned to overcome such occurrences. A few years later, his health much improved, his favorite activity is designing new survey questionnaires. A very generous man, he has given his oldest grandson and his wife a great deal of money so they can buy a house. ("You can't take it with you.") At age seventy-seven Phillip Stark says his goal for the rest of his life is to work in his office and "die with my boots on." He is not only an intelligent person but a wise one as well.

Self-Concept and Goal Satisfaction

Let us say that a friend of yours is very pleased with her accomplishments thus far. Would you expect her to have a positive image of herself? What about a man with few achievements? Would you expect him to have a poor opinion of himself? With respect to both of these questions, we would have said "yes, of course"—until we began to analyze the relationship between these two variables among our respondents. Here, as in Chapter Two, we use a simple dichotomy: positive and negative perspectives on the self.

Positive Image of Self. By the time of the third interview, the youngest people of both sexes have good opinions of themselves and are very satisfied with their goal achievements. At the final interview, however, somewhat fewer of the men's rated selves are on the plus side but they do continue to be satisfied with their achievements. Why some of them come to dislike themselves is an open question. The youngest women do not change at all in their positive concept of themselves, but their goal satisfaction deteriorates. Among both of the youngest groups, in other words, there is not a strong correlation between self-concept and goal satisfaction. Most of the second youngest men have good images of themselves at the third contact and about half of them are satisfied with their accomplishments.

Six years later, few rank themselves very positive on the Adjective Rating List and those satisfied with their goal achievements are very few indeed. As in other respects, these men are an enigma. In contrast, the second youngest women improve in self-esteem but rank by far the lowest of all subgroups in goal satisfaction. In their mid-thirties or so by the fifth contact, coping with adolescent children is their primary job and they no doubt have little time or energy for the pursuit of personal goals.

The self-views of older people, as we know, do not necessarily change for the worse, nor do their goal satisfactions, though some of these satisfactions may be retrospective. The second oldest men declined the most in self-esteem and also in goal satisfaction. By the third interview, making enough money for a comfortable retirement is the main preoccupation of these men and they feel they have not yet done so. It is no surprise to learn that their sense of goal achievement has declined commensurately. The second oldest women, as the reader may recall, have very positive opinions of themselves at the fifth contact and also appraise their goal achievements as very satisfying. Some have retired from full or part-time work and are now free to get involved with their favorite interests.

The oldest men maintain their positive self-concepts at the third and fifth contacts and satisfaction with goal achievement as well. The oldest women feel positive about themselves at both times, but their goal achievements are less satisfying than those of their male counterparts.

Negative Image of Self. People who check quite a few negative traits on the Adjective Rating List are, for the most part, not as satisfied with goal achievements as those who think well of themselves. Both men and women in the youngest group check several negative characteristics at the third contact and rate themselves low on goal achievement. By the fifth contact they are only a bit less negative about themselves and satisfaction with goal achievement remains low. Those "deviant" second youngest men rank the lowest of all the young subgroups in their self-views at both the third and fifth interviews. It is therefore befitting that their goal satisfaction is lowest of the four young subgroups in negative personal characteristics at both interviews, and their goal satisfaction declines precipitously as well. Women in the same life stage outdo men in both respects: more have negative self-views at both times and only two are satisfied with goal accomplishment at the end of the study. They lend strong support to the thesis that self-image is related to satisfaction with goal achievement, but they are paradoxical people.

The second oldest men are, at the third contact, the lowest-ranking people of all eight subgroups as far as self-image is concerned, but most of them feel good about their goal achievements. Over the next six years they deteriorate: even more negative about themselves, fewer of them are satisfied with goal achievements. Women in the same stage of life are not so extreme. Their self-views do not change much, nor does their goal achievement. They represent a sort of median of all eight subgroups. The oldest men and women have quite adverse self-concepts at the third contact but improve with time.

A majority of the oldest men are very satisfied with their goal achievements both times, but not so the oldest women: on a par with men at the third contact, only four of them are satisfied at the fifth. Increasingly aware of the brevity of life, these women seem to be saying, "now it's too late."

Examples of the Goal/Self Relationship. A few vignettes may bring to life the nature of the relationship between self-approval and goal satisfaction. One of the second youngest women, Carlene Masters, paints a very negative sketch of herself on the Adjective Rating List. Graduate of a junior college, she works as a typist. Her husband, a high school graduate, works for a warehouse company. The two do not have much rapport. Carlene has many goals—get more education, find a better job, have children, and buy a house—but she makes little effort to achieve them. The last time we see her she is even more disgusted with herself. She has left her husband because he would not see a marriage counselor. She divorced him, he remarried, and, still in the same year, she lost her job. Carlene has moved in with her mother and brother, looks for work, and has what she calls a "fragmented" relationship with another man. Except for the vague aim of finding a job, she has no goals and is now taking antidepression medication. One can only hope that she finds a better job, gets a new husband, sets realistic goals, and polishes her self-image.

Austin Linder is, as his mother used to say, "a different cup of tea." He has a good, but not an inflated, opinion of himself. Son of a stevedore, he considers himself a self-made man. He is a very successful accountant. His most important goal when we first meet is to help his college-age son and daughter to "find themselves." At our last meeting his daughter is about to graduate from an Ivy League college (one goal reached), but his son has serious psychological problems (goal not reached). Austin has a very jealous wife who envies his success; she was even jealous of the interviewer who spent two or three hours alone with him at each contact.

Eleanore Lang too has a good self-image. College educated and a grade school teacher, she loves her work. Her husband, a high school graduate, is a wine salesman and often comes home more than a little intoxicated. The Langs have one child, a daughter, and Eleanore's most important goal is to see her graduate from a good university. By the fifth interview her husband is no longer drinking (another goal achieved) and she finds his personality "much enhanced." Eleanore says each year is better than the year before. A sturdy optimist ("positive thinking" becomes her), she is also somewhat Pollyannaish.

Wilhelm Newstadt is extremely negative about himself. Painter for a tracking company, he has had only eight years of schooling and hates his work. His wife went to a business college and works as an army supply technician. Wilhelm himself feels he has a serious "inferiority complex." His only goal is that his two sons go to college. Dissatisfied with himself and life itself, he refuses to be interviewed at the second contact because he is "too busy." The last time we talk with him is at the third contact, and our conversation is via telephone; his wife has died and he is angry and depressed and has no goals whatsoever. A self-defeating man, Wilhelm is incapable of hope.

These short case studies well illustrate the symbiotic nature of self-concept and goals. They seem to suggest that people who have low self-esteem are often lacking in personal goals or tend to give them up readily.

Happiness and Goal Achievement

Happiness, as any good thesaurus explains, has many definitions: cheeriness, blitheness, euphoria, joyousness, ecstasy, and elatedness. In Chapter Three we reported on free-flowing self-descriptions and from them we find many synonyms used by our respondents in their self-descriptions (to which the reader should add the prefix "I am"): "fullfilled," "enjoyer of life," "ecstatic," "a laugher," "sunshine," "a bon vivant," "fully content." These are all nuances suggesting some of the meanings our respondents apply to happiness. Bear them in mind as we pursue the concept.

In this section we examine the thesis that goal satisfaction is without question correlated with happiness regardless of how it is defined. Logic tells us that goal achievement is a form of self-actualization, but that is hard work and an end in itself that has little to do with happiness. Was Einstein happy? Was Leo Tolstoy? Does it matter? Happiness is not the be-all and end-all of existence, though it may be a by-product. To explore this relationship, we first turn to the youngest men.

At the third interview many of the youngest men are very or fairly satisfied with their goal achievements, but a fourth of them are dissatisfied. Few are very happy; the majority are "pretty happy." Six years later, fewer are dissatisfied with goal achievements and many are now very happy. Among these men, then, there is a tenuous connection between the two variables. The youngest women do a bit better. The third contact finds more of them satisfied with goal achievement and more of them happy.

Six years later, differences between men and women are even stronger and favor the latter: more are "goal-satisfied" and twice as many women as men are "very happy." Perhaps the males of our species tend to find the word effeminate, especially when preceded by the adjective *very*. "Pretty happy" seems more acceptable to them. The second youngest people, however, do not confirm this thesis (though some older groups do). Well over half of both men and women are very satisfied with their goal attainments at the third contact, and about half of them are very happy. Their reports six years later are strikingly different. Only half as many of the men are goal-satisfied as before, and fewer are happy. Women in this group fare worse: only two are very pleased with their goal achievements, and not nearly so many are happy.

The second oldest men, often disgruntled, decline drastically in goal satisfaction between the third and fifth interviews; they do not change in happiness, but then few were very happy to begin with. The women in this second oldest group do not change much in goal satisfaction, and at the fifth contact twice as many are satisfied with goals as are the men. Happiness is another matter: the great majority of them are very happy at the third contact but only five are at the fifth. In addition five of them are "not too happy." One plausible explanation, considering their age, is that they have menopausal symptoms and are temporarily depressed.

The oldest men are rather better off than the second oldest ones. Most are very gratified with their achievements at the third contact and remain so through the fifth. About as many are very happy, too, and they do not change. The oldest women are just as happy as their male counterparts at the third contact, and as satisfied with goal achievement as well, but by the fifth interview most of them are only fairly satisfied and five are very or fairly dissatisfied. The only explanation for the differences between the oldest men and women is one used earlier: women live in the present, but men are prone to retrospection about the good old days.

A Pause for Review

What our respondents are telling us in this chapter says something about their emotions and philosophy of life. These range from cynical to optimistic and from complex to simple-minded, with a little buffoonery thrown in for good measure. They illustrate a variety of modes of human development or lack thereof. Some of the youngest people think "life is just a bowl of cherries" until they grow up a bit. Others sink into throes of despair when a girl- or boyfriend jilts them. Ten years later they may look back at their prior selves and laugh.

The second youngest people like to think of themselves as more sophisticated and less emotional. Their goals may be reappraised and sometimes changed. Heading toward young middle age by the fifth interview, they feel more mature and some begin to trust their intuition about what is good or not so good in their modes of thinking and feeling. Most important, they consider the future consequences of their present goals. These are generalizations, of course, and do not account for the goals, emotions, and behavior of everyone in this stage of life.

The people who, in the course of the study, move into late middle age vary more. Some cheerfully accept the facts of life; others would like to set back their clocks to the time when they were in their heyday. Generativity as a goal is present, too, though truly generative people are hard to find in this sample or any other. They are a very special breed. Generativity, as we define it, is a concern for posterity, the future of human beings and the world they live in, and doing something about it. Such people are altruistic in the best sense of the word. Their goals are symbols of legacy to forthcoming generations.

There is nothing unusual about Barney Martin and Jules Conan, two men in the oldest group. Neither is very well educated, nor do they have well-paid careers. But they are both insightful people, sensitive and instinctively aware of the world they live in. They have also done some serious reading on the issues that interest them. Barney's role model is John Muir (1838–1914), the naturalist who pioneered in saving the redwoods and other classic flora and fauna. Jules's ideal is Jacques Cousteau, the founder of undersea research. Jules would have liked to follow in his footsteps. In our interviews Barney says he would like to pass on his goals and ideals to his children, grandchildren, and great-grandchildren. Jules, a doer, wants to leave something behind before he dies, such as helping old people who cannot help themselves any more.

The Four

As one might have guessed, our stalwart machinist Olav Olavsen ranks such goals as personal growth, social service, philosophical/religious (he is both), and good personal relationships as very important. Not so important are hedonism and achievement (in the sense of economic rewards or social status).

Hazel Sutter's most important goal is good personal relations. She is the rather plodding school cafeteria cook (who does not plod at all once she finally falls in love). Her main goal at the final interview is good personal relations, presumably with her gentleman friend and the students she feeds. Ease and contentment are second on her list.

Ranked lowest are philosophical/religious goals. Hazel is not religious, nor is she the kind of person who thinks in philosophical terms. Social service ranks quite low on her list, perhaps because she plans to retire soon and thinks she has been doing social service in her work all along. Personal growth is not important to her because her major goal now is to make her close friend happy.

Max Schindler is the man whose favorite activity is hunting and shooting game, especially ducks. Now retired from his foreman job in the city, he has bought a ranch and is a part-time farmer. He takes the easy way out in ranking his seven goals: six of the seven are placed as number one; the exception, as we might expect, is social service. Typical of his expansive ego, he claims to have thirty-eight close friends.

Adelaide Stone finds it hard to decide how her goals should be ranked. At the first interview they include a better job (she was a secretary then) and a happy retirement with her second husband (whom she later divorces). Throughout the study she reports some anxiety about death because her family's genes are "not very good." Before her fourth interview she has a stroke; by the fifth she feels a little better but is pessimistic about her future. In fact, the interviewer has to do the goal ranking for her. "When I was twenty-five these would have been meaningful," Adelaide reports, "but it does not mean anything to me now." In any case, her three most important goals now are ease and contentment, good personal relations, and philosophical/religious. Adelaide is Catholic and manages to attend church every Sunday.

These four people, representing the four older groups, are a miniature cross section of the sample so far as goals are concerned. To make the cross section more representative, we add four alternates from the four older groups. Alfred Bryant is a well-educated and successful man who is well off financially—rather a rarity in this sample, but most of the money comes from his wife's inheritance. He thinks he has to make still more money, not for wealth itself but for security. (He was a child in the Great Depression.) Alfred is a supervisor for a utility company but would prefer to work in real estate. Fifty-two when we first meet, he hopes to retire at sixty. By the fourth interview he is more relaxed and spends more time with his family; he reports the change as being a result of learning to meditate, which his wife has encouraged him to do. Now very relaxed, his ranking of the goal cards seems appropriate (and very different from his list at the third contact). His three most important goals now are ease and contentment, good personal relations, and seeking enjoyment; lowest are philosophical/religious goals (despite his Zen) and social service, which he never has done.

Della Swanson is the former nurse whose husband refuses to let her work. Her main goal at the first interview is "to have the world a little better because of my having been in it." Another goal at that time is social service; Della likes to help people. She is also one of the few older women who are well informed about social problems. By the third contact her husband has retired. He is not very well but does allow her to do volunteer work now and then. By the fourth contact the Swansons have moved to a semiretirement area, where she continues to do volunteer work whenever her spouse lets her out of the house. He also allows her to continue her "reading and learning" by way of serious books. For the fifth interview Della mails the completed questionnaire to the office. Her top goals are ease and contentment and good personal relations. (She has found good friends in the retirement community.) Least important now are achievement and seeking enjoyment.

Abraham Brady will retire (as an electronics engineer) just after the first interview. His goals at this time are to be a good citizen, responsible, and God-fearing. (He is a devout Lutheran.) On our first acquaintance he is sixty-five; he is seventy-seven at the final session. He has few friends, if any, being as he says "family-oriented." Abraham, as the reader will recall, is a right-wing conservative, to put it mildly, and a tense person. His only yes on the list of psychological symptoms is in response to the question "Do you have to be on guard even with friends?" At the fifth interview, he says his most important goal is "the welfare of the family." Elaborating a little, he explains that in his will his "little wife is taken care of properly." His most important goals at this last interview are good personal relations (with family), achievement, and work rewards. (He has spent a lot of time fixing up his ample house in the country.) His next most important goal is philosophical/religious; in his case the emphasis is on religious. Social service, as for most oldest men, rates lowest.

Annabelle Whitman is the woman with an advanced degree in French. Age sixty at our first encounter, she calls herself a housewife. Her most important goal at this time is to "live life in a manner not offensive to others." The Whitmans have two married daughters but no grandchildren as yet. She feels much closer to her sister than to her husband; he knows it and is resentful. At the final interview Annabelle is seventy. In answer to the question "What are your goals now and for the next five years?" she says she is not sure she has any, but on the card sort she turns out to be the only person in the oldest group who ranks growth first.

Summing Up

Goals and values are rather elusive concepts. At the same time, they can provide a sense of continuity in the midst of change. Several of our participants commented on the sense of loss they experienced after achieving some long-sought-after goal: the birth of a child, graduation, even retirement. For them the quest had in some sense become the purpose, and the demand now was to reinstate some goal or direction to their lives.

We also encountered, in our participants' responses to questions about goals, an affirmation of the Jungian idea that there is a balancing out, in the second half of life, of those goals and values that predominate in the first half. For example, men in the oldest group placed less value on achievement goals and more on interpersonal; women, in contrast, seemed to place a higher value on achievement goals. Overall, the participants demonstrated considerable dexterity in changing their goals to match their circumstances.

11

Sense of Commitment:
A Fundamental Human Concern

In this chapter we look at another way in which people express their views of themselves and life in general: we look at their commitments. The concept of commitment has a long history and has been defined in diverse ways. However it is defined, the term generally connotes meaning, interest, value, engagement, and the choices and behavior associated therewith. For Gordon Allport (1939), a pioneer in the field, such concerns were initially seen as relating to functional autonomy. Later Allport (1955) introduced the term *proprium* to distinguish his idea from other concepts of motivation. Propriate striving, in his view, makes for unification of personality. People, as he studied them, were busy leading their lives into the future, whereas most of his contemporaries concentrated on tracing their pasts. Allport's thesis is echoed by Kurt Goldstein (1963, p. 201), who says the tendency to actualize oneself is the only motive by which human activity is "set going." Like many other contemporary scholars, Goldstein maintains that the individual's ongoing vision of self is to be found in the person's choices and behavior.

Life-course research requires an expansion of these assumptions to accommodate the older people who are becoming an increasingly large proportion of this country's population. (By the end of this century two-thirds will be over fifty.) Old people's concerns may be autonomous and self-actualizing, but they are not necessarily future-oriented. For them, a sense of satisfaction and meaning may draw upon a new awareness of inner states and modes of experiencing the present.

By the late 1950s the word *commitment* was surfacing increasingly in the scientific literature. Becker (1960) notes that it has both growing appeal and a notable lack of formal definition. Stemming from a bewildering array of humanistic and materialistic contexts, commitment was not a concept to gain much consensus. Some scholars described its meanings and trusted that the reader's interpretation would fit their own. Others focused on one or more self-defined dimensions and proceeded to develop a schema that best suited their objectives. To further obfuscate the issue, since the late 1970s commitment has been adopted by both the popular media and serious novelists. Both groups assume that its meaning is self-evident.

A number of theorists view commitment as underlying personality. Chein (1972) believes that the capacity for commitment is the essential human quality. He also discusses two important components: one is a time dimension that influences moment-by-moment decisions and behavior; the second relates to the complexity of interactions among the specific concerns of a commitment cluster. Chein himself is interested in the state of commitment: it must be wholehearted to be genuine. Marks (1977) introduces commitment as part of a comprehensive theory of human energy, one which includes the creation of energy. He contends that strong commitments expand both energy and time, and derive from the individual's assessments of the various performance clusters required in each arena within which they function. While any of these elements may inspire commitment, if a person values all of them, his or her commitment will be particularly strong. Klinger (1975, pp. 3-4) adopts a different approach. The commitment process, he holds, "must be inferred as a logically necessary antecedent of its presumed consequences." He postulates recurring cycles that have a beginning and a continuing state (both characterized by invigoration) and an end. During the life of a given incentive, it serves as an organizing force for thought, perception, behavior, and affect.

Defining and Measuring Commitments

Processes of the sort described by Klinger can be traced, but only with difficulty. The patterning of commitments may remain stable, for example, but the meaning ascribed to them may change. Or a person may still rank high, say, on mastery but the source of masterful feelings might change from external factors (a powerful and rich parent, for example) to inner satisfaction. In Kitchener's (1976, p. 208) terms, the components of commitment hierarchies can be reinterpreted, sometimes rearranged as well, and a different "whole" will emerge.

After reviewing the literature as well as in-depth protocols, including life histories, we identified four categories of commitment: moral, interpersonal, mastery, and self-concern. We validated the four categories by independent analyses of in-depth material undertaken by an interdisciplinary team including a psychoanalyst and a psychiatrist. Examined in relation to each other, the four commitments represented, as far as we could tell, at least a sampling of the fundamental concerns people harbored at each of the five contacts in the course of nearly twelve years.

Identifying the basic commitments was one thing; trying to develop a reasonable means of assessing them was another. This chapter is based on findings from the Adjective Rating List, which includes descriptive items that match quite well with the four basic commitments. Unlike goals, which are future-oriented, commitments are a pledging of the self, intrinsic states of being that may or may not be hierarchical. As the reader may recall, respondents were asked to check the adjectives most like themselves, those most unlike, and those about which they could not make up their minds.

How, then, did we define these four commitments? Mastery, we concluded, is an intrinsic interest derived from fulfilling personal standards and from perceived self-efficacy. The adjectives on which it is based include *energetic, imaginative, versatile,* and *persevering;* negative valences are assigned to *helpless, lazy,* and *uninterested.* There was little agreement about how to define moral commitment. For this study we concluded that it encompasses concerns that transcend the self and includes benevolence and integrity. Adjectives forming the cluster are positive on *fair-minded, idealis-*

tic, and *sincere* and negative (unlike self) on *guileful.* Interpersonal commitment, in turn, represents commitments ranging from dyadic to groups and social entities. Adjectives in this cluster are *sympathetic, warm, friendly, likable, considerate,* and *not hostile.* Self-concern is a more difficult commitment to define. It not only includes self-preservation, a sine qua non for survival, but also narcissism, a lifelong need for reinforcement so pressing that it precludes any serious commitments. Taken together, these components of self-concern seemed to be defined by the following adjectives: *cautious, self-indulgent, selfish,* and *inconsiderate.*

We do not claim that these four commitments are all-inclusive. For instance, in this mainstream sample we detect another, which might be called environmental sensitivity, one powerful enough to hamper other commitments at times. Such concerns, which may be traced through the life stories of the subjects, include a need for orderliness, quiet, and some sense of harmony with the world.

Commitment to Mastery

The youngest people do not seem very committed to being masterful. On the contrary, compared with some of the older groups, they rated that state of being quite low. Very few of the youngest men favored that category at the third and fifth contacts, and some ranked it very low. Jeff is quite typical: an efficient accountant who has certainly mastered his job, he does not consider it a state of being. One of very few people in the sample who have a good sense of humor, he feels it is the best way to cope with the inevitable ups and downs of life. His humor is not sarcastic or cynical, and for him it is a philosophy of life, a way of being.

The youngest women, perhaps because they are women, include several who are extremely low in mastery, and six years later their numbers have increased. The mastery concept does not seem to fit their self-image at all. Ella Trumbull, for example, might best be described as a "fraidy-cat." By nature a shy and timid senior in high school (first contact), she had blossomed a bit by the third interview, when she was a private secretary to a VIP who had confidence in her discretion. His encouragement gives her ego a boost

and she can chat with his visitors until he is free to see them. By
the fifth contact Ella has married one of her boss's clients and her
main commitment is to this husband and their eagerly awaited first
child.

The second youngest men feel more committed to mastery
with time—that is, as they became six years older at the fifth contact,
they came to feel at home in that state of being. To illustrate, take
Tony Hurt. He is a salesperson in an expensive women's shoe shop
where patrons are likely to try on as many as twenty or thirty pairs
before making a final decision. He has to be very patient with them,
which is no easy task toward the end of a busy day, but he is a master
of his trade and his boss sometimes gives him a bonus at the end
of a lucrative month. By the time he gets home, which takes almost
an hour in rush-hour buses, he is tired and plunks himself down
in front of TV until dinner is ready. After that he plays games with
his two young sons until it is time for them to go to bed. His
familial commitment (interpersonal) is strong indeed.

The second youngest women resemble the men, with more
favoring mastery at the fifth contact than at the third, but not really
very committed to it as a state of being. Still to some extent loving
newlyweds at the third interview, most of them have a child or two
by the fifth. Women's concerns have shifted to them, and husbands,
as noted earlier, feel neglected. Lena Weiner is a good example. She
is the daughter of a fireman who taught her how to protect herself
in the big city. Now grown up, married, and with one young son,
she tries to teach him the same lessons. Like most of the younger
women in the sample, her main commitment is interpersonal. Her
major concern now is to keep open house for her son and his
friends, noisy as it may be, an innovative idea in which mastery is
implicit.

The second oldest men and women differ from each other in
how they feel about mastery as commitment. The men have increased their sense of masterfulness considerably in the six years
between the third and fifth contacts. Paul Murphy, for example,
falls into the masterful category. A foreman for a public utility
company, he sees that the city streets are kept clean. Rather compulsive about doing a good job, he checks a different area of the city

each day of the week to make sure his employees have actually done the sweeping. He enjoys being masterful, and it comes close to being a strong commitment. After work he likes to be rather boastful in telling his wife about the events of his day.

In contrast to the men, the second oldest women stay about the same in their mastery scores over the course of the study and are not very high to begin with. The masterful state of being does not seem to appeal to them. Mary Brower illustrates this point. Mary has never been very masterful, nor does she wish to be. Her husband is an assistant in an accountant firm who spends his workdays adding and subtracting figures on a computer. Mary would be bored with that sort of job—when she was in high school, math was the class she least enjoyed. When her husband comes home she does not ask him if he had a good day but entertains him about how inept she has been in preparing dinner. She forgets to buy his favorite dessert, a neighbor came by and borrowed their electric mixer and has not yet returned it and she cannot remember where she put the old one—or did they throw it away? Mary may not be very masterful about anything, but she is very empathic.

The oldest men rank by far the highest one of any subgroup on mastery. At the first interview nearly half are in that state of being, and by the fifth interview well over half feel masterful. As we know from prior chapters, they have looked forward to retirement, when they can indulge in their favorite hobby, be it fishing, repainting a flat, or planting a vegetable garden that in the long run will save them money. Jim Long, for example, now retired, is a tall, rather husky man. He has not only repaired his own small apartment but that of two neighbors as well.

The oldest women present a somewhat startling contrast to their male counterparts. At both the first and last interviews, fewer than a fifth of them feel committed to mastery. It is as though they want to be taken care of. Ida Ames is a good example. Ida enjoys being "helpless," an antonym of mastery. A little hard of hearing, she refuses to wear a hearing aid because "it's too noisy." In consequence, she does not like to be with people. This makes life difficult for her husband not only because he has to shout to be heard but because she wants him to stay with her all the time.

Moral Commitment

We must emphasize from the outset that moral commitment is not synonymous with moral majority; the adjective cluster that represents moral commitment consists of *fair-minded, idealistic, sincere,* and *not guileful.* Rankings were high, medium, and low. Oddly, no one in the entire sample rated him- or herself high, and only six people ranked low; none of them did so at both the third and fifth interviews. A low rank implies immorality, of course, and who would wish to consider that as a state of being? A professional statistician might say "your cutoff points were wrong," but we tried them all and can only conclude that nearly everyone favors moral as a state of being (and that being at one extreme or the other does not suit them). There are no contrasts to be illustrated by particular people in the sample.

Interpersonal Commitment

Adjectives used to assess a person's stance toward relationships include *sympathetic, warm, friendly,* and *considerate,* on the positive side, and *affected* and *hostile,* on the negative. The theme of this commitment is "birds of a feather flock together." People within each of the eight subgroups are very much alike in regard to where they stand, but unlike moral commitment, each subgroup differs from the others. The youngest men differ from the youngest women quite strikingly: all but two of the men are highly committed to interpersonal relationships at both times, but all women cast themselves in the "medium" category. This runs contrary to the notion that men are the workers and women the socializers. The stereotypical example of this might be what happens when you call to invite a married couple to have dinner at your house: the man answers but then says, "Hold on a minute and I'll get my wife." In other words, the woman is often viewed as the person who arranges for socializing, sending birthday cards, keeping track of anniversaries, and the like.

To illustrate the differences between these youngest men and women, let us consider two of them. Archy Campbell's strongest commitment is to people. By the fifth interview he has become a successful social worker with a large clientele of mostly poor people. When he first sees clients he asks a lot of questions about what they like or dislike about themselves. Then he focuses on the "likes" for several sessions, strengthening egos to the point where "dislikes" can be tackled. He has never had a client he did not like. Ruthey Dishman, on the other hand, is less people-oriented. By the fifth contact she is married to a good-looking man who works at a bank. While he is at work she keeps thinking of all the pretty women who must be admiring him and trying to lure him away from her. Indirectly she is in fact oriented to interpersonal relations, but in a different way than we were measuring: jealousy seems to be her problem.

The second youngest men's commitment to people is almost a carbon copy of the youngest women's at both the third and fifth contacts: all but one of them is at the medium level of interpersonal commitment at both times. The second youngest women fit the stereotype: all but one of them rank high both times.

The next to oldest men change more than anyone else, but not to the degree we note in other sections of this chapter. A significant number of them rank high at the third contact, and a few more of them do so at the fifth. Some of them are in the medium range at both times, but only one ranks himself low. (He also reports being in the midst of a series of disagreements with his wife, which may have affected his scores.) Two of the second oldest women are in the medium range on interpersonal commitment at the third contact, but all are strongly committed at the fifth. The oldest men and women, to our surprise, are like the youngest ones: most men are in the high range; all women are in the middle.

Commitment to Self-Concern

This commitment is of course more self-centered than the rest and really deals with the basic survival qualities that Abraham Maslow listed at the fundamental end of his hierarchy of needs. The adjectives we used to assess commitment to self-concern are *cautious, self-indulgent, selfish,* and *considerate* (scored negatively). None of our respondents admits to ranking high on what is an extreme form of egotism. Some people in the sample have sought a therapist of one sort or another, but not for this kind of ailment. *Selfish* and *self-indulgent* are the most egocentric of the four adjectives, *cautious* and *inconsiderate* the least so.

Since no one ranks high on self-concerns, we concentrate on the middle range of being concerned with the self. Some people change for the better, others for the worse, and two subgroups do not change at all. Overall, both life stage and gender have a bearing on self-commitment. In the four younger groups, the women are more preoccupied with themselves than the men, while in the four older groups it is the men who tend to be selfish, self-indulgent, and inconsiderate.

The youngest men and women differ notably. Only a few of the men are self-protective at the first interview and none at the last, whereas more than a third of the women are self-committed both times. Silvia Fontana is one of those with a history of being high on self-protectiveness. About twenty-eight at the third contact, she is one of the most talkative people in the sample. She is a certified practical nurse, and one feels sorry for her patients, who probably cannot get a word in edgewise. A tall and seriously overweight young woman, by the fifth contact she has incredibly high blood pressure that cannot be controlled with medication. Moaning and groaning is her way of eliciting sympathy. By now her patients must be seeking another nurse.

The second youngest men and women, like the youngest, also have marked differences. Only two men are concerned with themselves at the third contact and only one at the fifth. The women resemble the youngest ones but manifest a slight decline in self-preoccupation at the final contact. Harold Burke is a good example of a man who is not at all concerned with himself. About thirty-two at the third contact, he is on his way up the ladder as general secretary of a YMCA in a middle-size town. Harold has two young children, a girl of seven and a boy of two. He works days and evenings six days a week. He loves his work and encourages his daughter to take lessons in the swimming pool and learn to do acrobatics in the gym. By the fifth interview he is the boss and has selected his co-workers very carefully. They find his enthusiasm contagious and work the same long hours he did. Harold does not have time to think about himself.

The second oldest men and women do not differ as much as the youngest ones, especially at the final interview. At the third contact, many more men than women are self-concerned, but by the fifth contact they are on a par. Jodey Robertson is a very self-preoccupied person. She works as manicurist in a beauty salon and has had the same job for more than twenty-five years at the third contact. Her two children are married and live far away, so she does not see them often. Since Jodey and her husband do not have a car, she walks to work. She envies her affluent clients, their chatter about trips they have taken, concerts they have been to, and grown children who are successful and making a lot of money. By the last encounter she is a widow, nervous, worried, and more self-protective than ever.

Every researcher is curious by nature, and we are no exception. Thus we wondered whether there is any evidence from the Twenty Statements Test (Chapter Three) that relates to self-concern. We found that indeed there is, with the interesting exception of the oldest men. The words that participants generally use to describe themselves in this test are not necessarily the same four terms we used to measure self-concern, but they can easily be translated into synonyms. The youngest men and women often describe themselves with words like *worrier* and *nervous*, which suggest a cautiousness and self-protective quality. The second youngest people freely admit to being self-indulgent and selfish. The second oldest people, apparently feeling their age, make "who am I" statements such as "defensive" and "meek," which makes them cautious too. That the oldest men list no statements related to self-concern is an anomaly. The oldest women, for the most part, use synonyms of *cautious*—for example, words like *anxious, timid,* and *nervous* were common in their self-descriptions. The one exception is a woman who said "I am a semiselfish person."

Stress and Commitment

In Chapter Six we discussed stress in the context of challenge or defeat. Here the purpose is to explore the impact of stress on commitment. Do highly committed people find that being moral buffers them from stress? Does ranking high on mastery ameliorate stress in the workplace? Does strong commitment to interpersonal relationships provide a resource when a person needs help? Finally, do people who are primarily concerned with themselves manage to avoid stress? Is it possible that stress avoidance is the main reason why people become self-concerned? We cannot say aye or nay to every aspect of these questions, but we may be able to offer some plausible explanations about levels and types of commitment and the extent to which they appear to mitigate or exacerbate stress.

First we should explain how our sample distributes itself in terms of change in level of stress at the third and fifth interviews. Here we are using responses to a general question concerning how stressed participants were; the response categories are "high," "medium," and "low." At the third contact only two of the youngest men ranked themselves high on stress. At that time they were as a group the lowest of all participants except for the oldest women, who were on a par with them. Six years later the youngest men were if anything even less stressed. Whereas at the third interview half of them said they were moderately stressed, that number was greatly reduced by the fifth contact and more of them ranked low than at the third contact.

The youngest women were quite different from the men: at both the third and fifth interviews about a fourth of them felt highly stressed, and, at the other extreme, those ranking low dwindled considerably. Turning to the second youngest group, we find that the men and women differ from each other more than the youngest ones do. More men are highly stressed at both times than are women, and fewer men than women rank low at both times.

While one might expect that the older people are under more stress than the younger ones simply because they are older, this is not the case. Most of the second oldest men and women rank low on stress at both times, and only three are high. The oldest people are very relaxed: the vast majority of them rank low or medium on stress.

To untangle the correlation between stress and commitment we now look at various combinations of stress and mastery. The logical alternatives are high stress and high mastery, low mastery and low stress, and high mastery and low stress. The youngest men become more stressed between the third and fifth interviews and about average on high mastery. At the fifth contact none of these men is low on mastery and several experience less stress than they had at the third. In other words, there is a modest correlation between being masterful and ranking low on stress. This is a rational and predictable correlation. Several of the youngest women feel they are very stressed at the third contact, and at the fifth they are only a bit less so. Their commitment to mastery at both times is weaker than that of any other subgroup. Conversely, these women rank lower than any other subgroup on stress except for the second oldest women at the third contact, but by the final interview the situation has changed: fewer of them rank low than those in any other group. Stress for these women correlates with lack of mastery and the correlation is thus an inverse one.

The second youngest men and women differ from each other somewhat more than the youngest ones in both degree of stress and strength of the mastery commitment. The men experience more stress than any others at the third contact, but by the fifth they are about on a par with the youngest men. The number of those ranking high on mastery at the third contact is very low, but by the fifth they are better off than the youngest people. Low stress for these men by the fifth interview correlates neatly with high mastery. As for the second youngest women, they are singularly lacking in stress and do not change at all between the third and fifth contacts. In regard to numbers ranking low on mastery, no other groups outdo them. The correlation between stress and mastery is almost perfectly inverse.

The older people fare somewhat better than the younger ones on the correlation between stress and mastery. The second oldest men rank lowest of all subgroups, except for the oldest men, who match them. Fewer rank low on mastery at both times, and they experience the least stress of any subgroup except the oldest men, who have the same score. The second oldest women rank fairly high on stress at the third contact, but fewer of them are stressed at the fifth. They do not change in mastery between the third and fifth contacts. In the low-stressed category they turn out to be the least stressed of all eight subgroups. In other words, lack of stress is inversely correlated with mastery. The fact that these women experience stress and rank low on the mastery commitment supports the thesis that lack of challenge can lead to defeat. The oldest men give us a different perspective. These men rank very low on stress at both times, and their commitment to mastery is the highest of all subgroups at the third and fifth contacts. In fact, their commitment to mastery becomes stronger in the six-year interval between the two contacts. Such men can become role models for the generation that succeeds them. The oldest women are less stressed at the third contact than all subgroups except the youngest men, and even at the fifth contact they are below average. They are not as committed to mastery as their male counterparts, but at the final contact they do better than the average of most other groups.

Thus far we have focused on how people who reported different levels of exposure to stress fared in terms of their commitments. The measure of stress was self-reported: we simply asked how much stress they felt they had been exposed to. There are many ways of defining and assessing exposure to stress, however, so before we abandon the topic of stress and commitments, we want to discuss one more set of findings.

In our exploration of stress in Chapter Seven, we found it useful to conceptualize stress in terms of both positive and negative life experiences. This was because even a clearly positive experience may entail some disruptions in life. We first noticed this when we found that our newlywed sample—perhaps the healthiest group during the year before their marriage—were among the sickest the following year. For our study of change in commitments, therefore, we included positive as well as negative indices as possible antecedents of change. We hypothesized that large numbers of negative life events would lead to more commitments to self-protection and fewer commitments to mastery and interpersonal relations. On the other hand, we also felt that large numbers of positive life events might well be associated with an increase in the commitment to mastery and interpersonal relations. It also seemed possible that positive and negative events would interact.

Using a repeated-measures ANOVA design with positive and negative events (both dichotomized) as main effects, we proceeded to examine change in the four commitment categories from the first interview all the way to the final one. We conducted separate analyses for men and for women and combined the empty nest and retirement groups into one older group since our initial reviews showed no significant differences between them. The life-events measure drew on data collected at the third contact pertaining to the year immediately preceding that interview.

Positive and negative life events alone did not affect the commitments of older men, but they did influence those of women. We found that women with more negative events generally demonstrated less commitment to interpersonal relations. These results suggest that stress may create interpersonal barriers—paradoxically at a time when perhaps they have the greatest interpersonal needs. In contrast to the problems imposed by negative events, women with more positive events were generally higher in commitment to moral issues and mastery but lower in self-protectiveness.

On Intimacy as Commitment

When Jean-Paul Sartre was interviewed on his seventieth birthday, he said that his hopes for the future of humanity center on an increased willingness of individuals to yield their subjective selves to others above and beyond any expectation of reciprocity. It remains to be seen whether Sartre is a true prophet, but he did seem to sense the winds of change. Research, the mass media, and, in between, the popularizers of psychology share an increasingly pervasive complaint: lack of genuine communication between the sexes, between generations, and between people in general. Indeed, the remarkable, if not frightening, proliferation of various encounter groups is perhaps the most dramatic consequence of the emotional frustration felt by middle-class Americans, especially women.

Almost no research has been devoted to close relationships in life crises as they are usually defined. One of our research-based observations is that losing a spouse is often more traumatic for men than for women because men are less likely to have really close relationships with anyone but their wives. In fact, men name their spouses as confidants far more often than women do. Some writers claim that men's inability to disclose themselves contributes to their shorter life expectancy. The capacity for intimacy, mutuality, and empathy is also useful in predicting outcomes—for example, the happiest people and those having the fewest symptoms at the third interview are those who ranked high on intimacy at the initial contact. Knowing through experience that one is capable of having an intimate relationship, romantic or otherwise, is expedient in a time of crisis: a former relationship is reinforced and at the same time sustains hope for a future bond. Sometimes it even happens for the first time in late life.

The Four

The theme of Olav Olavsen's entire adult life is wholehearted commitment. He represents a benchmark by which others can be assessed. He ranks high on mastery, as well as moral and interpersonal states of being, at both the third and fifth interviews. Even after he became a widower and lived alone, he refused to feel sorry for himself. (Self-pity would be anathema to him.) A growth-oriented person, he takes courses relevant to his interests whenever he can find them, cooking, woodcarving, needlepoint, gardening. Olav's strongest commitment is to his children and, by the fifth contact, to grandchildren as well.

Hazel Sutter could be called the diametric opposite of Olav. She is a persevering plodder and not at all creative, yet one cannot help but admire her stamina. At all interviews except the last one she ranks high on self-protection—mainly hoping to keep her good health. By the fifth contact, when she has a close male friend, she has transferred her commitment to him.

Max Schindler is the right-wing radical who is also a successful denier. He has had several coronary bypasses (and will have another soon) but feels "just fine." He is fixing up his ranch by himself, and it is hard physical work. If one thumbs through his five protocols, there is nothing about himself, his work, his family, his friends (he of course has no enemies), or anything else that is negative. Either he is making it all up or he is a perfect example of the power of positive thinking.

Adelaide Stone, like Olav, is a strong person and highly committed to those in her life. She was not interviewed at the third contact because she was hospitalized with a stroke that in the long run "made me a better person." Both of her parents died when they were quite young, and she herself has strong premonitions of mortality. Her husband, much older than she, works for a public utility company and will soon have to retire. She wants to get a better secretarial job than the one she has now. Adelaide does not feel committed to her drug-addicted son because he has to steal money, including his mother's, to support the addiction. Although Adelaide is committed to her daughter and proud of her, she has "her own life to live." By the final interview she feels fulfilled. She paints portraits, swims regularly, and considers her sister her closest friend. Adelaide looks forward to doing volunteer work with homeless and hungry people.

Summing Up

In the preceding chapter we saw how goals and values can shape the life course. With this chapter we introduce another factor that may direct people's efforts and, ultimately, their lives: the concept of commitment. Curiously, commitments are unrelated to goals and values. A commitment to mastery was highest in the oldest group of men, for example, but women in the two older groups generally did not feel themselves to have such a commitment. These findings stand in some contrast to the goal of achievement, which seems to become more valued by women in the two older groups.

12

Having Enough
Life Satisfactions:
The Measure of Life's Quality

Many readers will be familiar with such concepts as quality of life, morale, life satisfaction, and psychological well-being. These concepts assess whether a person is doing well or not, and a number of people have been trying to find out for many years. In a study of older men, for example, Ekerdt, Bosse, and Levcoff (1985) discerned two patterns that seem to emerge from the first three years of retirement: compared with those in the first six months of retirement, men retired thirteen to eighteen months had lower levels of life satisfaction and involvement in physical activities. These results were interpreted to indicate the existence of a period of letdown after the first year.

David Gutmann, writing about the trials and tribulations of people in the earlier stages of adulthood, finds that many young people do not expect to live very long; he calls them "presenile youth" (Gutmann, 1972). Drug addiction is only one of their many problems. He finds present-day adolescents, like very old people, to be often depressed. Similarly, Costa and McCrae (1976) report, on the basis of data from the Normative Aging Study, that young men are concerned with their feelings, middle-aged men with their thinking, and old ones try to integrate the two.

Majda Thurnher (1983) uses a very different approach to evaluate the well-being of people and the factors influencing this well-being. Her work is based on the same longitudinal study we use in this book, but it covers eight years instead of twelve. Only two questions were asked: Looking back over the past eight years, what have been the major turning points in your life? What effect did these turning points have on you? Responses were in three categories: positive, neutral, and negative. Only 6 percent felt they had no turning points, a third reported one or two, almost half had three or four, and the rest five or more. Young people averaged four; old people, between one or two. Three-quarters of the young people reported changes in themselves, whereas fewer than a third of the older ones did. Well over half of the sample reported positive change; a fourth were neutral and a fourth were negative.

All these studies—and many more we have not cited—are searching for some means of assessing the well-being of persons in a reasonably comprehensive manner. Although there is no single accepted method, the most likely choice is that of morale as measured by such instruments as the Bradburn (1969) Affect Balance Scale or the Lawton (1972) Philadelphia Geriatric Center Morale Scale. In this chapter we present information on another approach—one that has not received much attention to date but has yielded promising results. This approach is based on what we call the Enough Scale.

When Is Enough Enough?

In the mid-1970s, a member of our research team, Robert Pierce, undertook a cross-sectional study of how people view their lives. Searching for another means of expressing what quality of life is all about, he interviewed ninety-seven persons living in the San Francisco Bay Area and asked them to rate the relevance of 176 attributes to their work and to their favorite free-time activity. After considerable data analysis he came up with eighteen dimensions that were appropriate to both leisure and work. A subsequent study of 259 subjects established the replicability of these dimensions (Pierce, 1980). Based on Pierce's work we put together for our own study a somewhat shorter instrument that included eighteen items, one for each of the eighteen dimensions that emerged in the initial testing—for example, vigorous physical activity, relaxation, achievement, and excitement. At the fourth and fifth interviews, we asked participants whether they got "not enough," "barely enough," "enough," or "more than enough" of each dimension.

Here we will just consider stage differences in the eighteen dimensions as computed separately for men and women. By and large there is not much evidence of life-stage differences. Among the men three dimensions show significant life-stage variation: physical acitivity, play, and peace and quiet. In each case, the high school seniors and retired men were the most likely to feel their needs had been met; the newlywed men showed the least evidence of satisfaction. Among the women three significant differences were also found across the life stages. For both peace and quiet and flamboyance, the high school seniors and newlywed women had equally low satisfaction while the two older groups of women had higher and roughly equal satisfactions of needs. For sensuality, however, the high school women exhibited the greatest satisfaction, newlywed and retirement women had equally low satisfaction (that is, they did not get enough), and the former empty nesters fell in between. Interestingly, among the women the newlyweds tended to be the least satisfied on all dimensions, although this became a significant difference on only three occasions. The results do suggest that the newlywed women are at something of a nadir, and the trends for the newlywed men hint at much the same thing.

Getting Enough: How People Differ

The rest of the chapter is devoted to comparisons of the four young groups with the four older ones in terms of psychological characteristics, affect (mental attitude), intimacy, humor, power, sociability, and, among other items, the capacity for sharing thoughts with others. A few favored spare-time activities conclude this report, in which we find that gender differences are often greater than life-stage differences. As mentioned earlier, participants were instructed to rate themselves as having too much or more than enough, enough, barely enough, or not enough. Gender differences are most striking in the not enough ratings.

Affection. None of the youngest men said they did not have enough affection but five of the youngest women said they did not. The second youngest people were similar in pattern but not markedly so. The next to oldest men included only one who had not enough affection, but five women were in this category. The imbalance between the oldest people was in the same direction. At the other extreme, neither gender nor life stage seems to account for variations. Those rating themselves as having too much or more than enough affection reveal no consistent pattern, but the oldest men are more likely to have more than enough affection than any other group. Fourteen of the four younger groups are in the barely enough category, but only five of the older people are. What does it all mean? It is sobering that women of all ages consistently report feeling they lack sufficient affection, while men, especially the older men, sometimes even report they get too much affection. Such differences emphasize the potential for gender conflict and misunderstanding that has received wide attention in the popular press.

Intimacy. As in the preceding section, again we find that by and large gender differences are more dramatic than those of life stage. The youngest men outdo every other group in complaining about too much or more than enough intimacy. Machismo is what they represent, as do a few of the oldest men. At the not enough level of intimacy we find a similar trend: except for the second youngest people, many more women than men do not feel satisfied; the second oldest women are in the lead. People who complain of barely enough intimacy are mainly in the four younger groups, and more women than men make such complaints. Altogether there were twenty-three such people and they include a few more women than men. Only four older people are in this category, two women and two men. We have discussed this characteristic in another chapter, and the reader is reminded that the word *intimacy* is not limited to husbands and wives but includes friendship, both close and casual.

Humor. Our respondents, as noted elsewhere, do not have much of a sense of humor. Participants supply further evidence of this when asked whether they get enough humor in their lives. If we examine those who complain about too much or more than enough humor, however, we find notable life-stage and gender differences. Thirteen of the youngest people and nearly all of the second youngest men

are found in this category, but there is only one among the second
youngest women. Perhaps having two or three young children in
the house is no laughing matter, and fathers are more likely to
escape such situations except for evenings and weekends. If we add
up totals for the four young groups in the enough category and
compare them with the four older ones, we find they are identical—
rather a rarity in this sample. The barely enough and not enough
groups are relatively few in number among all eight groups except
for the second youngest women, of whom about a third feel they
lack sufficient opportunity to experience humor. Burdened with
young and growing families, but obligated to work in order to
maintain a reasonable standard of living, life for these young
women is noteworthy for its demands, not for its frivolity.

Power. In the competitive world Americans live in, nearly everyone
admires or envies power. That the people in our primarily middle-
class and lower-middle-class sample think they have it, even too
much of it, is an eye-opener. The word *power* itself is ambiguous,
and one thesaurus gives eighteen definitions. To avoid overwhelm-
ing the reader, we will provide just a few examples: authoritative-
ness, control, eloquence, influence, prerogative, and supremacy.
Perhaps *influence* is the synonym most of the sample would select.
A few people confess that they have too much or more than enough
power. Presumably they do not mean that they misuse it but that
they dislike it (something like a bad conscience). That this is a likely
interpretation is supported by the fact that fifteen women and only
seven men have more than enough power.

      People who say they have enough power are not very evenly
distributed either. In each of the four young groups more men than
women vote for power, but the second oldest women feel more
powerful than men. The reverse holds true for the two older groups,
where more men than women say they have enough power. Those
who report "barely enough" are very few and tend to be young.
Only two women in the four younger groups, and no younger men,
did not have enough. The oldest men feel more powerful than their
female counterparts do.

Sociability. Here the findings are a bit enigmatic, especially at the
extremes. Sociability involves associational, communicative, and

friendly associations. Too much or more than enough implies some sort of coercion, perhaps by relatives or friends. More young people than older ones say they have too much or more than enough sociability; the ratio is sixteen to ten. The second youngest women complain more than people in other groups. At the other end of the spectrum only nine people say they do not have enough, and they are rather evenly distributed in terms of young and old people. Those having enough social interaction show very few life-stage differences and include a majority of all subgroups except for the second oldest men, of whom only two socialize enough and about half are in the barely enough category. In many other contexts as well, they seem to complain a lot, especially about working too long and hard.

Superiority. Considering the demographics of our sample, that so many of them feel superior is an unexpected surprise. At the fourth interview nearly all of the youngest men feel that way, and a few years later (final interview) only two have dropped out of this category. The youngest women are only a bit more modest. In fact, at the fourth interview most members of each subgroup are what may be called egotists, which may be a conscious or unconscious way of boosting their morale. By the final interview men and women in the youngest group have become more modest, but the second youngest ones feel even more superior. The egos of the four older groups are by no means weakened by age, except that the women do not feel quite so superior as the men at the third contact. The final interview finds the second oldest women feeling more superior than men do, but the oldest men are superior to the oldest women: the ratio is seventeen to twelve. Those indicating barely enough and not enough show a different pattern: the youngest men all feel superior at the fourth contact, but a few years later a few of them are more modest. Quite a few of the youngest women do not feel superior at the fourth contact, and even more of them are in that category at the fifth. The next to youngest people reveal sharper gender differences: only two men but six women say they have barely enough or not enough at the fourth contact, but by the fifth the ratio has improved for women.

The older groups distribute themselves a bit differently. At

the fourth interview a few of the second oldest men and women say
they have barely enough or not enough superiority, and at the fifth
contact the women have doubled (but not the men). The oldest
people differ by gender: several men feel superior at the fourth contact, and a few years later only three feel they have not enough or
barely enough superiority. The women do not change: at both times
only three of them fall in the barely enough or not enough category.
As noted in other chapters, the oldest women become more self-
confident and assertive with time.

Sensuality. Myth and fact tend to agree that both age and gender
make a difference in regard to sensuality and love. Our respondents
may or may not have defined sensuality in terms of sexuality. Judging from how the data are distributed, they may have even defined
it in terms of making love. When we examine the distribution on
these psychological needs at both the fourth and fifth contacts, we
will see there is quite a lot of change in most of the eight groups.
In this section both life stage and gender are significant.
     A majority of the youngest men have enough or more than
enough sensuality at the fourth contact, and at the final interview
there are even more of them. Conversely, very few rate themselves as
having barely enough or not enough at the third contact, and only
two of them do so at the fifth contact. The youngest women may be
more bashful than men. For whatever reason, at the third contact well
over a third of them check the too much or more than enough category; at the last session fewer of them do so. Perhaps as they grow
older they become better acquainted with their interviewer and can
say what they really think. As for the other extreme (barely enough
or not enough), the two youngest groups do not disagree: there are
very few of them in that category. The second youngest people also
have important gender differences. At the third contact the majority
of men and women alike have enough sensuality. A few years later
(final interview) men dominate the scene: half or more have enough
sensuality, but only six women feel that way. Most of these women
have two or more almost adolescent children, and the devout Cathol-
ics among them think that is enough. No more sensuality is appropriate. The other end of the continuum gives us complementary
information. A few of the second youngest men have barely enough

or not enough sensuality at the fourth contact, but most of their female counterparts feel that way. At the fifth contact the gender gap is even wider: nearly twice as many women as men have barely enough or not enough sensuality.

The older people are not much different than the younger ones. At the fourth interview just about as many next to oldest men as women have enough or more than enough sensuality, and they add up to about half of the people in each subgroup. At the fifth contact the women outnumber men on this score. The other side of the coin is obvious: barely enough or not enough accounts for only five men and four women at the fourth interview, but there is a change at the fifth—distinctly more women than men have enough sensuality. There is a slight difference between the sexes as to barely enough or not enough at the fourth contact, but at the fifth the women far outnumber the men. The oldest people are not uninterested in sensuality. At both times their interest is only slightly less than that of the second oldest group. Men and women, at both times, do not differ more than one digit. On the other side of the scale, barely enough or not enough sensuality, ten men and nine women complain at the fourth contact, but the ratio is only six to four at the final contact. There are many ways of making love.

Risk. Risk implies that a person likes to court danger, peril, and uncertainty. One would not expect danger to appeal to any subgroup in our sample except, perhaps, the youngest men when they were seniors in high school (first contact) and ony a few of the second youngest men. Yet at the fourth contact fourteen of the youngest men and eighteen women say they take enough or more than enough risks. Obviously these youngest people enjoy taking chances. A few years later (fifth contact) there is no change among the youngest men, but quite a few of the youngest women feel less inclined to take risks. Conversely, at the fourth contact a few of the youngest men and women say they are not risky enough. Perhaps they are timid or irresolute. At the final interview the timidity ratio is six men to seven women. The second youngest people are more fickle. At the fourth contact only twelve men but seventeen women are risk-takers, and by the fifth they have declined to ten and twelve. At the other end of the scale (barely or not enough), there are more

men than women at the fourth contact but the genders are equal by
the final interview. By adding up these four young groups we can
later compare them with the older ones. To simplify the matter we
use data from the final interview only. In this way we learn that the
younger women take more risks than men and do not have enough
opportunity to do so.

Among the older men and women there is a wider difference
both by gender and by life stage. Only two of the second oldest men
think they take too many risks, while three times as many women
do so. The oldest men far outrank the women in taking risks—quite
the opposite of the second oldest people. Adding it all up we find
that the four younger groups reveal only slight differences, but there
are more older women than older men who take chances. Statistics
garnered from states where gambling is legal indicate that at least
as many women as men devote themselves to winning the jackpot.

Transcendence. This concept has a long history. Ralph Waldo
Emerson (1803–1882), the leading spokesperson for transcendental-
ism in this country and England, emphasized the intuitive and spiritual above the empirical. Transcendence is defined on the Enough
Scale as "experiences where you lose track of time, get entirely absorbed, and get outside of yourself." It includes something like
Transcendental Meditation. Our data suggest there are enough
changes in our sample to make it worthwhile to include the fourth
as well as the fifth interview. At the fourth contact the youngest men
and women consider transcendence in both enough and not enough
terms, but the barely and not enough categories predominate for
both men and women. At the fifth contact there is little change
except that one woman reports a transcendental experience. Perhaps during the three and a half years between interviews they have
been obliged to become more practical. The next to youngest respondents are very different from each other. At the fourth contact
over half of the men say they have more than enough and nearly
all the women report barely enough or not enough. Their adolescent children require a watchful eye, and that usually takes some
doing. By the fifth interview life is different. Of the second youngest
men three-fourths say they feel transcendent. Most of them by now
have had promotions; many are so absorbed in their work that they

lose track of time. The second youngest women at the fourth contact include a majority who do not achieve a transcendent state of being, but a few years later they outdo their male counterparts. By this time several have part-time jobs that keep them engrossed.

There are generational chasms in regard to transcendence among the older groups compared to the younger ones, but before we analyze them we should review the facts. At the fourth contact a majority of the second oldest men are in the enough category; only a few report barely enough or not enough. Their female counterparts are equally divided: one half report enough or more than enough, the other half barely or not enough. The oldest men feel much more transcendent than any other group, whereas the oldest women feel the least so. Most of them experience barely or not enough transcendence. In Emerson's terms, they are neither intuitive nor spiritual. A few years later (final interview) we find significant changes in some but none to speak of in others. The second oldest men change very little and for the better. Their female counterparts change a great deal: more than twice as many of them rank higher transcendence at the fifth contact than at the fourth. Perhaps they realize they are not going to live forever and have become more spiritual. The oldest men change very little: only two of them feel less transcendent. Twice as many of the oldest women feel transcendent at the fifth contact as did so at the fourth.

Sharing with Others. Sharing may best be defined as having a harmonious relationship with at least one other person. It may involve harmony, sympathy, empathy, mutuality, reciprocity, compatibility, or all of the above. We look first at all the subgroups at the fourth interview. Most of the youngest men feel they have done enough sharing; only six of them report barely or not enough. The youngest women are rather different: most of them feel they have had enough or more than enough sharing. The second youngest men rank themselves considerably lower on sharing than do the youngest ones. Women in the same stage of life, for the most part, rate themselves high but not quite so high as the youngest women. In both of these younger groups women surpass men. The second oldest men and women make identical ratings of themselves, but there are fewer sharing types among them than in the younger groups. The oldest men rank higher than any other group on sharing; the oldest women lag far behind them.

The final interview reveals some changes. Fewer of the youngest men rank high on sharing but more of the youngest women do so. The second youngest men rank lower on sharing at the fifth interview than at the fourth and so do women. On the other hand, the second oldest men become more inclined to share than at the fourth contact and so do their female counterparts, but the oldest men and women are a bit less inclined to do so.

New Experiences. New experiences probably include a great variety of novelties. We can only speculate about their substance. Almost certainly men seek out different experiences than do women, and younger people look for different ones than their elders. The youngest men who know how to play baseball might decide to try football. The youngest women might decide to have a child or learn how to use a computer. The oldest men may get tired of their hobbies and decide to take a trip to a place they have never been. The oldest women may shift from doing volunteer work—say at an SPCA—to taking a course in literature at a junior college.

All we can assume is that people reporting barely or not enough new experiences at the fourth contact will be in the enough category at the final interview. Beginning as usual with the youngest men, at the fourth contact thirteen of them (a good majority) have had enough new experiences but nine have not. They have not changed much by the fifth contact except that two of them have shifted from enough to barely enough, suggesting that they have become less enterprising. At the fourth contact the youngest women are somewhat more stimulated to seek new experiences than their male counterparts, but by the fifth they lag far behind them—no doubt because the full-time job of mothering infant children leaves them no time to seek novelty. Most of the second youngest men have had enough novelty in their lives at both times. Women in the same life stage are exactly the same as men at the fourth contact but lag behind them a little at the fifth. Overall, these four younger groups enjoy new experiences.

Some of the older people find new experiences challenging; others, more set in their ways, do not. At the fourth contact most of the second oldest men are challenged by new experiences, but by the fifth contact only five of them are in that category. As noted in other contexts, presumably they are working hard at their jobs and trying for promotions so their retirement pay will provide enough money to live comfortably. The trend is similar among the second oldest women, but their changes are not so drastic. Nearly all of the oldest men have retired by the fourth contact, and at both times all but a handful are enjoying new experiences and do not change at all. The women in this group are very similar to the men and do not change much either.

Intellectual Challenge. It might be more appropriate to call this section challenging the intelligence because there are only four or five bona fide intellectuals in the sample. Nevertheless, there are many intelligent people here, though some of them have had only a high school education. We do not know their intelligence quotients. What we do know is that any organ that does not get used wears out. Apparently the youngest men do exercise their brains, since more of them feel challenged at the fifth contact than at the fourth. Conversely, twice as many of them feel they have had barely enough or not enough challenge at the fourth contact as at the fifth. Again, the youngest women resemble the men in some respects but not in others. At the fourth contact their ratio of too much versus too little is fourteen to eleven; at the fifth contact it is seven to fourteen. Apparently their brains need more exercise. Few of the second youngest men have had enough mental challenge at the fourth contact (the ratio is seven to fourteen), but they have turned themselves around by the fifth contact, when the balance is fifteen to four. Most of the women in the same stage of life have had too little challenge at the fourth contact: their ratio of enough versus not enough is nine to thirteen. They are still on the down side at the fifth interview.

The older people on the whole are less well educated than the younger ones, but many of them told us they learned much more in high school than their children did in a two-year college. At the fourth contact the second oldest men include a slight majority who feel challenged, but several report barely enough or not enough challenge. They of course are still working, but many have boring jobs and nine do not feel intellectually challenged. At the fifth contact fewer of them answer the question, perhaps because some have retired. Yet there are other modes of challenge having nothing to do with work. Reading good books is one way to feel mentally stimulated; watching stimulating television programs, doing crossword puzzles, and learning to play chess are other ways. At the fourth contact the second oldest women are evenly divided: half of them have had enough mental stimulation, half barely or not enough. Three years later a majority of them are dissatisfied with the amount of mental stimulation they are getting. Most of the oldest people are retired by the fourth contact and doing "their own thing," which may not have anything to do with mental challenge. In any case, most of the oldest men have had enough mental challenge at both times. The oldest women feel differently: well over half have had barely enough or not enough mental challenges at both times. That they can do something about it does not seem to occur to them.

Excitement. Excitement is an emotional characteristic that may be positive or negative—never neutral. It is yet another word that is ambiguous and therefore difficult to analyze. It includes stimulation, exhilaration, sensation, and titillation but also agitation, perturbation, and trepidation. Here we assume that our respondents interpret it simply as having fun. At the fourth contact the youngest men's ratio of enough versus not enough is thirteen to nine; they obviously have had more fun by the fifth contact, when it is fifteen to four. The youngest women's ratio at the fourth contact is similar to the men's, but, unlike them, by the fifth contact several have infants to care for, which they may or may not consider fun.

The second youngest men are not quite as fun-loving: at the fourth contact their ratio is twelve to nine, but it has increased considerably three years later—no doubt because their children are getting old enough to play with. The second youngest women have had little time for fun. At the fourth contact their ratio is fourteen to eight and has deteriorated to ten to eleven by the fifth contact. Unlike the men, as their children grow older they are too busy for fun; grandparents are people who have fun with the children. The second oldest men seem to enjoy life more. At the fourth contact their ratio is fifteen to seven and a few years later it is even better.

The second oldest women are much like their male counterparts: the majority of them are having fun at both times.

The oldest people have more time to have fun. We find the oldest men with a ratio of twenty to three at the fourth contact and seventeen to four at the fifth. The oldest women are a contrast to the men, representing the negative states listed earlier—agitation, perturbation, and trepidation—at both the fourth and fifth interviews.

Relieving Tension. As we discussed in Chapter Seven, certain activities can help an individual vent his or her frustrations and defuse stress. Many of the same activities also serve to enhance an individual's physical fitness, while others may provide a more quiet and contemplative means of stress reduction. Here we will consider four topics from the Enough Scale that may help individuals relieve their tensions. The younger and older groups are considered separately, to accentuate not only age differences but also common characteristics within these two broad age groupings. The topics we include are:

- Vigorous exercise
- Flamboyance
- Peace and quiet
- Play

We begin, then, with the younger groups and vigorous exercise. At the fourth contact, the youngest and second youngest men are very similar: about a third of each group have barely enough or not enough exercise. By the last interview there are only five who have barely or not enough. On the other hand, at both the fourth and fifth contacts about a third feel they get "too much" or "more than enough" exercise. This is in part due to work and life-style. Some of these men have jobs that involve lifting heavy machinery or packing boxes for shipping. While the youngest and second youngest women cook, clean house, and nurture children, they are more sedentary than the men; they entertain only vague hopes of even being able to take a walk. More than two-thirds of them have barely or not enough exercise at the fourth contact, and three years later sixteen out of twenty-two report having barely or not enough.

Flamboyant people are eager, zestful, and energetic, and some of them like to show off a little. At the fourth contact six of the youngest men think they are not flamboyant enough and there are seven who think so at the last interview. The youngest women report a greater deficit: at both interviews about a third of these women wish they were more flamboyant. Of the second youngest men, about three-fourths feel sufficiently flamboyant at both the fourth and final contacts, suggesting that it may be a permanent characteristic. Their female counterparts are different: more than half of them do not feel flamboyant at either interview.

Although one might assume that flamboyance is an antonym of peace and quiet, we found that both qualities are valued in fairly equal proportions by our younger participants. For example, looking only at data from the final interview, we find, among the youngest men, thirteen enjoy flamboyance and fourteen like peace and quiet. Thirteen of the youngest women prefer flamboyance and fifteen favor peace and quiet. Most of the second youngest men like being flamboyant, but half need peace and quiet as well. Half of the second youngest women are in the flamboyant category and more than half need peace and quiet. Rather than being contradictory, this evidence could confirm the hypothesis that perhaps a person who is flamboyant by day might like to have peace and quiet in the evening.

We turn now to the category of play. When asked, people in our sample define play as an activity they undertake in order to have fun. The kinds of playful activities they actually participate in vary widely: the youngest men may like to play baseball; the middle-aged women may prefer bridge; the oldest men might like to take the bus to Reno and play the slot machines. Nine of the youngest men have enough time to play; eight do not. By contrast, a significant majority of the youngest women have enough playtime, perhaps teaching their young children how to use crayons or playing the games given them by doting grandparents.

The children of the second youngest people are too old to need help in playing. Ten of the second youngest men think they play enough; eight do not. The enterprising men who get to play enough may take advantage of free tennis courts available in the neighborhood in which they live, or use a nearby swimming pool.

Almost half of the second youngest women do not get to play enough. With their children now in school some of them do part-time work.

Recapitulating, we find that the four youngest groups differ most by gender. For convenience we summarize here using only information from the final interview and focus on people who report getting barely or not enough. The youngest and second youngest people are combined—that is, we add up the scores of the youngest and second youngest men and then do the same for the women. Many more women than men complain of lack of exercise. As to flamboyance, almost twice as many women as men claim they do not have enough. The situation is reversed when it comes to peace and quiet: almost twice as many men as women do not have enough. Play is the only category in which they are in complete agreement.

Turning to the second oldest and oldest groups, we find that most of the second oldest and oldest men do not have enough exercise at the fourth interview but by the final interview more of them not only are satisfied but are doing work-outs by themselves or at a local gym. They apparently are paying heed to the message of health promotors: one of these men attributed his increased activity to "post-middle-aged spread" that had become the subject of jokes at the office.

All but one of the second oldest men feel flamboyant at the fourth contact, but three years later there are several who do not feel that way at all. They begin to suffer from what, in the vernacular, are called the insults of aging. Women in the same stage of life provide an interesting contrast: at the fourth interview nearly all of them feel flamboyant and only a few are dropouts at the final contact. The oldest people must have discarded their inhibitions: most of them, including women, seem to revel in flamboyance.

Peace and quiet and play are the two variables left to analyze, and in a way they complement each other. Most of the second oldest men at both times have enough peace and quiet, but six of them do not. All six are still working and the lack of peace and quiet seems to originate at work. The second oldest women at the fourth contact resemble men: the great majority of them have enough peace and quiet. By the fifth interview these women have the advantage: several more of them have enough peace and quiet. It seems to be that when men say they do not have enough peace and quiet, they mean at work, not at home. Once they get home, they want to be pampered.

Very old people, folklore tells us, need lots of peace and quiet, but our respondents belie the myth. At the fourth contact only three of the twenty-four oldest men have barely or not enough peace and quiet and three years later only two of them feel that way. At the fourth contact the oldest women differ from the men in that six out of twenty women do not have enough quiet. However, by the fifth contact this gender difference evaporates and only one of them complains about lack of peace and quiet.

As to play, interpreted here simply as having fun, the second oldest and oldest men are like the younger people: at the fourth contact only five of them complain about not having enough fun and games, and a few years later only three do so. The older women are a bit more extreme, but their overall pattern is similar. Seven complain of barely enough or not enough play at the fourth contact but only four of them voice a similar complaint three years later. It is good to know that for many people growing old does not necessarily preclude playing, whether it is sedentary, such as checkers or chess, or physical activity, such as fishing, hiking, or golf.

As we review these findings on whether people get more or less than enough in basic dimensions of life, the message, it seems to us, is to stay alert to the possibilities of the givens. Whether sick or well, young or old, rich, poor, or overworked, our participants are making the best of what they are given, whether they are getting more or less than enough.

Relation of Enough to Morale

We wanted to find out, of course, whether our new measure of satisfaction might be tapping a meaningful aspect of life. One way of finding out was to consider the relationship of the Enough Scale's items to the morale of respondents. To do this we developed a comprehensive measure of morale that summed information from three instruments: the "dissatisfied" and "unhappy" items from the Adjective Rating List, the Bradburn Morale Scale's overall happiness question, and the participant's rating of satisfaction with the present year of life (Lowenthal, Thurnher, Chiriboga, and Associates, 1975). Overall, our findings suggest that satisfaction of needs has very little to do with morale among our younger participants but has a lot to do with it in the two older stages.

The Youngest and Second Youngest Groups. The only significant relationship (using analysis of variance) was found for the youngest men: those who reported they got more than enough flamboyance in their lives were the happiest. This finding makes sense in light of what we already know about these young men.

For the second youngest men we found two dimensions of satisfaction to relate to overall happiness: peace and quiet and relaxation. The formerly newlywed men could not get enough relaxation; those who reported they had more than enough relaxation were the happiest. None of these men reported they had more than enough peace and quiet, but those with enough of it were happiest. Another look at the data suggests at least a partial explanation: most of these men were now parents, and it appears that a major accomplishment during the parental years may be getting enough peace and quiet to restore one's sanity.

For the second youngest group of women the message is somewhat different. It seems important for these women to get enough, but not more than enough, of feelings of superiority over others and feelings of self-sufficiency. These women seem to be struggling to establish an independent identity of worth akin to Erikson's stage of industry versus inferiority. The only dimension for which these women evidently could not get enough satisfaction was sensuality: here the women who reported "more than enough" were happiest.

The Second Oldest Group. There were strikingly different patterns of satisfaction between the second oldest men and women. These middle-aged men could not get enough peace and quiet; they also could not get enough sensuality, transcendence (or engrossment), and achievement. Reading the cases suggests that these men are facing the beginning of a gradual decline, both physical and social. Achievements at work, for example, are harder and harder to come by. On the other hand, enough was indeed enough for the dimensions of creative activity and spirituality, where those who reported getting enough were definitely happier than those who got either more than enough or less than enough.

Among the second oldest group of women, in contrast, happiness declines with increased peace and contentment; the happiest were those with not enough peace and quiet. Moreover, they could not get enough novelty and new experiences. Many of these were women presiding over the so-called empty nest. One gets the sense that for years they have been constrained by tradition and family obligations but suddenly find themselves freed of many responsibilities in a society that now accepts women as equals.

This surge of excitement and interest in the world does not, however, seem to hold true for their male counterparts. In fact, although the relationship reached only the trend level of probability ($p = .10$), men who get not enough or barely enough novelty were the happiest. Moreover, unlike the men, these women could not get enough intellectual challenge, creative activity, or excitement. And, like their male peers, they could not get enough achievement and sensuality.

The Oldest Group. Among the oldest people, all of whom had entered their years of retirement, the differences between men and women are less obvious. For the oldest men there is a continuation of the trend, found among the second oldest men, toward not being able to get enough relaxation. Similarly, those with enough play in their activities were the happiest. (None of them reported more than enough, while nineteen of the twenty-four reported having just enough play.) Novelty is important for these men, but in moderation: barely enough seems better than enough. Feeling superior, on the other hand, is definitely a dimension on which they cannot get enough, as is the case for sensuality (refuting for the nth time the myth about the lack of sensuality and sexuality in older persons).

For the oldest group of women, the need dimensions are more frequently associated with happiness than for any other group. Physical activity plays a role in their morale, but the association is complex. Those who do not get enough physical activity are actually the happiest, although those with enough come in a close second. No one reports having more than enough. Enough is enough, however, for peace and quiet: those with more than enough peace and quiet are less happy than those who simply report enough. While this finding strikes us as reinforcing what we reported for the second oldest women, the oldest group is not as enthusiastic and venturesome. The findings suggest that these women, unlike the second youngest, might have too much novelty and new experiences. Play is now an important factor: the more play, the higher the morale.

Similarly, the oldest women find that enough is enough in regard to creativity, self-sufficiency, and transcendence (or engrossment in self or situation). Like the oldest men, they apparently cannot get enough feelings of superiority—a pair of findings that suggests this is a dimension of growing importance for people in later life. Activities that provide feelings of superiority may therefore combat the usual connotations of aging.

Finally, the dimension of sharing presents a dramatic variation from the usual pattern of relationships: the oldest women are happier when they have less of it. The happiest, in fact, are those with not enough sharing, and the least happy are those with enough or more than enough. An examination of the cases reveals that many of those who feel they have enough or more than enough sharing are those who are having to contend with newly retired husbands. Thus having to share may become a source of marital discord among those who are making the transition into the retirement years.

The Four

Although Olav Olavsen is one of the most genuinely religious persons we encounter in the study, at the last two contacts he reports not having enough opportunity for spirituality. He also feels consistently in need of more opportunity for sharing with others, achievement, and creative activity. Generally he reports more of his needs being met at the fifth contact (twelve items) than at the fourth (three items). The lack of satisfaction reported at the fourth contact, of course, may well have involved his wife's prolonged hospitalization and comatose state. Thus, once again, we find evidence of Olav's movement toward a resolution of his wife's illness and subsequent death.

Hazel Sutter's life is "on a roll" as we follow her in our study. Filling out the Enough Scale for the first time in the next-to-last interview, she reports having enough in fourteen of the eighteen items. She gets more than enough vigorous physical exercise and not enough play and sharing with others. By the fifth and final interview she is still reporting enough in fourteen items, but the pattern is now slightly different. She is now getting enough play and sharing with others, but she is getting "more than enough" self-sufficiency, riskiness, and transcendence. In other comments we learn that she is definitely the boss in her newfound relationship but rather wishes that this, and the self-sufficiency it demands, were not the case. On the whole, though, Hazel is one of the most satisfied of all our participants, young or old.

If Hazel is one of the top five most satisfied participants, Max Schindler is one of the top one or two. At the fourth interview he rates himself as getting enough on sixteen items and more than enough on two: vigorous physical activity and transcendence. Both the physical activity and the transcendence draw from his experiences on the farm he has purchased recently. Farm work, Max has discovered, is seemingly endless and draining. By the fifth interview Max reports getting too much in one area, vigorous physical activity, and more than enough creative activity. Again the farm is proving to be a physical and now a creative challenge. Otherwise we see a very satisfied man who has probably realized his life ambition: he has bought the farm in the best sense of that expression.

From the fourth to the fifth contacts, Adelaide Stone reports that her unmet needs have increased from seven to nine. Even more sobering, at both times this formerly exuberant and outgoing woman reports not getting enough of a number of activities that used to be an important part of her life: play, new experiences, intellectual challenge, sensuality, and riskiness (that is, taking chances). From the fourth to fifth contacts she moves from reporting not enough to barely enough creative activity, but when we last see her she feels she does not get enough physical activity, achievement, or excitement. At both points she reports getting too much relaxation and peace and quiet. All in all, the information on the

Enough Scale substantiates what we have already surmised: Adelaide Stone is being constrained by a life-style in fundamental opposition to her needs and temperament.

Summing Up

We have touched on a number of points in this chapter, all of them bearing on how our participants feel about their lives, and conclude with a brief discussion of two issues. The first concerns the differences in what is most salient for morale among the second oldest group of men and women. The second issue concerns the oldest people and the fine line they must walk between peace and quiet, on the one hand, and boredom, on the other.

The differences between the second oldest men and women are particularly intriguing because they reflect two very different orientations to activities and perhaps to life in general. The middle-aged men are very concerned with the reduction of stimulation and change. Many of them seem to want only peace and quiet, with just enough creative activity to keep life from becoming boring. In contrast, the middle-aged women can hardly get enough novelty, intellectual challenge, excitement, and creativity. The case histories suggest that these gender differences are associated with certain realities of middle age. For the men, a growing sense of stalled careers, declining achievements, and impending retirement is leading to a growing dissatisfaction with the demands of the workaday world. The middle-aged women, on the other hand, are experiencing the departure of their children as an opportunity to seek new challenges. There is a growing recognition of one's potential—particularly for those who have, until now, dedicated their lives to caring for others.

Whether or not these opposing directions will lead to marital conflict and misunderstanding seems to depend on the individuals and how well they know each other. Certainly these opposing directions of development are not something we alone have discovered—they have been talked about in the literature for some time. The work of Carl Jung, as expanded in the writings of Gutmann and others, reinforces the idea that men and women may make substantial changes in their interests and activities as they enter the second half of life. We should emphasize, though, that the reasons for these changes seem embedded in the experiential histories of the people themselves and do not occur in some preordained fashion.

Turning to another topic—the configuration of needs we found to be most associated with morale among the oldest subjects—we find a different message. For these persons there is apparently a fragile balance between the peace and quiet they seem to value and boredom. The finding among both men and women that some degree of novelty or creative activity (but not much) is enough implies that these dimensions provide the minimal stimulation necessary to keep tranquillity from translating into what seems to be a prime stressor of later life: boredom.

13

Epilogue:
Charting Change and Continuity
over the Life Course

As we look back over the many topics and lives introduced in this book, we find ourselves concluding that the trajectory of life, after the early biological imperative plays itself out, may lie increasingly at the mercy of what Shakespeare called the "slings and arrows of outrageous fortune." This in itself is certainly not a new conclusion. As early as the 1970s Bernice Neugarten (1977) was advancing the notion that social stressors are an appropriate topic for life-course research, and chance events have been suggested as important contributors to development (Gergen, 1975; Baltes and Baltes, 1980). In his landmark work on children of the Great Depression, moreover, Glen Elder (1974) clearly demonstrated the salience of societal upheaval for the life course.

Our research, however, has focused on the ordinary, day-to-day stresses that affect people's lives in unspectacular but very real ways. While we have certainly included the catastrophic stressors like bereavement and retirement and the Great Depression, our objective has been to examine a wide variety of stressors, some major and some minor, representing all levels of the stress paradigm: micro, meso, and macro. Such stressors are conventionally examined solely for their immediate impact on mental health, especially depression. What we have sought to evaluate is the idea that ordinary

281

stressors may not only exert an immediate effect on well-being but may lead to enduring alterations in the life course.

It may seem to the reader that any compelling evidence that day-to-day stressors can affect the trajectory of life would make non-sense of the idea of adult development. In other words, if our lives are indeed shaped by seemingly random events, there can be no predictability to life. And if there is no predictability to life, what need is there for a science of human development?

What we found, however, is that an emphasis upon the role of social and health stressors does not necessarily imply that adult development is chaotic. For one thing, stressors are not necessarily random events but exhibit levels of continuity over time—suggesting either that certain people may be predisposed to certain kinds of stress or that there is continuity in the kinds of conditions that generate stress. Max Schindler, for example, felt hassled for many years by the same kind of stress at work: the presence of poorly trained minority workers, what he considered unfair hiring practices, and general mismanagement higher up. Olav Olavsen, in contrast, for many years went through life without any major stress.

Our analyses also suggest that continuity is more or less the norm for most variables relating to personal functioning and, moreover, that continuity is evident in the absence of disruptive factors. This conclusion is based on our finding that for personal characteristics as diverse as psychological symptomatology and morale and self-concept, people exhibited substantially greater continuity over time if they experienced little exposure to stress. Stressors, in other words, disrupt continuity; depending on the circumstances, they are catalysts for change.

The role of stress may become greater at those times when the sources of continuity lose their strength—and the key sources of continuity may begin to wane in importance during the middle and later years. Consider, for example, William Henry's (1971, p. 126) suggestion that work is "the central and most binding continuity of the years between age twenty and seventy." We would agree that work is an important source of continuity, as is the family, but there is evidence that both family and work may gradually weaken as binders of continuity during middle age as children leave and the worker nears retirement (Neugarten, 1969; Chiriboga, 1989). Health also seems to be a binder of continuity. Consider where Adelaide Stone might have been at the fifth interview were it not for her massive and crippling stroke, or where Max Schindler might be if he had in fact suffered such a stroke.

In the following pages we want to discuss several themes that emerge from our study—all of which underscore the pivotal role of stress in adult development. Keep in mind that developmental studies of stress cannot readily be made with the typical short-term study, since the significance of exposure to stress may only become evident when people are followed over considerable lengths of time. As Elder and Clipp (1988, p. 133) note, "the full consequences of human experience, especially extremely traumatic ones, are often expressed across the life span and even into successive generations."

The Study of Change

A focus upon the disruptive potential of stress, as we have suggested, does not negate the considerable evidence of regularity in people's progression from one stage of life to the next. As we followed the lives of our participants, we too found evidence suggesting the evolution of behavior and sense of self and supporting the works of such theorists as Jung and Erikson. At the same time, our study enables us to trace reciprocal interactions among several aspects of living and to view life as process. The majority of our older men, for example, reached their occupational peak in middle age. By late middle age they were thoroughly bored with their work routines and looking forward to rest, relaxation, recreation, pampering by their wives, and often a degree of hedonism. During the same span of time many of their female counterparts manifest signs of growth, including increased autonomy and independence, and a sometimes exuberant quest for new experiences.

The evidence for continuous and reciprocal transactions between the person and the environment, which we have found in both quantitative data and the study of cases, does not cast the person into a passive role at all. Rather, the evidence supports in many ways the viewpoint of Albert Bandura (1978, p. 356): "People are not only perceivers, knowers, and actors. They are also self-reactors with capacities for reflective self-awareness that are generally neglected in information-processing theories based on computer models of human functioning." Consider, for example, the many years of effort that Max Schindler devoted to his quest for not only an early retirement but a life that in fact proved compatible with his needs and desires: his dream. At the same time, life can certainly deal an uneven hand on occasion. As in the case of Adelaide Stone, the notion of a "kicked in the butt" syndrome does seem to explain why at times people are forced into a more accommodating and reactive role. Among our participants this syndrome seemed most likely to appear when the stressor was secondary to a major health problem such as stroke or cancer.

Physical Versus Social Stress. One theme we found in our research was that health problems are not only major stressors in and of themselves but tend to precipitate a chain of secondary stressors. The onset of a serious health problem, especially during the later years, leaves a characteristic signature: the loss of a sense of personal security, a heightened sense of vulnerability, acceleration of the psychological process of aging. Here is Adelaide Stone's response when asked, at the final interview, what things she does really well: "I don't think I do anything really well anymore. Since the stroke . . . it took something away from me. I don't know what I can do really well." Her personal insecurity, still growing some three years after the stroke, is revealed in many ways. Adelaide now adds "driving" to the Hassles Checklist, for example. When asked why, she replies: "I know I can drive but now it scares the hell out of me." One gets the sense that the stroke precipitated a downward spiral in self-esteem and self-confidence that continues unchecked and is a major reason why Adelaide now considers life in a retirement home to be a reasonable option.

In contrast, it appears that a lifetime of experience in dealing with social stressors often results in some expertise in coping with problems—or at least a habitual approach to dealing with them, whether it be to indulge in an alcoholic binge or take direct action. Olav Olavsen is a man whose characteristic approach to stress exposure can be classified as challenged. He never seeks or creates problems, but when they present themselves he deals with them simply and directly and effectively. Faced with the extremely grave health problems of his beloved wife, and her subsequent death, Olav reacts with uncharacteristic depression and other symptoms of psychological disturbance. Three years later he still mourns her loss but is putting together a new life and is actually beginning to enjoy it.

Social Change and the Life Course. Understanding the lives of people in any age group is certainly not a simple matter. Curiously, we found that the normative transitions defining the study did not themselves provide much in the way of a catalyst for change. Normative transitions, by their very nature, can be anticipated long before they occur and thus give people ample time to prepare. Moreover, most normative transitions are either ambiguous or positive— and as we found in our research, positive stressors have a generally weaker effect overall, one that is restricted basically to increments in positive affect. Thus it was the unanticipated events that most often brought upheaval and change.

At the same time, as we looked at our data and examined individual cases, it was evident that even among this relatively stable, lower-middle-class group of people, social trends were having an impact. Apparently even the timing of normative transitions is becoming more variable now than in the past. We can see this even in the age distribution of our subgroups: while the high school seniors exhibit a tight age clustering, the spread of years represented in each successive transition group (newlyweds, empty nesters, and retirement stagers) is much more extensive. This wider age range for the same normative transition is a reflection of our changing world. Over the past two decades, social and technological changes have caused dramatic shifts in the way adults around the world live out their lives.

Three social trends often cited are those reflected in marriage, divorce, and death rates. The marriage rate per thousand persons in the United States has shown a zigzag pattern of decline ever since the beginning of our study, while the divorce rate continued a dramatic increase but then leveled off. The death rate, on the other hand, has demonstrated minor but reasonably steady increments. These social indicators tell us that the social dimension of adult life is gradually changing and that a variety of new patterns may be emerging in American society. We are witnessing, for example, a steady increase in the prevalence of adults who are divorced. In the long run, this trend may lead to greater numbers of older adults without social supports, since their remarriage rates are quite low, especially among older women like Adelaide Stone.

The emerging patterns are not necessarily consistent. Among certain socioeconomic groups, for example, there is a trend toward earlier marriage and parenthood. In fact, one out of every five children born in America today is born to a teenage mother (Jones and others, 1986). One long-term consequence has been that grandparenthood for many is commencing in the middle forties or even earlier. At the same time, growing numbers of adults, interested in furthering themselves personally or professionally, are marrying later, having children in their later twenties and early thirties, and can expect to become grandparents much later in life. The result is an increasing diversity in progress through the life course—due in part to greater participation by women in the labor force as well as to the development of birth control pills and other contraceptive devices.

As Neugarten and Neugarten (1986, p. 33) have noted, we are witnessing "the blurring of life periods." The next time you visit the supermarket, you may encounter, while strolling down the aisles, newborn infants with mothers who are aged fifteen and sixteen and newborn infants with mothers aged thirty-five to forty. At vacation resorts you may encounter newlyweds in their late teens as well as newlyweds in their fifties and sixties and seventies. You may encounter, in fact, grandparents in their early forties as well as parents in their sixties and seventies who are still waiting for their children to settle down and get married.

Too Many Options, Not Enough Choices. The implications of this blurring of age distinctions are immense. One way of interpreting the situation, for example, is that there is now at least the appearance of a greater individualization of the life course, with each of us having access to more options and choices. But the greater availability of options has a downside as well. In the *Rime of the Ancient Mariner,* the protagonist speaks of "water, water every where, nor any drop to drink." And like the Ancient Mariner, we in modernized society are surrounded by a sea of options but few real choices. One reason is that our options have been ripped away from the bedrock of tradition and ritual. We sometimes, if we are lucky, have the options but may lack certainty about how they can be organized into a coherent life pattern. Perhaps more tellingly, often we have no control over the options either.

Each of us is now faced with the challenge of putting together into the semblance of a pattern all the options that seem to make sense. We must decide on certain questions: Will I be a worker, a professional, a parent, a jogger, a vegetarian? Should I marry early or late? At what time of life should I have children? The challenge is that we must make these decisions before we ourselves have experience; the irony is that we never seem to listen to those who do. We decide to have children, for example, without fully understanding the time and energy demands this decision entails over the next fifteen to twenty years. We decide to become a lawyer before having lived the life of a lawyer for sufficient years to really understand the role. We put selected options together like building blocks into a pattern that can rechart our lives. But the glue of tradition that holds such patterns together may not be as strong as before, due to the uniqueness of these new patterns. And thus, also like building blocks, the whole can come tumbling down or result in a masterpiece. For Adelaide Stone, the whole came tumbling down; for Max Schindler, the later years seem directed toward, if not a masterpiece, at least a substantial creation. The importance of the unexpected means that we cannot be sure of the trajectory our lives will take.

In short, the growing number of life options has a dark side: the frequent absence of any sense of integration or coherence in our lives. And if our lives lack coherence, it is because many of the choices available to us in the developed nations have been stripped of their articulation with a meaningful pattern of living. (See Antonovsky, 1987.) We are becoming social smorgasbords. The background against which the life course is played, moreover, has in some respects reduced the number of choices available. The increasing numbers of older people who need care, as we have seen, are exerting a powerful demand on their adult children. Even the *meaning* of having options and alternatives may be questioned. For in

today's age of nuclear armament, terrorism, civil strife, and technological pollution, the very future of the human race may seem open
to question. Certainly we found among our older participants a
much stronger concern with public affairs than we had anticipated.

Social Upheaval and Personal Loss

The years spanned by this study have given us a rare opportunity to assess the impact, on four life-stage groups, of an unprecedented series of social stressors: Vietnam and its sequelae, women's
liberation, religious revival and innovation, new life-styles, Watergate, inflation, recessions, acts of terrorism, increases in suicide
among the young, shortages of natural resources, health threats
from the food we eat and the environment we live in, implicit
threats of nuclear war, and more. Certainly we could not have asked
for a better climate in which to study personal change in the context
of societal transformation.

News of such events has produced an almost unavoidable
impact upon our participants. Their sense of personal immortality,
for example, often seems sundered from its usual sources: the presence of children, a legacy of work and accomplishment, possibly
even the sense of being one with the human race. Today the continuation of any aspect of life—even the human race itself—is no
longer a certainty. And not only because of the bomb, but because
of the host of factors, including nuclear technology, to which we
have just alluded. In our study, the impact of macro-level stressors
seems most evident among those in the two older groups. Even a
tough old bird like Max Schindler registers dismay over where the
world seems headed.

The sense of loss—loss of self and of society—is not restricted
to the middle-aged and elderly. In the long run it may affect the
younger participants most strongly. Robert Lifton (1987) thinks
today's young adults suffer from a kind of double vision in which
images of marriage and a successful life are overlaid with images of
the final holocaust. A similar phenomenon is reported by Greenwald and Zeitlin (1987). Using family interviews, these therapists
discovered that adolescents are finding it harder to undertake adult
commitments due in part to their underlying fear of nuclear dev-

astation. Such blurring of images may well account for the disturbing concern many of our younger respondents seem to show for material things, their determination to have it all and have it now, and their lack of a secure identity.

Gender and Social Concerns. Women, we found, may be especially vulnerable to social stressors. At the first contact, back in 1968–1969, women in the two oldest groups far outrank their male counterparts with regard to a concern with social issues. These older women also posit quite different solutions for what they perceive as negative social changes: as a group they advocate that people should be more responsive to national and international problems. The few men who are troubled by social change tend to place responsibility squarely on the government and not on themselves. For them the government should be more assertive in the enforcement of law and order and in the control of technology and change generally.

As the study continued, people showed greater and greater concern over where the country—and the world—are headed. By the fourth contact, approximately seven years into the study, worries about social issues have doubled. Among the retirement-aged subjects, women account for most of the increase, but among the middle-aged parents, both men and women show greater concern.

When we look at the responses to our checklist of specific socioenvironmental issues, we find that among both groups of older adults the majority have become more worried about war at the final contact, and women's concern with the Vietnam disaster doubles between the fourth and fifth interviews. Worry about the dangers of nuclear war and nuclear plants is widespread, but the women are far more worried about such risks than the men.

These sex differences are particularly strong when one considers that the men and women in our sample closely resemble each other on all demographic characteristics. The differences seem to parallel changes in the sense of commitment that we also found. Over the eleven to twelve years of study, for example, women generally become less self-concerned and more altruistic. They also score lower on commitment to mastery or autonomy, perhaps registering a sense of defeat. Among their male counterparts, on the other hand, there is increasing evidence of indifference and self-interest.

Identity Lost. Another dimension in which we explored the impact of our social environment was that of the self-concept. Changes in self-concept can be a bellwether of alterations in personal functioning, as Elder (1981) has discussed so eloquently in the context of the Great Depression. When we first began interviewing our subjects, we were fascinated but not surprised to find that the younger subjects seem very unsure of their personal identity. On our seventy-item Adjective Rating List, for example, they show a significantly greater tendency to place themselves in the neutral region on personal characteristics compared to our middle-aged and older subjects. That is, they register a more diffuse self-image and in open-ended discussions present a less certain image of who they are and who they want to be. Their quest for identity seems predicated on value returned: "If I become a lawyer, will I make more money and be more happy?" The image of Protean Man (Lifton, 1971), shifting identities to fit the times, and of what Rosow (1978) has called a "chameleon-like" ability to shift persona in midstream, seems to characterize many.

Twelve years later, the younger groups still appear to be groping toward an identity (or leaning toward identity diffusion as a way of life). Our group of retirement subjects, however, who ranked lowest on self-diffusion at the initial contact, continue to rank lowest on self-diffusion at each interview. Middle-aged parents of both sexes had changed very little up to the third contact, but by the final interview they are more certain about themselves.

The Interplay of Self and Society

In this book we have spent a lot of time evaluating the continuities and changes among our various participants. In some chapters we focused on their specific characteristics such as self-concept, goals and values, satisfactions in life, and commitments. We also spent time demonstrating that stressors come in all sizes and shapes: some are cataclysmic and others remind us of T. S. Eliot's apocalyptic saying, "This is the way the world ends, not with a bang but a whimper." The importance of a stressor, we found, can often be understood only in the context of other stressors as well as the presence or absence of such mitigating factors as social supports, experience, and the like. We also found it fascinating that life events, the supposedly random and adventitious accidents of life, in fact correlate significantly with the experiencing of subsequent life events. The bottom line, however, whether one is talking about childhood stressors or current stress in adulthood, is that multiple causation is the basic rule in trying to understand the life-course implications of any experience.

We have attempted, in the various chapters, to illustrate that the lives of people change or indeed remain stable due to a host of conditions. In discussing The Four we sought to demonstrate how a personal style (commitment to self-concern) interacts with the social environment. One thing we learned from these cases is that even these commitments, although they are among the most stable of our personal indicators, themselves interact with the social context. Adelaide Stone, for example, maintained a commitment to openness until a series of physical and social stresses forced her into a self-protective mode. In contrast, Hazel Sutter progressed from a relatively self-protective way of life to a more open and accepting one that can be traced to the establishment of a very satisfying relationship with a male friend. Max Schindler, discontented with his situation in life, rails against minorities and a host of other societal problems. But when, after considerable perseverance and planning, he actually achieves his life goals, we find a very different man—a man who now seems remarkably unperturbed by minority rights issues and who has become quite accepting and caring of other people. In Olav Olavsen we see yet another aspect of social stress. Olav's life illustrates the tremendous importance of bereavement, a social loss that can disturb the equilibrium of even the staunchest coper. Even Olav was crushed, at least temporarily, by the loss of the central person in his life.

With the life of Adelaide Stone we see yet another issue: the importance of health problems as a stressor. Adelaide's stroke was certainly a crippling event, but, what is worse, it seems to have changed the way she views the world and herself. The world is now a threatening place. In search of what she calls "a niche" for herself, the only thing she can think of is an institutional setting: safe and secure. Significantly, she has labeled herself "disabled." Adelaide's life is also a good illustration of multiple causation. It was not just the stroke that created the massive change in Adelaide's life. And it was not just the long-standing problem with her drug-addicted son or the low-grade but long-term problems with her husband. It was in fact the overlapping occurrence of all these stressors—her addicted son, the disruptive presence of grandchildren in the house, the unhappy marriage and subsequent divorce—culminating in, and magnifying the effect of, her stroke. In a sense the stroke was the straw that broke the camel's back. Although a stroke is certainly not an insignificant event, without the other stressors one senses that the outcome might have been very different.

Summing Up

We have seen that the everyday stressors of life are strongly and significantly associated with levels of change and continuity. We have also seen that stressors themselves do not really tell us why certain lives head in certain directions. It is in fact the interweaving of personal and social circumstances that gives us some sense of why. Naturally, not everything is predictable or even understandable. We find, for instance, that among our older respondents the loss of a loved one or the onset of a serious and chronic health problem can rewrite an individual's life script in completely unexpected ways.

As we read case after case, we also encounter an impressive number of people whose true potential remains submerged for extended periods as a result of social constraints. Daphne Randall spent all but the last two or three years of her life trapped in a world that demanded subservience to the needs of others. With her husband's death and the departure of her son, she suddenly gained a freedom she vigorously pursued until her untimely death. Similarly but more fortunately, Max Schindler's more tolerant and giving side emerged only after he was freed of the world of work.

One conclusion we come to after reviewing such findings is that the study of adult development requires a substantial commitment of time by investigators. The trajectory of the individual life course is frequently masked by false starts and detours and becomes visible only to those willing to grow old along with their subjects. Even with a commitment of time, the clarity of focus depends on the adequacy and breadth of measures, as well as on the social context. Our study sought to identify some of the factors underlying change and continuity in the adult years. We were fortunate to have available a number of indices of stress that first appeared in the behavioral science literature in the mid-1960s, and also to have sufficient years in which to see a variety of personal and social forces play themselves out.

Resource A
Publications
Resulting from the Study

Please note that bibliographic citations in the text refer to works listed in References, not to works listed here.

Books

Fiske, M. *Middle Age: The Prime of Life?* Life Cycle Series. New York: Harper & Row, 1979.

Lowenthal, M. F., Thurnher, M., Chiriboga, D. A., and Associates. *Four Stages of Life: A Comparative Study of Women and Men Facing Transitions.* San Francisco: Jossey-Bass, 1975.

Articles

Chiriboga, D. A. "Life Event Weighting Systems: A Comparative Analysis." *Journal of Psychosomatic Research,* 1977a, *21,* 415–422.

Chiriboga, D. A. "Personality in Adults and Aged." In B. B. Wolman (ed.), *International Encyclopedia of Neurology, Psychiatry, Psychoanalysis, and Psychology.* New York: Van Nostrand Reinhold, 1977b.

Chiriboga, D. A. "Evaluated Time: A Life Course Perspective." *Journal of Gerontology,* 1978, *33* (3), 388–393.

Chiriboga, D. A. "Conceptualizing Adult Transitions: A New Look at an Old Subject." *Generations,* 1979, *4* (1), 4–6.

Chiriboga, D. A. "Middle Age." In *Academic American Encyclopedia.* Princeton, N.J.: Arete, 1980a.

Chiriboga, D. A. "Stress and Coping: An Introduction and Overview." In L. Poon (ed.), *Aging in the 1980s: Selected Contemporary Issues in the Psychology of Aging.* Washington, D.C.: American Psychological Association, 1980b.

Chiriboga, D. A. "The Developmental Psychology of Middle Age." In J. Howell (ed.), *Modern Perspectives in the Psychiatry of Middle Age.* New York: Brunner/Mazel, 1981.

Chiriboga, D. A. "Consistency in Adult Functioning: The Influence of Social Stress." *Aging and Society,* 1982a, *2* (1), 7–29.

Chiriboga, D. A. "An Examination of Life Events as Possible Antecedents to Change." *Journal of Gerontology,* 1982b, *37,* 595–601.

Chiriboga, D. A. "Social Stressors as Antecedents of Change." *Journal of Gerontology,* 1983, *39,* 468–477.

Chiriboga, D. A. "The Longitudinal Study of Transitions." In S. A. Mednick, M. Harway, and K. M. Finello (eds.), *Handbook of Longitudinal Research.* Vol. 2: *Teenage and Adult Cohorts.* New York: Praeger, 1984.

Chiriboga, D. A. "Personality in Later Life." In P. Silverman (ed.), *The Elderly as Modern Pioneers.* Bloomington: Indiana University Press, 1987.

Chiriboga, D. A. "Stress and Loss in Middle Age." In R. Kalish (ed.), *Coping with Loss in Middle Age.* Newbury Park, Calif.: Sage, 1988.

Chiriboga, D. A. "Mental Health at the Midpoint: Crisis, Challenge, or Relief?" in S. Hunter and M. Sandel (eds.), *Midlife Myths: Coping Strategies.* Newbury Park, Calif.: Sage, 1989.

Chiriboga, D. A., and Cutler, L. "Stress and Adaptation: A Life Span Study." In L. Poon (ed.), *Aging in the 1980s: Selected Contemporary Issues in the Psychology of Aging.* Washington, D.C.: American Psychological Association, 1980.

Chiriboga, D. A., and Dean, H. "Dimensions of Stress: Perspectives from a Longitudinal Study.'" *Journal of Psychosomatic Research,* 1978, *22,* 47–55.

Chiriboga, D. A., and Pierce, R. C. "The Influence of Stress upon Symptom Structure." *Journal of Clinical Psychology,* 1981, *37* (4), 722–728.

Fiske, M. "Interpersonal Relationships and Adaptation in Adulthood." In P. F. Ostwald (ed.), *Communication and Social Interaction: Clinical and Therapeutic Aspects of Human Behavior.* New York: Grune & Stratton, 1977.

Fiske, M. "The Reality of Psychological Change." In L. F. Jarvik (ed.), *Aging into the 21st Century: Middle-Agers Today.* New York: Gardner Press, 1978.

Fiske, M. "Changing Hierarchies of Commitment in Adulthood." In N. Smelser and E. Erikson (eds.), *Themes of Work and Love in Adulthood.* Cambridge, Mass.: Harvard University Press, 1980a.

Fiske, M. "Tasks and Crises of the Second Half of Life: The Interrelationship of Commitment, Coping and Adaptation." In J. E. Birren and R. B. Sloane (eds.), *Handbook of Mental Health and Aging.* Englewood Cliffs, N.J.: Prentice-Hall, 1980b.

Fiske, M. "Challenge and Defeat: Stability and Change in Adulthood." In L. Goldberger and S. Breznitz (eds.), *Handbook of Stress.* New York: Free Press, 1982.

Fiske, M., and Chiriboga, D. A. "The Interweave of Societal and Personal Change in Adulthood." In J.M.A. Munnichs, P. Mussen, E. Olbrich, and P. G. Coleman (eds.), *Life Span and Change in a Gerontological Perspective.* New York: Academic Press, 1985.

Krystal, S., and Chiriboga, D. A. "The Empty Nest Process in Midlife Men and Women." *Maturitas,* 1979, *1,* 215–222.

Lowenthal, M. F. "Intentionality: Toward a Framework for the Study of Adaptation in Adulthood." *Aging and Human Development,* 1971, *2* (2), 79–95.

Lowenthal, M. F. "Some Potentialities of a Life Cycle Approach to the Study of Retirement." In F. Carp (ed.), *Retirement.* New York: Behavioral Publications, 1972.

Lowenthal, M. F. "Psychosocial Variations Across the Adult Life Course: Frontiers for Research and Policy." *Gerontologist,* 1975, *15* (1), 6–12.

Lowenthal, M. F. "Toward a Sociopsychological Theory of Change in Adulthood and Old Age." In J. E. Birren and K. W. Schaie (eds.), *Handbook of the Psychology of Aging.* New York: Van Nostrand Reinhold, 1977.

Lowenthal, M. F., and Chiriboga, D. A. "Transition to the Empty Nest: Crisis, Challenge, or Relief?" *Archives of General Psychiatry,* 1972, *26,* 8-14.

Lowenthal, M. F., and Chiriboga, D. A. "Social Stress and Adaptation: Toward a Life Course Perspective." In C. Eisdorfer and M. P. Lawton (eds.), *The Psychology of Adult Development and Aging.* Washington, D.C.: American Psychological Association, 1973.

Lowenthal, M. F., and Robinson, B. "Social Networks and Isolation." In R. H. Binstock and E. Shanas (eds.), *Handbook of Aging and the Social Sciences.* New York: Van Nostrand Reinhold, 1976.

Lowenthal, M. F., and Weiss, L. "Intimacy and Crises in Adulthood." *Counseling Psychologist,* 1976, *6* (1), 10-15.

Lurie, E. "Sex and Stage Differences in Perceptions of Marital and Family Relationships." *Journal of Marriage and the Family,* 1974, *36* (2), 260-269.

Pierce, R. C. "Missing Data in Tryon's Cluster Analysis." *Perceptual and Motor Skills,* 1978, *47,* 1039-1043.

Pierce, R. C. "Dimensions of Leisure, I: Satisfaction." *Journal of Leisure Research,* 1980a, *12* (1), 5-19.

Pierce, R. C. "Dimensions of Leisure, II: Descriptions." *Journal of Leisure Research,* 1980b, *12* (2), 150-163.

Pierce, R. C. "Dimensions of Leisure, III: Characteristics." *Journal of Leisure Research,* 1980c, *12* (3), 273-284.

Pierce, R. C., and Chiriboga, D. A. "Dimensions of Adult Self-Concept." *Journal of Gerontology,* 1979, 34 (1), 80-85.

Robinson, B., and Thurnher, M. "Taking Care of Aged Parents: A Family-Cycle Transition." *Gerontologist,* 1979, *19* (6), 586-593.

Spence, D. L. "Life Satisfactions: A Basis for Programming for the Older Person." In *Statewide Education and Training Program in Gerontology.* Sacramento: Department of Recreation and Leisure Studies, San Jose State College, and California Commission on Aging, 1969.

Spence, D. L., and Lonner, T. D. "The 'Empty Nest': A Transition Within Motherhood." *Family Coordinator*, 1971, *20* (4), 369-375.

Spence, D. L., and Lonner, T. D. "Career Set: A Resource Through Transitions and Crises." *International Journal of Aging and Human Development*, 1978, *9* (1), 51-65.

Suzman, R. "Social Change in America and the Modernization of Personality." In G. DiRenzo (ed.), *We, the People: American Character and Social Change*. Westport, Conn.: Greenwood Press, 1977.

Thurnher, M. "Adaptability of Life History Interviews to the Study of Adult Development." In L. F. Jarvik, C. Esidorfer, and J. E. Blum (eds.), *Intellectual Functioning in Adults: Psychological and Biological Influences*. New York: Springer, 1973.

Thurnher, M. "Goals, Values, and Life Evaluations at the Preretirement Stage." *Journal of Gerontology*, 1974, *29* (1), 85-96.

Thurnher, M. "Midlife Marriage: Sex Differences in Evaluations and Perspectives." *International Journal of Aging and Human Development*, 1976, *7* (2), 129-135.

Thurnher, M. "Gender Experience and Later Life Transitions." *Generations*, 1979, *4* (1), 9-10.

Thurnher, M. "Family Patterns Vary Among U.S. Ethnic Groups." *Generations*, 1982, *7* (2), 8-9.

Thurnher, M. "Turning Points and Developmental Change: Subjective and 'Objective' Assessments." *American Journal of Orthopsychiatry*, 1983, *53* (1), 52-60.

Thurnher, M., Spence, D., and Lowenthal, M. F. "Value Confluence and Behavioral Conflict in Intergenerational Relations." *Journal of Marriage and the Family*, 1974, *36* (2), 308-319.

Resource B
Demographic Questions

Please note that we have omitted several standard questions dealing with such issues as the identification of age, gender, and ethnicity. To preserve overlap with the original instruments, we have retained the original numbering system and therefore begin with question 9 instead of question 1. Those interested in obtaining a more complete description of this or any other section of the interview are encouraged to write Dr. Chiriboga, School of Allied Health Sciences, Rt. J28, UTMB, Galveston, TX 77550.

9.   Are you working at present?

Yes, full time	4	[Ask 9A–G.]
Yes, part time	3	[Ask 9A–G.]
No, unemployed	2	[If no, go to Question 10.]
No, retired	1	[If no, go to Question 10.]

[If working, ask Question 9A–G.]

A.   What kind of work do you do? _____

_____ [Probe for specific occupational category.]

B.   How long have you been at your present job?

    C.   How do you feel about your job?   [Read:]

Very satisfied	4
Fairly satisfied	3
Fairly dissatisfied	2
Very dissatisfied	1

    D.   What do you find most satisfying in your present work?
    E.   What do you find least satisfying in your present work?
    F.   What part do you feel work plays in your life?
    G.   If you gave up your present job, what would you miss?

[If *R* is not working or is retired, ask Question 10.]

10.   Would you like to be working now?

No	1
Yes	2 [Ask A.]

    A. [If yes.]   What would you like to be doing?

[Ask Questions 11 and 12 if *R* is working or planning to work.]

11.   At what age do you plan to retire?   Age _____

    A.   Why at that age?

12.   Are you doing anything to prepare for retirement?

No	1
Yes	2 [If yes.] What? _____.

[Ask Questions 13–15 if *R* is retired.]

13.   When did you retire?   Year _____
    How old were you when you retired?   Age _____

14.   Was your retirement voluntary or mandatory?

Voluntary	1
Mandatory	2

15.   If you could do it over again, would you retire earlier or later than you did?

Earlier	1 [Ask A.]
Later	2 [Ask A.]

A. Why?

16. What is your present marital status?

Married	1
Separated	2
Divorced	3
Widowed	4
Never married	5
Living together	6

17. Have there been any changes in your marital status during the last years? (Circle all categories that apply and give date.)

No change	1	Date
Married/remarried	2	_____
Separated	3	_____
Divorced	4	_____
Widowed	5	_____
Reconciled	6	_____

18. If married or living together within the past three years:

A. When did you marry (start living together)? _____ (month and year)

B. Age of spouse (partner) at marriage _____

C. Education of spouse (partner)

None	00
1–6 years	01
7–8 years	02
9–12 years	03
High school graduate	04
Business, vocational, or technical school past high school	05
Some college (but not college graduate)	06
College graduate	07
Some graduate work, but no degree; teacher's credential; university nurse's training	08
M.A. or M.S.	09
Ph.D., M.D., D.D.S., L.L.B., M.B.A.,	

Pharmacist or equivalent	10	
Other	11	

D. Occupation of spouse (partner) _____

E. Number of spouse's (partner's) previous marriages ___

F. Number of spouse's (partner's) children from previous marriage _____

[If *R* is married or living together, ask Question 19.]

19. Is your spouse (partner) working at present?

Yes, full time	4	[Ask A–C.]
Yes, part time	3	[Ask A–C.]
No, unemployed	2	[Ask B–C.]
No, retired	1	[Ask B–C.]

A. [If yes.] What kind of work does he/she do?

_____

[Probe for specific occupational category.]

B. [Ask all Rs.] How do you feel about your spouse's (partner's) work situation?

C. [Ask all Rs.] When does your spouse (partner) plan to retire?

Plans to retire at	Age _____	Year _____
Already retired at	Age _____	Year _____

Resource C
Health Section

1. About how many times have you seen a doctor within the past year?

    _____ times

2. Have you had any serious illness or been hospitalized during the past three years?

    No   1
    Yes   2

[If yes.] What was the nature of the problem then, how long, and current status?

3. How many cigarettes do you smoke per day?

    Number _____ [If none, ask Question 4.]

4. [If R is a nonsmoker, ask Question 4A-B.]

    A. Were you ever a smoker?

        No   1
        Yes   2   [Ask B.]

    B. [If yes.] When did you quit?   _____ (year)

5. Has anyone in your immediate family had a serious illness or disability in the past three years? [Circle all that apply.]

No one	0
Spouse	1
Son	2
Daughter	3
Grandchild	4
Father	5
Mother	6
Brother	7
Sister	8
Other relative or in-law	9

[For each person mentioned, probe for nature of problem and current status.]

6. During the past three years, has anyone in your immediate family had emotional or mental problems? [Circle all that apply.]

No one	0
Spouse	1
Son	2
Daughter	3
Grandchild	4
Father	5
Mother	6
Brother	7
Sister	8
Other relative or in-law	9

7. During the past three years, did you have any emotional or mental problems that interfered with what you wanted to do?

No	1	
Yes	2	[Ask A–B.]

A. [If yes.] Probe for the nature of the problem; then ask how long and current status.

B. [If yes.] What sort of things helped you deal with the problem?

Resource D
California
Symptoms Checklist

I shall now ask you a series of questions to which you are to answer yes or no. [Write down spontaneous comments to items, but do not probe.]

Yes = 1   No = 2

1. Do you ever have times when you're moody and blue for no reason?
2. Does criticism always upset you?
3. Do you find that little things bother you?
4. Have you felt that different parts of your body were not under your control or have become disconnected somewhat?
5. Do you fairly often lose or misplace things?
6. Do you ever get the feeling that people are watching you or talking about you?
7. Have you suffered from loss of memory?
8. Do you usually keep in the background on social occasions?
9. Do you often shake and tremble?
10. Do you flare up in anger if you can't have what you want right away?

11. Have you had any unusual experiences of seeing or hearing things that no one else saw or heard?

12. Do you usually get up tired and exhausted in the morning?

13. Do frightening things keep coming back in your mind?

14. Are you troubled with headaches or pains in the head?

15. Do you find you are less interested than you used to be in things like personal appearance, table manners, and the like?

16. Are you sometimes worried or apprehensive for no reason?

17. Have you ever been so depressed that it interferes with what you want to do?

18. Do you ever have trouble getting to sleep and staying asleep?

19. Do strange people or places make you afraid?

20. Do you ever have the feeling that the world is very unreal to you?

21. Is it always hard for you to make up your mind?

22. Do you have any specific things that tend to terrify you such as the dark, heights, snakes, etc.?

23. Do you ever have loss of appetite?

24. Have you ever felt a lump in your throat for no reason?

25. Do people often annoy and irritate you?

26. Do you keep a very strict schedule and are you uncomfortable if you can't maintain it?

27. Are your feelings easily hurt?

28. Do you have hot spells or cold spells?

29. Are you constantly keyed up and jittery?

30. Do you have to be on guard even with friends?

31. Do you have constant tightness or numbness in any part of your body?

32. Do you ever have spells of dizziness?

33. Are you considered a nervous person?

34. Do you worry a lot about your health?

35. Have you ever contemplated suicide?

36. Do you go to pieces if you don't constantly control yourself?

37. Do you become scared at sudden movements and noises at night?

38. Do you ever get short of breath without having done heavy work?

39.   Must you do things slowly in order to make them without mistakes?
40.   Have you felt that life is not worth living?
41.   Has drinking at any time been a problem for you?
42.   Are you scared to be alone when there are no friends near you?

Resource E
The Enough Scale

Here are some things that some people have found to be important in their lives. Would you indicate how much of these things you feel that you get in your life?

	Too much	More than enough	Barely enough	Enough	Not enough
Vigorous physical activity	5	4	3	2	1
Relaxation	5	4	3	2	1
Opportunity to be mean or destructive and get away with it	5	4	3	2	1
Flamboyance (extravagance)	5	4	3	2	1
Peace and quiet	5	4	3	2	1
Play	5	4	3	2	1
Spirituality	5	4	3	2	1
Sharing with others	5	4	3	2	1
Achievement	5	4	3	2	1
Novelty (new experiences)	5	4	3	2	1
Intellectual challenge	5	4	3	2	1
Excitement	5	4	3	2	1

Chance to feel superior	5	4	3	2	1
Creative activity	5	4	3	2	1
Self-sufficiency	5	4	3	2	1
Sensuality (including sex)	5	4	3	2	1
Riskiness (taking chances)	5	4	3	2	1
Transcendence (the kind of experiences where you lose track of time, get entirely absorbed, and get outside yourself)	5	4	3	2	1
Affection	5	4	3	2	1
Intimacy	5	4	3	2	1
Solitude	5	4	3	2	1
Humor	5	4	3	2	1
Power	5	4	3	2	1
Sociability	5	4	3	2	1

Resource F
Goals Section

1. What goals or objectives do you have from now to the next five years or so?

[Probe for specific list.]

2. Of the goals you have mentioned, which would you say is *most important* to you?

3. In terms of your goals for the next five years, how satisfied are you with your progress?   [Read:]

Very satisfied	4
Fairly satisfied	3
Somewhat dissatisfied	2
Dissatisfied	1

Rank Order of Goal Areas—Present

Please number these goals in terms of how important they are to you *now*. (Put a 1 next to your most important goal, a 2 next to your second most important goal, etc.)

A. ACHIEVEMENT AND WORK REWARDS
    (This goal includes such things as competence, economic rewards, success, social status.)

B.   GOOD PERSONAL RELATIONS
        (This goal includes such things as love and affection, happy
        marriage, having good friends, belonging to groups.)
C.   PHILOSOPHICAL AND RELIGIOUS GOALS
        (This goal includes such things as living a spiritual life,
        doing God's will, having a philosophy of life, seeking the
        meaning of life, being wise, being morally good.)
D.   SOCIAL SERVICE
        (This goal includes such things as helping others, serving
        the community, contributing to the welfare of mankind or
        some part of mankind.)
E.   EASE AND CONTENTMENT
        (This goal includes such things as freedom from hardship,
        security, self-maintenance, peace of mind, health, simple
        comforts.)
F.   SEEKING ENJOYMENT
        (This goal includes such things as recreation, exciting ex-
        periences, entertainment, seeking pleasurable sights,
        sounds, feelings, tastes, and smells.)
G.   PERSONAL GROWTH
        (This goal includes such things as self-improvement, being
        creative, learning new things, "knowing yourself," meeting
        and mastering new challenges.)

Resource G
Evaluation of Past Life

I. Best and Worst Periods of Life

Instructions to Interviewer: The chart "Best and Worst Periods of My Life" will be mailed to respondent with request that he or she complete it before the interview. At the time of the interview, the interviewer should mark the present year and age of the respondent on the chart. The interviewer should first examine the chart made out by respondent to make sure that all years of past and future life have been scored. The interviewer should assist respondent in filling out any gaps he or she may have left or, if respondent has not yet done anything with the chart, give him or her time to fill it out. After completion, note here:

    1.   A.   Score for present year of life: _____
           B.   [Ask:] Please tell me some of the reasons why you gave the present year that particular score.

II. Life Evaluation (Open-Ended Questions)

    1.   Looking back, what do you think were the periods of major change, the turning points in your life?
    2.   When you have the chance to think about yourself and your life, would you say you tend to think or daydream more about the past or the future?

Past	0
Past and present	1
Present	2
Present and future	3
Future	4
All (or past and future)	5

3. Tell me the last important or interesting event in your life. [Probe for time of occurrence.]
4. What will be the next important or interesting event in your life? [Probe for time of occurrence.]
5. Viewing your life today, what sort of things give you the greatest satisfaction?
6. Viewing your life today, what do you see as your major difficulties or frustrations?
7. Looking *back* over your life, how successful would you say you have been in getting the things you wanted out of life? Would you say you have been: [Read:]

Very successful	4
Fairly successful	3
Somewhat successful	2
Not successful	1

Resource H
Stress Section

1. There are certain ages by which people are expected to have experienced such things as graduation from school, marriage, retirement, etc. Are there any areas of your life in which you feel yourself to be *behind* compared to most people your age?

2. A. What situation or event in the *past year* caused you the most stress?

   B. What did you do about it? (How did you cope?) [Probe for full response.]

   C. Is this the usual way you handle stress?

No	1	[Ask a.]
Yes	2	

   a. [If no.] What other things do you usually do?

   D. How much control did you have over the occurrence of this situation or event?   [Read:]

Complete	4
A lot	3
Some	2
None	1

   E. How did you feel about it?

3.   What kinds of situations usually cause you the most stress?

4.   Are there any stressful situations or events that you anticipate happening to you in the *next three years*?

Resource I
Life Events Questionnaire

INSTRUCTIONS: This is a checklist of important events or changes. We would like to know:

1. Which of these events happened to you within the past year
2. How you felt about the event when it occurred
3. How much you still think about it now

Please read down the list and for each event that happened to you within the past year indicate three things:

1. Whether it happened in the past year.
2. Your feelings about the event when it occurred—that is, whether you felt very happy, somewhat happy, somewhat unhappy, or very unhappy.
3. Indicate whether you still think about the event a lot, some, or not all.

A. EVENTS CONCERNING YOUR HEALTH

1. A major change in eating habits
2. A major change in sleeping habits
3. A major change in smoking habits
4. A major change in drinking habits

317

5. A change in your physical appearance
6. A change in your usual level of physical activity

B. EVENTS CONCERNING YOU AND YOUR WORK

1. Success and/or awards at work
2. A change to a new type of work
3. More responsibilities
4. Fewer responsibilities
5. A promotion
6. A demotion
7. A transfer
8. Spent more time at work
9. Spent less time at work
10. Salary increase
11. Spouse fired or having problems at work
12. A business failure
13. Trouble with your boss
14. Trouble with other workers
15. Not being able to work because of a disability
16. Being fired or laid off work
17. Quitting your job
18. Problems getting a new job
19. Retirement from work

C. EVENTS CONCERNING YOUR FEELINGS AND
    THOUGHTS

1. Feelings of being overwhelmed by difficult life situations
2. The realization that you will never attain an important goal
3. Unpleasant thoughts or images that keep coming back
4. Feelings of intense dislike for someone you deal with often
5. Feelings of intense loneliness

D. EVENTS CONCERNING YOUR DATING LIFE OR
    MARRIAGE

1. Getting engaged
2. Breaking up an engagement

3. Falling in love
4. Falling out of love
5. Sexual difficulties
6. Breaking up with steady
7. Getting married or beginning to live with someone
8. More arguments than usual with your spouse
9. In-law problems
10. Getting along better with your spouse
11. Minor problems of adjustment in your marriage
12. Separation from your spouse because of job demands
13. Spouse beginning or stopping work outside the home
14. Spouse retires and begins to stay at home more
15. Separation from your spouse due to marital problems
16. Going back to your spouse after separation
17. Divorce
18. Your spouse died
19. Your spouse was hospitalized
20. An extramarital affair
21. An unwanted pregnancy

E. EVENTS CONCERNING YOUR FAMILY

1. More family responsibilities than usual
2. Fewer family responsibilities than usual
3. Health problem of a family member (major illness, accident, etc.)
4. A miscarriage or abortion experienced by you or your spouse
5. Birth of a child, adopting a child
6. Your child did very poorly in school
7. Your child persistently disobeyed
8. Your child ran away or got into serious trouble (drugs, crime, etc.)
9. Your child got married
10. Your child got divorced
11. Loss of child by death
12. Intense arguments or disagreements with older children
13. Loss of contact with (or separation on bad terms from) your children

14.   A child moving out of the home
15.   More family get-togethers than before
16.   Fewer family get-togethers than before
17.   Relative moving in with you
18.   The death of a parent, brother, or sister
19.   Giving up a child (for adoption or to a divorced spouse)
20.   Birth of a grandchild

F.   EVENTS CONCERNING YOU AND PEOPLE NOT OF
     YOUR FAMILY

1.   Doing something that alienated you from your friends
2.   Fewer problems with friends
3.   Feelings of being seriously disliked by someone
4.   Loss of a close friend by death
5.   Separation from a close friend
6.   Fewer social contacts than before
7.   More social contacts than before
8.   A new close friendship
9.   Friend moving in with you

G.   OTHER IMPORTANT EVENTS

1.   A move of your home to another town or city
2.   A move within the same town or city
3.   Problems finding a new home or apartment
4.   Home improvement
5.   Lowering in value or condition of your house property
6.   Involvement in a lawsuit (other than divorce)
7.   Discrimination because of your sex, race, age, religion, or
     appearance
8.   Minor violations of the law
9.   A court appearance for a serious violation
10.   Being the victim of a criminal act (rape, assault, theft)
11.   Witnessing violence
12.   Being held in jail
13.   Purchases (or loans) of more than $10,000 (home, business,
     property, etc.)

14. Purchases (or loans) of more than $100 but less than $10,000 (TV, car, etc.)
15. Financial difficulties
16. Received an inheritance, scholarship, bonus, or cash award
17. Dependency on welfare or Social Security
18. A natural disaster (earthquake, fire, etc.)
19. Loss of a personally valued object
20. A change in your religious beliefs
21. Going to church more often
22. Going to church less often
23. An accident (automobile, at work, home, etc.)
24. Giving up a hobby, sport, etc.
25. Becoming more involved in hobbies or sports
26. A change in your political beliefs
27. Experimenting with drugs other than marijuana
28. Entering military service
29. Leaving military service
30. A major decision regarding your immediate future (retirement, etc.)
31. An outstanding personal achievement
32. A vacation
33. A long trip
34. Beginning to live alone
35. The loss or death of a loved pet
36. Obtaining a pet
37. Any other event of importance to you (please specify)

H. FOR THOSE OF YOU WHO HAVE BEEN ATTENDING SCHOOL

1. A great deal of academic pressure
2. Unusually good grades
3. Poor grades or failing an important exam
4. Dropping out of school
5. Reentering school after a period of absence
6. Graduation from high school or college
7. Beginning college

References

Allport, G. W. *Personality: A Psychological Interpretation.* New York: Holt, Rinehart & Winston, 1939.

Allport, G. W. *Becoming.* New Haven, Conn.: Yale University Press, 1955.

Antonovsky, A. *Unraveling the Mystery of Health: How People Manage Stress and Stay Well.* San Francisco: Jossey-Bass, 1987.

Baltes, P. B., and Baltes, M. "Plasticity and Variability in Psychological Aging: Methodological and Theoretical Issues." In C. Guerski (ed.), *Aging and the CNS.* Berlin: Schering, 1980.

Bandura, A. "The Self System in Reciprocal Determination." *American Psychologist,* 1978, pp. 344–358.

Becker, H. S. "Notes on the Concept of Commitment." *American Journal of Sociology,* 1960, *66,* 32–40.

Beiser, N. "A Study of Personality Assets in a Rural Community." *Archives of General Psychiatry,* 1971, *24,* 244–254.

Bengtson, V. L., Furlong, M. J., and Laufer, R. S. "Youth, Generation, and Social Change." *Journal of Social Issues,* 1974, *30* (2), 189–201.

Bengtson, V. L., Reedy, M. N., and Gordon, C. "Aging and Self-Conceptions: Personality Processes and Social Contexts." In J. E. Birren and K. W. Schaie (eds.), *Handbook of the Psychology of Aging.* (2nd ed.) New York: D. Van Nostrand, 1985.

Block, J. *Lives Through Time*. Berkeley, Calif.: Bancroft Books, 1971.

Bornstein, P. E., and others. "The Depression of Widowhood After Thirteen Months." *British Journal of Psychiatry*, 1973, *122*, 561-566.

Bowlby, J. "The Making and Breaking of Affectional Bonds. Part I: Aetiology and Psychopathology in the Light of Attachment Theory." *British Journal of Psychiatry*, 1977, *130*, 201-210.

Bradburn, N. *The Structure of Psychological Well-Being*. Chicago: Aldine, 1969.

Bradburn, N., and Caplovitz, D. *Reports on Happiness*. Chicago: Aldine, 1965.

Brenner, M. H. "Economic Change and the Suicide Rate: A Population Model Including Loss, Separation, Illness, and Alcohol Consumption." In M. R. Zales (ed.), *Stress in Health and Disease*. New York: Brunner/Mazel, 1985.

Brody, E. M. *Women in the Middle: Their Parent Care Years*. New York: Springer, 1990.

Burke, K. *Permanence and Change: An Anatomy of Purpose*. Indianapolis: Bobbs-Merrill, 1977.

Buss, A. R. "Generational Analysis: Description, Explanation and Theory." *Journal of Social Issues*, 1974, *30*, 55-71.

Chein, I. *The Science of Behavior and the Image of Man*. New York: Basic Books, 1972.

Chiriboga, D. A. "Social Stressors as Antecedents of Change." *Journal of Gerontology*, 1984, *39* (4), 468-477.

Chiriboga, D. A. "Stress and Loss in Middle Age." In R. Kalish (ed.), *Midlife Loss*. Newbury Park, Calif.: Sage, 1989.

Chiriboga, D. A., Catron, L., and Weiler, P. G. "Precursors of Adaptation: A Study of Marital Separation." *Family Relations*, 1987, *36*, 164-167.

Chiriboga, D. A., and Cutler, L. "Stress and Adaptation: Life Span Perspectives." In L. Poon (ed.), *Aging in the 1980s: Psychological Issues*. Washington, D.C.: American Psychological Association, 1980.

Chiriboga, D. A., and Fiske, M. "Recharting Adult Life." Plenary address at the First International Conference on the Future of Adult Life, The Netherlands, 1987.

Chiriboga, D. A., and Pierce, R. C. "The Influence of Stress upon Symptom Structure." *Journal of Clinical Psychology*, 1981, *37*, 722–728.

Costa, P. T., and McRae, R. R. "Age Differences in Personality Structure: A Cluster Analytic Approach." *Journal of Gerontology*, 1976, *31* (5), 564–570.

Ekerdt, D. J., Bosse, R., and Levcoff, S. "An Empirical Test for Phases of Retirement: Findings from the Normative Aging Study." *Journal of Gerontology*, 1985, *40* (1), 95–101.

Elder, G. H., Jr. *Children of the Great Depression*. Chicago: University of Chicago Press, 1974.

Elder, G. H., Jr. "Historical Experience in the Later Years." In T. K. Hareven (ed.), *Patterns of Aging*. New York: Guilford Press, 1981.

Elder, G. H., Jr., and Clipp, E. C. "Combat Experience, Comradeship, and Psychological Health." In J. P. Wilson, Z. Harel, and B. Kahana (eds.), *Human Adaptation to Extreme Stress: From the Holocaust to Vietnam*. New York: Plenum, 1988.

Erikson, E. H. *Life History and the Historical Moment*. New York: Norton, 1975.

Erikson, E. H. *The Life Cycle Completed*. New York: Norton, 1982.

Fiske, M. "Changing Hierarchies of Commitment in Adulthood." In N. J. Smelser and E. H. Erikson (eds.), *Themes of Work and Love in Adulthood*. Cambridge, Mass.: Harvard University Press, 1980.

Fiske, M., and Chiriboga, D. A. "The Interweave of Societal and Personal Change in Adulthood." In J. Munnichs, P. Mussen, E. Olbrich, and P. G. Coleman (eds.), *Life-Span and Change in a Gerontological Perspective*. New York: Academic Press, 1985.

Flavell, J. H. "Cognitive Changes in Adulthood." In L. R. Goulet and P. B. Baltes, (eds.), *Life-Span Developmental Psychology: Research and Theory*. Orlando, Fla.: Academic Press, 1970.

Freud, S. "An Outline of Psychoanalysis." In J. Strachey (ed.), *The Complete Psychological Works of Sigmund Freud*. Vol. 23. London: Hogarth Press, 1969.

Gergen, K. J. "Stability, Change, and Change in Human Development." In N. Datan and L. H. Ginsberg (eds.), *Life Span Developmental Psychology*. Orlando, Fla.: Academic Press, 1975.

Goldstein, K. *Human Nature.* New York: Schocken Books, 1963.

Greenwald, D. S., and Zeitlin, S. J. *No Reason to Talk About It.* New York: Norton, 1987.

Gubrium, J. F. "Being Single in Old Age." *International Journal of Aging and Human Development,* 1975, *6,* 29–41.

Gutmann, D. "The Premature Gerontocracy: Themes of Aging and Death in the Youth Culture." *Social Research,* 1972, *39* (3), 416–448.

Gutmann, D. L. "The Parental Imperative Revisited." In J. Meacham (ed.), *Family and Individual Development.* Basel, Switzerland: Karger, 1985.

Hagestad, G. O. "The Aging Society as a Context for Family Life." *Daedalus,* 1986, *115* (1), 119–139.

Havighurst, R. J. *Developmental Tasks and Education.* New York: McKay, 1953.

Henry, W. E. "The Role of Work in Structuring the Life Cycle." *Human Development,* 1971, *14,* 125–131.

Holmes, R. S., and Holmes, T. H. "Short-Term Intrusions into the Life Style Routine." *Journal of Psychosomatic Research,* 1970, *11,* 213–218.

Holmes, T., and Rahe, R. "The Social Readjustment Rating Scale." *Journal of Psychosomatic Research,* 1967, *11,* 213–218.

Jones, E. F., and others. *Teenage Pregnancy in Industrialized Countries.* New Haven, Conn.: Yale University Press, 1986.

Kagan, J. "Perspectives in Continuity." In O. G. Brim, Jr., and J. Kagan (eds.), *Constancy and Change in Human Development.* Cambridge, Mass.: Harvard University Press, 1980.

Kahana, E., Kiyak, A., and Liang, J. "Menopause in the Context of Other Life Events." In A. Dan, E. Graham, and C. Beecher (eds.), *The Menstrual Cycle.* New York: Springer, 1980.

Kahn, R. L., and Antonucci, T. C. "Convoys over the Life Course: Attachment, Roles, and Social Support." In P. B. Baltes and O. G. Brim (eds.), *Life-Span Development and Behavior.* Orlando, Fla.: Academic Press, 1980.

Kitchener, R. F. "Emergence: How to Get Something from Nothing." Unpublished doctoral dissertation, Colorado State University, 1976.

Klinger, E. "Consequences of Commitment to and Disengagement from Incentives." *Psychological Review,* 1975, *82* (1), 1–25.

Kohut, H. *The Restoration of Self.* New York: International Universities Press, 1977.

Kroeber, T. C. "The Coping Functions of the Ego Mechanisms." In R. W. White (ed.), *The Study of Lives.* New York: Atherton Press, 1963.

Krystal, S., and Chiriboga, D. A. "The Empty Nest Process in Midlife Men and Women." *Maturitas,* 1979, *1,* 215–222.

Kuhlen, R. G. "Aging and Life Adjustment." In J. E. Birren (ed.), *Handbook of Aging and the Individual.* Chicago: University of Chicago Press, 1959.

Kuhn, M. H., and McPartland, T. S. "An Empirical Investigation of Self Attitudes." *American Sociological Review,* 1954, *19,* 68–75.

Kuypers, J. A., and Bengtson, V. L. "Social Breakdown and Competence." *Human Development,* 1973, *16* (3), 181–201.

Lasch, C. *The Minimal Self.* New York: Norton, 1984.

Lawton, M. P. "The Dimensions of Morale." In D. P. Kent, R. Kastenbaum, and S. Sherwood (eds.), *Research Planning and Action for the Elderly.* New York: Behavioral Publications, 1972.

Lazarus, R. S., and Folkman, S. *Stress, Appraisal, and Coping.* New York: Springer, 1984.

Lifton, R. J. "Protean Man." *Archives of General Psychiatry,* 1971, *24,* 298–404.

Lifton, R. J. *The Broken Connection.* New York: Harcourt Brace Jovanovich, 1979.

Lifton, R. J. *The Future of Immortality: Essays for a Nuclear Age.* New York: Basic Books, 1987.

Lowenthal, M. F. *Lives in Distress: The Paths of the Elderly to the Psychiatric Ward.* New York: Basic Books, 1964.

Lowenthal, M. F. "Intentionality: Toward a Framework for the Study of Adaptation." *Aging and Human Development,* 1971, *2,* 79–95.

Lowenthal, M. F., Berkman, P. L., and Associates. *Aging and Mental Disorder in San Francisco: A Social Psychiatric Study.* San Francisco: Jossey-Bass, 1967.

Lowenthal, M. F., and Chiriboga, D. A. "Transition to the Empty

Nest: Crisis, Challenge or Relief?" *Archives of General Psychiatry,* 1972, *26,* 8–14.

Lowenthal, M. F., and Chiriboga, D. A. "Social Stress and Adaptation: Toward a Lifecourse Perspective." In C. Eisdorfer and M. P. Lawton (eds.), *The Psychology of Adult Development and Aging.* Washington, D.C.: American Psychological Association, 1973.

Lowenthal, M. F., and Haven, C. "Interaction and Adaptation: Intimacy as a Critical Variable." *American Sociological Review,* 1968, *32,* 20–30.

Lowenthal, M. F., Thurnher, M., Chiriboga, D. A., and Associates. *Four Stages of Life: A Comparative Study of Women and Men Facing Transitions.* San Francisco: Jossey-Bass, 1975.

McCrae, R. R., and Costa, P. T. *Emerging Lives, Enduring Dispositions: Personality in Adulthood.* Boston: Little, Brown, 1984.

Marks, S. R. "Multiple Role Models: Some Notes on Human Energy, Time, and Commitment." *American Sociology Review,* 1977, *42* (6), 921–936.

Marris, P. *Loss and Change.* Garden City, N.Y.: Anchor Press, 1975.

Michels, R. "Psychoanalytic Perspectives on Normality." In D. Offer and M. Sabshin (eds.), *Normality and the Life Cycle: A Critical Integration.* New York: Basic Books, 1984.

Neugarten, B. L. "The Awareness of Middle Age." In B. L. Neugarten (ed.), *Middle Age and Aging.* Chicago: University of Chicago Press, 1968.

Neugarten, B. L. "Continuities and Discontinuities of Psychological Issues into Adult Life." *Human Development,* 1969, *12,* 121–130.

Neugarten, B.L. "Personality and Aging." In J. E. Birren and K. W. Schaie (eds.), *Handbook of the Psychology of Aging.* New York: D. Van Nostrand, 1977.

Neugarten, B. L., and Datan, N. "Sociological Perspectives on the Life Cycle." In P. B. Baltes and K. W. Schaie (eds.), *Life-Span Developmental Psychology: Personality and Socialization.* New York: Basic Books, 1973.

Neugarten, B. L., Crotty, W. J., and Tobin, S. S. "Personality Types in an Aged Population." In B. L. Neugarten and Associates (eds.), *Personality in Middle and Late Life: Empirical Studies.* New York: Atherton Press, 1964.

Neugarten, B. L., and Neugarten, D. A. "Age in the Aging Society." *Daedalus,* 1986, *115* (1), 31–49.

Norton, D. *Personal Destinies: A Philosophy of Ethical Individualism.* Princeton, N.J.: Princeton University Press, 1976.

Persson, G. "Relation Between Early Parental Death and Life Event Ratings Among 70 Year Olds." *Acta Psychiatrica Scandinavia,* 1980, *62,* 392–397.

Pierce, R. C. "Dimensions of Leisure, I: Satisfactions." *Journal of Leisure Research,* 1980, *12* (1), 5–19.

Pierce, R. C., and Chiriboga, D. A. "Dimensions of Adult Self-Concept." *Journal of Gerontology,* 1979, *34* (1), 80–85.

Riegel, K. F. "Personality Theory and Aging." In J. E. Birren (ed.), *Handbook of Aging and the Individual.* Chicago: University of Chicago Press, 1959.

Robinson, B., and Thurnher, M. "Taking Care of Aged Parents: A Family Cycle Transition." *Gerontologist,* 1979, *19* (6), 586–593.

Rosenberg, M. *Conceiving the Self.* New York: Basic Books, 1979.

Rosow, I. "What Is a Cohort and Why?" *Human Development,* 1978, *21,* 65–75.

Rutter, M. "Individual Differences." In M. Rutter and L. Hersov (eds.), *Child Psychiatry: Modern Approaches.* Oxford, England: Blackwell Scientific, 1977.

Rutter, M. "Stress, Coping and Development: Some Issues and Some Questions." *Child Psychological Psychiatry,* 1981, *22* (4), 323–356.

Schaie, K. W. "Rigidity-Flexibility and Intelligence: A Cross-Sectional Study of the Adult Life Span from 20 to 70 Years." *Psychology Monographs,* 1958, *72* (9), 1–26.

Schulz, R., and Rau, M. T. "Social Support Through the Life Course." In S. Cohen and S. L. Syme (eds.), *Social Support and Health.* Orlando, Fla.: Acadmic Press, 1985.

Selye, H. *The Stress of Life.* New York: McGraw-Hill, 1956.

Smelser, N. J. "Issues in the Study of Work and Love in Adulthood." In N. J. Smelser and E. H. Erikson (eds.), *Themes of Work and Love in Adulthood.* Cambridge, Mass.: Harvard University Press, 1980.

Spitzer, S. P. "Test Equivalence of Unstructured Self Evaluation Instruments." *Sociological Quarterly,* 1969, *10,* 204–215.

Suzman, R. "Effects of Employment and Occupation on Ego-Level." Paper presented at 30th annual scientific meeting of the Gerontological Society, San Francisco, Nov. 17–22, 1977.

Thurnher, M. T. "Turning Points and Developmental Change: Subjective and 'Objective' Assessments." *American Journal of Orthopsychiatry,* 1983, *53,* 52–60.

Vaillant, G. "Natural History of Male Psychological Health: VI. Correlates of Successful Marriage and Fatherhood." *American Journal of Psychiatry,* 1978, *135* (6), 653–659.

Whitbourne, S. K. *Adult Development.* (2nd ed.) New York: Praeger, 1986.

Will, G. E. "The Networks' Evening Blues." *Newsweek,* Mar. 30, 1987, p. 86.

Zurcher, L. *The Mutable Self: A Self-Concept for Social Change.* Newbury Park, Calif.: Sage, 1977.

Index

ies, 116; stress, 117–118; influence upon development, 115

Chiriboga, D. A., 2, 3, 24, 25, 33, 54, 117, 120, 140–141, 142, 149, 150, 151, 156, 166, 172, 175, 191, 275, 282

Choices too few, 286–288

Clark, Irma, negative self-concept, 33–35, 71

Clipp, E. C., 283

Cohen, Forrest, moderate impact person, 104–105

Cole, Susie, strong impact person, 101–102

Collins, Robbie, overwhelmed by stress, 200

Commitment: defined 243–244; human concern, 242–257

Complexities, 1–16

Compulsive caregiver, relationships development, 117

Compulsive support seeker, relationships development, 117

Concepts, flexible vs. rigid personality, 74–77

Confidantes, 190

Confused and conflicted, unusual people, 53–54

Consequences of childhood: deprivation, 120–123; psychological symptoms, 122–123

Consequences of social change, 109–111

Constriction vs. expansion, spontaneity, 44–46

Continuity: goals and values, 215; and stress, 149–150

Costa, P. T., 7, 20, 75–76, 94–95, 258

Crotty, W. S., 74

Crime, older group concern, 99

Crisis vs. challenge, life stress, 136–167

Cross-generation contact: older group, 169–171; younger group, 169–171

Cutler, L., 149, 166, 175

Cutting, Audrey, goals and values, 222–223

D

Daily hassles, momentary stress, 179–186

Datan, N., 144

Davis, Christina, not enough solitude, 207–208

Death, social changes effects, 285–286

Demographic questions, 300–303

Deprived: changes, 120–121; feelings about parents, 122; perceived change in self, 123

Derogatory self-concept, 110

Development: midlife crisis effects, 171; role of stress, 144–147; stress effects, 137–139

Dishman, Ruthey, interpersonal commitment, 249

Divorce, social changes effects, 285

Dogmatism, rigid personality increases, 75

Dunlap, Margy, stress symptoms, 193

Dysphoria, adjective cluster, 24

E

Economy, younger group concern, 99

Education, lack of and rigidity, 91–92

Egos in older group, 263

Eiler, Frederic: high school senior and life circumstances, 124–125; too much solitude, 206–207

Ekerdt, D. J., 258

Elder, G. H., 281, 283

Emotions, respondents, 237–238

Employment, younger group concern, 99

Empty nest group: focus on the concrete, 65–66; respondent group, 3, 10–11; unanimity in statements, 62

Enough Scale questions, 309–310

Erikson, Arnold: older person and life circumstance, 125; rigid person, 90–91, 94

Erikson, E. H., 94, 110, 115, 283

Erwin, Bart, deficits, 198–199

Estes, Carroll, core staff of study, 2

67620

67620